INDIA BOOKVARSITY

LOTUS CHOICES

Editor: Mahendra Kulasrestha

COLOSSUS
Vivekananda Select

'He was a born king and nobody ever came near him either in India or America without paying homage to his majesty!'

—*Romain Rolland*
French Nobel
Laureate

One circle more the spiral path of life ascends
And Time's restless shuttle – running back & fro
through maze of warp and woof – of shining
threads of life, spins out a stronger piece
Hand in hand they stand – and try to fathom the depths whence
spring eternal love; each in other's eyes
And find no hold that age but brings the youth anew to them
And time, the good the pure the true.

So wrote Vivekananda

4735/22, Prakash Deep Building
Ansari Road, Darya Ganj,
New Delhi - 110002

COLOSSUS
Vivekananda Select

Lotus Press : Publishers & Distributors
Unit No. 220, 2nd Floor, 4735/22, Prakash Deep Building,
Ansari Road, Darya Ganj, New Delhi- 110002
Ph.: 41325510, 98118-38000
• E-mail : lotuspress1984@gmail.com
www.lotuspress.co.in

Colossus Vivekananda Select

ISBN: 81-8382-163-6

Printed & Published by : **Lotus Press Publisher & Distributors,** New Delhi-02

Editorspeak

Swami's Agenda

The great Swami Vivekananda holds an extremely significant place in the modern history and culture of India. He passed away at an astonishingly early age—thirty-nine (may I ask the Goddess whom he and his Master worshipped, the reason for not giving him even the normal life-span, as also tolerable health? Which, in its turn, reminds me that Rabindranath Tagore did not like Shakti worship, especially in the form of Kali, the fearful goddess; he instead preferred Lakshmi, the gentle goddess of love and good fortune.) — but he rose like a golden phoenix in the utterly dark firmament of India's situation of those times, and for the first time after several centuries, filled it with immense light, which transcended all over the West, influencing the highest minds, including scholars like the old Max Muller and philosophers like Paul Deussen, and Nobel Laureates like Romain Rolland; and in the process sowing seeds of a universal religion inspired by the ideas of Adviata — which could most probably have succeeded if he were given two or so more decades to live, if not 80 to 90 as many of us have now. Had it been so—I put the question to students of history and intellectuals in general, to surmise how the present-day world would have benefitted, how there would have been harmony and peace, how human beings would be living in a soft-and-smooth environment of fellowship, how wars and terrorism would have died their natural death and been cremated perhaps for ever, how... etc... etc... etc.

I have a question to the gentlemen of the Ramakrishna Mission also: Why did they not carry the real mission of Vivekananda to its fulfilment? It is an absolute surprise to me that the inheritor Swamis did utterly fail in even recognising this great aim and purpose, despite their being some of the best, suitably educated—more than the Swami himself—and even inspired persons of their times? I am disappointed that I find no talk of this purpose in any of the Mission activities—in fact I find no visible or audible activity of the Mission other than selling books in exhibitions—; the great idea with the spirit and the energy of the phoenix is totally extinct. History should take note of it.

As I now find time—as a retired editor of books—to collect all the material published in the name of the Swami and go through it thoroughly and in perspective—I am amazed at the extremely wide range of his scholarship, his clear understanding of not only his own country's philosophies and religions, including the much derided Buddhism, which, according to the Swami himself, had no follower in India at that time; but those of other lands, their critical analysis—of Islam and Christianity in particular—; his views of history, Western culture, its strong points as well as weaknesses; his understanding of human behaviour in various lands and situations; his treatment of women; and, above all, his ideas about a universal religion—on which he seems to have started working since he was quite young. I am flabbergasted that he could earn all this before he was thirty, when he appeared at the Parliament of Religions in Chicago in 1893. Many more credits could be added to these, and what is yet more amazing is that he could acquire all this in face of hard travels all over the country, foodless, clothless, friendless— in a way, running away from a family-situation which was terrible and for which he could do nothing. No wonder, he gave the greatest value to removing the poverty of the country even above the winning of freedom from the British. The fact should be underlined that his chief aim in visiting America was to collect enough money to feed his countrymen. On many an occasion he bombarded the West for sending missionaries to India and China, and instead of giving them the much needed food, converting them to Christianity, a decrepit religion in comparison to Indian religions.

My reading into the works of Vivekananda leads me to the conclusion that he had a quite clear and definite agenda of the work he wanted to do, most of which was of an original nature. I'll try to pinpoint some of the main ideas here:

— To develop a universal religion — which has already been underlined. This in fact is the idea which attracted the highest minds of the West, and which made them visit India and write about the lives of the Swami and his Master, as well as the philosophy he wanted to promote. In this respect the second part of Romain Rolland's biography of the Swami is noteworthy, where he presents and discusses the philosophical aspects in quite some detail.

— To bring Religion closer to Science, and to further develop the Vedanta theories to make them thoroughly scientific. I find some interesting material in this area in one of Sister Nivedita's books, nowhere else. The Mission swamis did not realise the significance of work in this area, a pity indeed. Shouldn't they have developed an independent institute to further this most significant work?

— To develop Science in the country and to industrialise. It is a relatively lesser known fact that the idea of starting an institute of science was given to Jamshedji Tata by him. Tata wanted to start a science university but because the British did not permit him to do so, he had to contend with the Indian Science Institute, at Bangalore, which is still regarded as the best in the whole country. I feel that if not in the area of Science the Mission could have easily worked in the area of Industry.

The story of the Swami's deliberations with Jamshedji is not properly known and one might ignore it as mere gossip, but to me it was confirmed by a note on the Institute published in a well known magazine a couple of years ago, in which its then head, Dr. Mehta, did mention, though in passing, this fact.

But the Swami was not overawed by rich men and could tell them what he wanted to, is clear from his meeting with the first Rockefeller, a stingy person, whom the Swami made to offer his first charity cheque. An interesting episode, I'm tempted to give it here in full detail, as given in 'Complete Works of Swami Vivekananda' and quoted in 'New Discoveries, Vol.1'. The reader will find it illuminative of Swami Vivekananda's nature.

Rockefeller's First Donation to Public Welfare

Mr. X, in whose home Swamiji was staying in Chicago, was a partner or an associate in some business with John D. Rockefeller. Many times John D. heard his friends talking about this extraordinary and wonderful Hindu monk who was staying with them, and many times he had been invited to meet Swamiji but, for one reason or another, always refused. At that time Rockefeller was not yet at the peak of his fortune, but was already powerful and strong-willed, very difficult to handle and a hard man to advise.

But one day, although he did not want to meet Swamiji, he was pushed to it by an impulse and went directly to the house of his friends, brushing aside the butler who opened the door and saying that he wanted to see the Hindu monk.

The butler ushered him into the living room, and, not waiting to be announced, Rockefeller entered into Swamiji's adjoining study and was much surprised, I presume, to see Swamiji behind his writing table not even lifting his eyes to see who had entered.

After a while, Swamiji told Rockefeller much of his past that was not known to any but himself, and made him understand that the money he had already accumulated was not his, that he was only a channel and that his duty was to do good to the world—that God had given him all his wealth in order that he might have an opportunity to help and do good to people.

Rockefeller was annoyed that anyone dared to him that way and tell him what to do. He left the room in irritation, not even saying goodbye. But about a week after, again without being announced, he entered Swamiji's study and, finding him the same as before, threw on his desk a paper which told of his plans to donate an enormous sum of money toward the financing of a public institution.

"Well, there you are," he said. "You must be satisfied now, and you can thank me for it."

Swamiji didn't even lift his eyes, did not move. Then taking the paper, he quietly read it, saying: "It is for you to thank me." That was all. This was Rockefeller's first large donation to public welfare.

•

That the Swami's attitude was basically scientific, need not be emphasised. His presentation of the Raja Yoga practices to his

Western disciples was scientific, also explained by psychology. He was deeply influenced by the theory of evolution and wanted to apply it to Yoga. It may be said that a few years later Sri Aurobindo took it up in right earnest and the hardcore revolutionary developed his philosophy and practice of Integral Yoga to which he devoted forty long years of his life. Here was an unbelievable experiment to evolve human being to the next possible species of evolution through severely practising a completely new kind of Yoga. It immediately drew worldwide attention and his ashrama in Pondicherry was crowded with those who not only wanted to know more about it, but were willing to undertake the practices, however difficult these may be, and come up as the first such evolved species. But unfortunately, the experiment did not succeed as Sri Aurobindo suddenly passed away in Dec. 1950. After him, the Mother tried some other methods to achieve the aim, but she too did not succeed. It may happen some other day.

It has been noted that the Swami did not keep good health almost all his life, and was also quite disappointed at the response he got from his countrymen as well as his Indian comrades. On occasions he furiously expressed his frustrations and wanted to retire or quit. His foreign followers, including Sister Nivedita, stood by him as much as they could. To them goes the entire credit of noting down his lectures and speeches which are now with us to study and discover. The ashrama at Almora was also their contribution.

Although it would seem that the present-day spread of yoga in the West is a direct outcome of the seed sown by Swami Vivekananda more than a century ago, but this should not be taken as a satisfactory and even the right outcome. Much more should have been expected of it. To the present writer it seems that religion is fast losing its ground in modern times and its better part is totally dead. Its uglier aspect is far more expressive, resulting in unbelievably gory acts and attacks in many parts of the world. We all know about it.

The Swami, though admiring highly the equality-supporting aspect of Islam, had severely criticised its fundamentalist attitudes in several of his speeches. It may surprise many that he regarded the Islamic practice of social equality as an expression of Vedanta, and once desired that he would start a Vedanta Institute with a

Muslim at its head. If we study his views about Buddhism in specific details, we will conclude that his understanding of this world religion was correct, exact and worthy of emulation. This is the reason why he could declare that all religions are true but all have errors in them. The debate he had started, would have certainly resulted in an eclectic religion, if not a universal fellowship religion.

Once again, I am given to think that had the Swami been given some more years to live, the conflict of civilisations, which is essentially religious, could have been prevented. The age of religion, in which the Swami lived, is now over, and as Karen Armstrong in her 'History of God' has predicted, something totally new may eventually arise. I also feel that the Swami himself was also not very happy about the results of religion; there are signs that on occasions he was quite critical and furiously reprimanded those facing him. But times were different and he could not go beyond a point; and he was too young to take very radical steps. Had he been living in mid-twentieth century, he might even have started a totally different and new religion, based on some new Jnana discovered by him, for which the Indian tradition has immense scope.

Interesting things are happening in the arena of God in the present times, the latest being the truly venerable Mother Teresa questioning the existence of God, and arguing that if He does exist, why does He not intervene in removing the poverty and misery of human beings. Poverty was the chief problem with Swami Vivekananda also and perhaps he would also have reacted similarly.

Netaji Subhas and the Swami, and to some extent Tagore also, all giants from Bengal, have so far remained ignored and their contribution has not been suitably recognised, much less carried out. The Swami's mission remains incomplete and is awaiting our attention especially from the new generation, fortunately spreading all over the world for a variety of reasons. They are looking for their cultural roots to strengthen their identities in a fast globalising world. If they thumb through the Swami's work they will find lots of humanitarian material which already runs through their, our, veins, and which is able to stand on its own against the frightening fundamentalism we are facing today, as also the clash of civilisations, to which also it is the answer. Fortunately, again, Indian diaspora is very well educated and is capable of handling and providing leadership in the difficult situation.

Swamispeak

Agenda for a World Religion

Religion is the highest plane of human thought and life, and herein we find that the workings of these forces have been most marked. The intensest love that humanity has ever known has come from religion, and the most diabolical hatred that humanity has known has also come from religion. The higher the object of any religion and the finer its organisation, the more remarkable are its activities. Nothing has brought into existence so many hospitals and asylums for the poor; no other human influence has taken such care, not only of humanity, but also of the lowest of animal, as religion has done.

This has been so in the past and will also, in all probability, be so in the future. Yet out of the midst of this din and turmoil, there have arisen, from time to time, potent voices, drowning proclaiming peace and harmony. Will it ever come?

Is there one universal philosophy? Not yet. Each religion brings out its own doctrines and insists upon them as being the only true ones. And not only does it do that but it thinks that he who does not believe in them must go to some horrible place. Some will even draw the sword to compel others to believe as they do. This is not through wickedness, but through a particular disease of the human brain called fanaticism.

All religions have their own mythology.

Next come the rituals. In rituals there is no universal symbol which can command general recognition and acceptance.

It is hard to find any universal features in regard to religion, and yet we know that they exist. We are all human beings, but are we all equal? Certainly not. Are we all equal in our brains, in our powers, in our bodies? Yet we know that the doctrine of equality appeals to our heart.

Unity in variety is the plan of the universe. As a man you are separate from the animal, but as living beings, man, woman, animal, and plant are all one; and as existence, you are one with the whole universe. That universal existence is God, the ultimate Unity in the universe.

What then do I mean by the ideal of a universal religion? I do not mean any one universal philosophy, or any one universal mythology, or any one universal ritual held alike by all.

What can we do then? We can make it run smoothly, we can lessen the friction. How? By recognising the natural necessity of variation. We must learn that truth may be expressed in a hundred-thousand ways. I would ask mankind to recognise this maxim, "Do not destroy. Iconoclastic reformers do no good to the world. Break not, pull not anything down but build. Secondly, take man where he stands, and from there give him a lift. If it be true that God is the centre of all religions, then it is certain that all of us must reach that centre.

What I want to propagate is a religion that will be equally acceptable to all minds; it must be equally philosophic, equally emotional, equally mystic, and equally conducive to action.

To become harmoniously balanced in all these four directions is my ideal of religion. And this religion is attained by what we, in India call Yoga—union. The worker is called the Karma-Yogi. He who seeks the union through love is called the Bhakti-Yogi. He who seeks in through mysticism is called the Raja-Yogi. And he who seeks it through philosophy is called the Jnana-Yogi. So this world Yogi comprises them all.

•

After long study and experience, I have come to these conclusions that—

1. All religions, those of reason as well as of faith, are true;
2. All religions have some error in them;
3. All religions are almost as dear to me as my own Hinduism.

4. **Consequently, the thought of conversion is impossible.** The object of the Fellowships ought to be to help a Hindu to be a better Hindu, a Mussalman to become a better Mussalman, a Christian to become a better Christian.
5. **An attitude of protective tolerance is opposed to the spirit of International Fellowship.**
6. **Every faith has an equal right to live, and that there is an equal duty incumbent upon every man to respect that which his neighbour respects.**

Contents

1. **The First Words: Addresses at the Parliament of Religions** 17

• Response to Welcome • Break Down the Barriers • The Basic Ideas of Hinduism • Religion Not the Crying Need of India • Buddhism, the Fulfilment of Hinduism • Address at the Final Session

2. **Reports in American Newspapers** 43

• After the Parliament • Before the Parliament

3. **The Swami Who Shook America** 75

• India's Warrior-Saint • Vivekananda's Contribution to World Culture

4. **A Wreath of Poems** 95

• The Hymn of Creation • India Awake • Nirvana • Kali the Mother • Hold on Yet a While, Brave Heart • Angels Unawares • O Sannyasin • The Hymn of Samadhi • The Cup • On the Seas • The Living God • To an Early Violet • To My Own Soul • In Memorium • Now Sister Mary • Peace • My Play is Done • A Hymn to Shri Ramakrishna • Light

5. **Selected Lectures and Writing** 131

• My Life and Mission • What is Religion? • The Hindu Theories of God, Life and Karma • The Vedanta Philosophy • Reason-Checking of Religion • Practical Vedanta • The Social Ideal of Vedanta • Towards a Universal Religion • India: My Analysis • Christ, the Messenger of Life • The Ether • The Four Paths of Yoga

"The going abroad of the Master to take the world in his two hands, was the first sign that India was awake not only to survive but to conquer."

—Sri Aurobindo

THE FIRST WORDS

that, over a century ago, started the spread of India's unique religio-philosophical ideas in the West. It was a veritable revolution—which is still awaiting its completion.

Addresses at the Parliament of Religions, Chicago

11-27 Sept. 1893

Response to Welcome

The Idea of Toleration

11th September, 1893

Sisters and Brothers of America,

It fills my heart with joy unspeakable to rise in response to the warm and cordial welcome which you have given us. I thank you in the name of **the most ancient order of monks in the world;** I thank you in the name of the mother of religions; and I thank you in the name of **millions and millions of Hindu people of all classes and sects.**

My thanks, also, to some of the speakers on this platform who, referring to the delegates from the Orient, have told you that these men from far-off nations may well claim the honour of bearing to different lands the idea of toleration. I am proud to belong to a religion which has taught the world both tolerance and universal acceptance. **We believe not only in universal toleration, but we accept all religions as true. I am proud to belong to a nation which has sheltered the persecuted and the refugees of all religions and all nations of the earth.** I am proud to tell you that we have gathered in our bosom the purest remnant of the Israelites, who came to Southern India and took refuge with us in the very year in which their holy temple was shattered to pieces by Roman tyranny. **I am proud to belong to the religion which has sheltered and is still fostering the remnant of the grand Zoroastrian nation.** I will quote to you, brethren, a few lines from a hymn which I remember to have repeated from my earliest boyhood, which is every day repeated by millions of human beings:

As the different streams having their sources in different places all mingle their water in the sea, so, O Lord, the different paths which men take through different tendencies, various though they appear, crooked or straight, all lead to Thee.

The present convention, which is one of the most august assemblies ever held, is in itself a vindication, a declaration to the world of the wonderful doctrine preached in the Gita:

Whosoever comes to Me, through whatsoever form, I reach him; all men are struggling through paths which in the end lead to me.

Sectarianism, bigotry, and its horrible descendant, fanaticism, have long possessed this beautiful earth. They have filled the earth with violence, drenched it often and often with human blood, destroyed civilisation and sent whole nations to despair. Had it not been for these horrible demons, human society would be far more advanced than it is now. But their time has come; and **I fervently hope that the bell that tolled this morning in honour of this convention may be the death-knell of all fanaticism, of all persecutions with the sword or with the pen, and of all uncharitable feelings between persons wending their way to the same goal.**

Break Down the Barriers

15th September, 1893

I will tell you a little story. You have heard the eloquent speaker who has just finished saying, "Let us cease from abusing each other," and he was very sorry that there should be always so much variance.

But I think I should tell you a story which would illustrate the cause of this variance. A frog lived in a well. It had lived there for a long time. It was born there and brought up there, and yet was a little, small frog. Of course the evolutionists were not there then to tell us whether the frog lost its eyes or not, but, for our story's sake, we :must take it for granted that it had its eyes, and that it every day cleansed the water of all the worms and bacilli that lived in it with an energy that would do credit to our modern bacteriologists. In this way it went on and became a little sleek and fat. Well, one day another frog that lived in the sea came and fell into the well.

"Where are you from?"

"I am from the sea."

"The sea! How big is that? Is it as big as my well?" and he took a leap from one side of the well to the other.

"My friend," said the frog of the sea, "how do you compare the sea with your little well?"

Then the frog took another leap and asked, "Is your sea so big?"

"What nonsense you speak, to compare the sea with your well!"

"Well, then," said the frog of the well, "nothing can be bigger than my well; there can be nothing bigger than this; this fellow is a liar, so turn him out."

That has been the difficulty all the while.

I am a Hindu. I am sitting in my own little well and thinking that the whole world is my little well. The Christian sits in his little well and thinks the whole world is his well. The Mohammedan sits in his little well and thinks that is the whole world. I have to thank you America for the great attempt you are making to break down the barriers of this little world of ours, and hope that, in the future, the Lord will help you to accomplish your purpose.

The Basic Ideas of Hinduism

Paper read on 19th September, 1893

Three religions now stand in the world which have come down to us from time prehistoric—Hinduism, Zoroastrianism and Judaism. They have all received tremendous shocks and all of them prove by their survival their internal strength. But while **Judaism failed to absorb Christianity and was driven out of its place of birth by its all-conquering daughter, and a handful of Parsees is all that remains to tell the tale of their grand religion,** sect after sect arose in India and seemed to shake the religion of the Vedas to its very foundations, but like the waters of the seashore in a tremendous earthquake it receded only for a while, only to return in an all-absorbing flood, a thousand times more vigorous, and when the tumult of the rush was over, these sects were all sucked in, absorbed, and assimilated into the immense body of the mother faith.

From the high spiritual flights of the Vedanta philosophy, of which the latest discoveries of science seem like echoes, to the low ideas of idolatry with its multifarious mythology, the agnosticism of the Buddhists, and the atheism of the Jains, each and all have a place in the Hindu's religion.

Where then, the question arises, where is the common centre to which all these widely diverging radii converge? Where is the common basis upon which all these seemingly hopeless contradictions rest? And this is the question I shall attempt to answer.

The Hindus have received their religion through revelation, the Vedas. They hold that the Vedas are without beginning and without end. It may sound ludicrous to this audience, how a book can be without beginning or end. But **by the Vedas no books are meant. They mean the accumulated treasury of spiritual laws discovered by different persons in different times.** Just as the law of gravitation existed before its discovery, and would exist if all humanity forgot it, so is it with the laws that govern the spiritual world. The moral, ethical, and spiritual relations between soul and soul and between individual spirits and the Father of all spirits, were there before their discovery, and would remain even if we forgot them.

The discoverers of these laws are called Rishis, and we honour them as perfected beings. I am glad to tell this audience **that some of the very greatest of them were women.** Here it may be said that these laws as laws may be, without end, but they must have had a beginning. The Vedas teach us that creation is without beginning or end; Science is said to have proved that the sum total of cosmic energy is always the same. Then, if there was a time when nothing existed, where was all this manifested energy? Some say it was in a potential form in God. In that case **God is sometimes potential and sometimes kinetic, which would make Him mutable.** Everything mutable is a compound, and everything compound must undergo that change which is called destruction. So God would die, which is absurd. Therefore, there never was a time when there was no creation.

If I may be allowed to use a simile, creation and creator are two lines, without beginning and without end, running parallel to each other. **God is the ever active providence, by whose power systems after systems are being evolved out of chaos, made to run for a time and again destroyed.** This is what the Brahmin boy repeats every day: *"The sun and the moon, the Lord created like the suns and moons of previous cycles."* **And this agrees with modern science.**

Here I stand and if I shut my eyes, and try to conceive my existence, "I", "I", "I", what is the idea before me? The idea of a body. Am I, then, nothing but a combination of material substances? The Vedas declare, "No". I am a spirit living in a body. I am not the body. The body will die, but I shall not die. Here am I in this body; it will fall, but I shall go on living. I had also a past. The soul was not created, for creation means a combination which means a certain future dissolution. If then the soul was created, it must die. Some are born happy, enjoy perfect health, with beautiful body, mental vigour and all wants supplied. Others are born miserable, some are without hands or feet, others again are idiots and only drag on a wretched existence. Why, if they are all created, **why does a just and merciful God create one happy and another unhappy,** why is He so partial? Nor would it mend matters in the least to hold that those who are miserable in this life will be happy in a future life. Why should a man be miserable even here in the reign of a just and merciful God?

In the second place, the idea of a creator God does not explain the anomaly, but simply expresses the cruel fact of an all-powerful being. **There must have been causes, then, before his birth, to make a man miserable or happy and those were his past actions.**

Are not all the tendencies of the mind and the body accounted for by inherited aptitude? Here are two parallel lines of existence—one of the mind, the other of matter. If matter and its transformations answer for all that we have, there is no necessity for supposing the existence of a soul. But it cannot be proved that thought has been evolved out of matter, and if a philosophical monism is inevitable, spiritual monism is certainly logical and no less desirable than a materialistic monism; but neither of these is necessary here.

We cannot deny that bodies acquire certain tendencies from heredity, but those tendencies only mean the physical configuration, through which a peculiar mind alone can act in a peculiar way. There are other tendencies peculiar to a soul caused by its past actions. **And a soul with a certain tendency would by the laws of affinity take birth in a body which is the fittest instrument for the display of that tendency. This is in accord**

with science, for science wants to explain everything by habit, and habit is got through repetitions. So repetitions are necessary to explain the natural habits of a new-born soul. And since they were not obtained in this present life, they must have come down from past lives.

There is another suggestion. Taking all these for granted, how is it that I do not remember anything of my past life? This can be easily explained. I am now speaking English. It is not my mother tongue, in fact no words of my mother tongue are now present in my consciousness; but let me try to bring them up, and they rush in. That shows that **consciousness is only the surface of the mental ocean, and within its depths are stored up all our experiences.** Try and struggle, they would come up and you would be conscious even of your past life.

This is direct and demonstrative evidence. Verification is the perfect proof of a theory, and here is the challenge thrown to the world by the Rishis. We have discovered the secret by which the very depths of the ocean of memory can be stirred up—try it and you would get a complete reminiscence of your past life.

So then the Hindu believes that he is a spirit. Him the sword cannot pierce—him the fire cannot burn—him the water cannot melt—him the air cannot dry. The Hindu believes that **every soul is a circle whose circumference is nowhere, but whose centre is located in the body, and that death means the change of this centre from body to body.** Nor is the soul bound by the conditions of matter. In its very essence it is free, unbounded, holy, pure, and perfect. But somehow or other it finds itself tied down to matter, and thinks of itself as matter.

Why should the free, perfect, and pure being be thus under the thraldom of matter, is the next question. How can the perfect soul be deluded into the belief that it is imperfect? We have been told that the Hindus shirk the question and say that no such question can be there. Some thinkers want to answer it by positing one or more quasi-perfect beings, and use big scientific names to fill up the gap.

But naming is not explaining. The question remains the same. How can the perfect become the quasi-perfect; how can the pure, the absolute, change even a microscopic particle of its nature? But the Hindu is sincere. He does not want to take shelter under sophistry. He is brave enough to face the question in a manly fashion; and his answer is: "I do not know. I do not know how the perfect being, the soul, came to think of itself as imperfect, as joined to and conditioned by matter." But the fact is a fact for all that. It is a fact in everybody's consciousness that one thinks of oneself as the body. The Hindu does not attempt to explain why one thinks one is the body. The answer that it is the will of God is no explanation. This is nothing more than what the Hindu says, "I do not know."

Well, then, the human soul is eternal and immortal, perfect and infinite, and death means only a change of centre from one body to another. **The present is determined by our past actions, and the future by the present. The soul will go on evolving up or reverting back from birth to birth and death to death.** But here is another question: Is man a tiny boat in a tempest, raised one moment on the foamy crest of a billow and dashed down into a yawning chasm the next, rolling to and fro at the mercy of good and bad actions—a powerless, helpless wreck in an ever-raging, ever-rushing, uncompromising current of cause and effect; a little moth placed under the wheel of causation which rolls on crushing everything in its way and waits not for the widow's tears or the orphan's cry?

The heart sinks at the idea, yet this is the law of Nature. Is there no hope? Is there no escape?—was the cry that went up from the bottom of the heart of despair. It reached the throne of mercy, and words of hope and consolation came down and inspired a Vedic sage, and he stood up before the world and in trumpet voice proclaimed the glad tidings: "Hear, ye children of immortal bliss! even ye that reside in higher spheres! I have found the Ancient One who is beyond all darkness, all delusion: knowing Him alone you shall be saved from death over again."

"Children of immortal bliss"—what a sweet, what a hopeful name! Allow me to call you, brethren, by that sweet name—heirs of immortal bliss—yea, the Hindu refuses to call you sinners. **Ye are the Children of God, the sharers of immortal bliss, holy and perfect beings. Ye divinities on earth—sinners! It is a sin to call a man so; it is a standing libel on human nature. Come up, O lions, and shake off the delusion that you are sheep; you are souls immortal, spirits free, blest and eternal; ye are not matter, ye are not bodies; matter is your servant, not you the servant of matter.**

Thus it is that the Vedas proclaim not a dreadful combination of unforgiving laws, not an endless prison of cause and effect, but that at the head of all these laws, in and through every particle of matter and force, stands One "by whose command the wind blows, the fire burns, the clouds rain, and death stalks upon the earth."

And what is His nature? He is everywhere, the pure and formless One, the Almighty and the All-merciful. "Thou art our father, Thou art our mother, Thou art our beloved friend, Thou art the source of all strength; give us strength. Thou art He that beareth the burdens of the universe; help me bear the little burden of this life." Thus sang the Rishis of the Vedas. And how to worship Him? Through love. "He is to be worshipped as the one beloved, dearer than everything in this and the next life."

This is the doctrine of love declared in the Vedas, and let us see how it is fully developed and taught by Krishna, whom the Hindus believe to have been God incarnate on earth.

He taught that a man ought to live in this world like a lotus leaf, which grows in water but is never moistened by water; so a man ought to live in the world—his heart to God and his hands to work.

It is good to love God for hope of reward in this or the next world, but it is better to love God for love's sake, and the prayer goes: "Lord, I do not want wealth, nor children, nor learning. If it be Thy will, I shall go from birth to birth, but grant me this, that I may love Thee without the hope of reward—love unselfishly for love's sake." One of the disciples of Krishna, the then Emperor of India, was driven from his kingdom by his enemies and had to take shelter with his queen in a forest in the Himalayas, and there one day the queen asked him, how it was that he, the most virtuous of men, should suffer so much misery. Yudhishthira answered, "Behold, my queen, the Himalayas, how grand and beautiful they are; I love them. They do not give me anything, but my nature is to love the grand, the beautiful, therefore I love them. Similarly, I love the Lord. He is the source of all beauty, of all sublimity. He is the only object to be loved; my nature is to love Him, and therefore I love. I do not pray for anything; I do not ask for anything. Let Him place me wherever He likes. I must love Him for love's sake. I cannot trade in love."

The Vedas teach that the soul is divine, only held in the bondage of matter; perfection will be reached when this bond will burst, and the word they use for it is, therefore, Mukti—freedom, freedom from the bonds of imperfection, freedom from death and misery.

And this bondage can only fall off through the mercy of God, and this mercy comes on the pure. So purity is the condition of His mercy. How does that mercy act? He reveals Himself to the pure heart; the pure and the stainless see God, yea, even in this life; then and then only all the crookedness af the heart is made straight. Then all doubt ceases. He is no more the freak of a terrible law of causatian. This is the very *centre,* the very vital conception of Hinduism. The Hindu does not want to live upon words and theories. If there are existences beyond the ordinary sensuous existence, he wants to come face to face with them. If there is a soul in him which is not matter, if there is an all-merciful universal Soul, he will go to Him direct. He must see Him, and that alone can destroy all doubts. So the best proof a Hindu sage gives about the soul, about God, is: "I have seen the soul; I have seen God." And that is the only condition of perfection. **The Hindu religion does not consist in struggles and attempts to believe a certain doctrine or dogma, but in realising—not in believing, but in being and becoming.**

Thus the whole object of their system is by constant struggle to become perfect, to become divine, to reach God and see God, and thus reaching God, seeing God, becoming perfect even as the Father in Heaven is perfect, constitutes the religion of the Hindus.

And what becomes of a man when he attains perfection? He lives a life of bliss infinite. He enjoys infinite and perfect bliss, having obtained the only thing in which man ought to have pleasure, namely God, and enjoys the bliss with God.

So far all the Hindus are agreed. This is the common religion of all the sects of India; but then, perfection is absolute, and the absolute cannot be two or three. It cannot have any qualities. It cannot be an individual. And so when a soul becomes perfect and absolute, it must become one with Brahman, and it would only realise the Lord as the perfection, the reality, of its own nature and existence, the existence absolute, knowledge absolute and bliss absolute. We have often and often read this called the losing of individuality and becoming a stock or a stone.

"He jests at scars that never felt a wound."

I tell you it is nothing of the kind. If it is happiness to enjoy the consciousness of this small body, it must be greater happiness to enjoy the consciousness of two bodies, the measure of happiness increasing with the consciousness of an increasing number of bodies, the aim, the ultimate of happiness being reached when it would become a universal consciousness.

Therefore, to gain this infinite universal individuality, this miserable little prison-individuality must go. Then alone can death cease when I am one with life, then alone can misery cease when I am one with happiness itself, then alone can all errors cease when I am one with knowledge itself; and this is the necessary scientific conclusion. Science has proved to me that physical individuality is a delusion, that really my body is one little continuously changing body in an unbroken ocean of matter; and Advaita (unity) is the necessary conclusion with my other counterpart, soul.

Science is nothing but the finding of unity. As soon as science would reach perfect unity, it would stop from further progress, because it would reach the goal. Thus Chemistry could not progress farther when it would discover one element out of which all others could be made. Physics would stop when it would be able to fulfil its services in discovering one energy of which all the others are but manifestations, and **the science of religion become perfect when it would discover Him who is the one life in a universe of death,** Him who is the constant basis of an ever-changing world. One who is the only Soul of which all souls are but delusive manifestations. Thus is it, through multiplicity and duality, that the ultimate unity is reached. Religion can go no farther. This is the goal of all science.

All science is bound to come to this conclusion in the long run. **Manifestation, and not creation, is the word of science today, and the Hindu is only glad that what he has been cherishing in his bosom for ages is going to be taught in more forcible language,** and with further light from the latest conclusions of science.

•

Descend we now from the aspirations of philosophy to the religion of the ignorant. At the very outset, I may tell you **that there is no polytheism in India. In every temple, if one stands by and listens, one will find the worshippers applying all the**

attributes of God, including omnipresence, to the images. It is not polytheism, nor would the name henotheism explain the situation. **"The rose called by any other name would smell as sweet." Names are not explanations.**

I remember, as a boy, hearing a Christian missionary preach to a crowd in India. Among other sweet things he was telling them was that if he gave a blow to their idol with his stick, what could it do? One of his hearers sharply answered, "If I abuse your God, what can He do?" "You would be punished," said the preacher, "when you die." "So my idol will punish you when you die," retorted the Hindu.

The tree is known by its fruits. When I have seen amongst them that are called idolaters, men, the like of whom in morality and spirituality and love I have never seen anywhere, I stop and ask myself, "Can sin beget holiness?"

Superstition is a great enemy of man, but bigotry is worse. Why does a Christian go to church? Why is the cross holy? Why is the face turned toward the sky in prayer? Why are there so many images in the Catholic Church? Why are there so many images in the minds of Protestants when they pray? **My brethren, we can no more think about anything without a mental image than we can live without breathing. By the law of association, the material image calls up the mental idea and *vice versa*. This is why the Hindu uses an external symbol when he worships.** He will tell you, it helps to keep his mind fixed on the Being to whom he prays. He knows as well as you do that the image is not God, is not omnipresent. After all, how much does omnipresence mean to almost the whole world? It stands merely as a word, a symbol. Has God superficial area? If not, when we repeat that word "omnipresent", we think of the extended sky or of space, that is all.

As we find that somehow or other, by the laws of our mental constitution, we have to associate our ideas of infinity with the image of the blue sky, or of the sea, so we naturally connect our idea of holiness with the image of a church, a mosque, or a cross.

The Hindus have associated the idea of holiness, purity, truth, omnipresence, and such other ideas with different images and forms. But with this difference that while some people devote their whole lives to their idol of a church and never rise higher, because with them religion means an intellectual assent to certain doctrines and doing good to their fellows, **the whole religion of the Hindu is centred in realisation. Man is to become divine by realising the divine.** Idols or temples or churches or books are only the supports, the helps, of his spiritual childhood, but on and on he must progress.

He must not stop anywhere. *"External worship, material worship,"* say the scriptures, *"is the lowest stage, struggling to rise high, mental prayer is the next stage, but the highest stage is when the Lord has been realised."* Mark, the same earnest man who is kneeling before the idol, tells you, *"Him the sun cannot express, nor the moon, nor the stars, the lightning cannot express Him, nor what we speak of* as *fire; through Him they shine."* **But he does not abuse anyone's idol or call its worship sin.** He recognises in it a necessary stage of life. *"The child is father of the man."* Would it be right for an old man to say that childhood is a sin or youth a sin?

If a man can realise his divine nature with the help of an image, would it be right to call that a sin? Nor even when he has passed that stage, should he call it an error. To the Hindu, man is not travelling from error to truth, but from truth to truth, from lower to higher truth. To him all the religions, from the lowest fetishism to the highest absolutism, mean so many attempts of the human soul to grasp and realise the Infinite, each determined by the conditions of its birth and association, and each of these marks a stage of progress; and every soul is a young eagle soaring higher and higher, gathering more and more strength, till it reaches the Glorious Sun.

Unity in variety is the plan of nature, and the Hindu has recognised it. Every other religion lays down certain fixed dogmas, and tries to force society to adopt them. It places before society only one coat which must fit Jack and John and Henry,

all alike. If it does not fit John or Henry, he must go without a coat to cover his body. The Hindus have discovered that the absolute can only be realised, or thought of, or stated, through the relative, and the images, crosses, and crescents are simply so many symbols—so many pegs to hang the spiritual ideas on. It is not that this help is necessary for every one, but those that do not need it have no right to say that it is wrong. Nor is it compulsory in Hinduism.

One thing I must tell you. **Idolatry in India does not mean anything horrible. It is not the mother of harlots. On the other hand, it is the attempt of undeveloped minds to grasp high spiritual truths.** The Hindus have their faults, they sometimes have their exceptions; but mark this, they are always for punishing their own bodies, and never for cutting the throats of their neighbours. **If the Hindu fanatic burns himself on the pyre, he never lights the fire of Inquisition. And even this cannot be laid at the door of his religion any more than the burning of witches can be laid at the door of Christianity.**

To the Hindu, then, the whole world of religions is only a travelling, a coming up, of different men and women, through various conditions and circumstances, to the same goal. Every religion is only evolving a God out of the material man, and the same God is the inspirer of all of them. Why, then, are there so many contradictions? They are only apparent, says the Hindu. The contradictions come from the same truth adapting itself to the varying circumstances of different natures.

It is the same light coming through glasses of different colours. And these little variations are necessary for purposes of adaptation. But in the heart of everything the same truth reigns. The Lord has declared to the Hindu in His incarnation as Krishna, *"I am in every religion as the thread through a string of pearls. Wherever thou seest extraordinary holiness and extraordinary power raising and purifying humanity, know thou that I am there."* And what has been the result? **I challenge the world to find, throughout the whole system of Sanskrit philosophy, any such**

expression as that the Hindu alone will be saved and not others. Says Vyasa, *"We find perfect men even beyond the pale of our caste and creed."* One thing more. How, then, can the Hindu, whose whole fabric of thought centres in God, believe in Buddhism which is agnostic, or in Jainism which is atheistic?

The Buddhists or the Jains do not depend upon God; but the whole force of their religion is directed to the great central truth in every religion, to evolve a God out of man. They have not seen the Father, but they have seen the Son. And he that hath seen the Son hath seen the Father also.

This, brethren, is a short sketch of the religious ideas of the Hindus. The Hindu may have failed to carry out all his plans, but if there is ever to be a universal religion, i**t must be one which will have no location in place or time; which will be infinite like the God it will preach, and whose sun will shine upon the followers of Krishna and of Christ, on saints and sinners alike; which will not be Brahminic or Buddhistic, Christian or Mohammedan, but the sum total of all these, and still have infinite space for development;** which in its catholicity will embrace in its infinite arms, and find a place for every human being, from the lowest grovelling savage not far removed from the brute, to the highest man towering by the virtues of his head and heart almost above humanity, making society stand in awe of him and doubt his human nature. It will be a religion which will have no place for persecution or intolerance in its polity, which will recognise divinity in every man and woman, and whose whole scope, whose whole force, will be created in aiding humanity to realise its own true, divine nature.

Offer such a religion, and all the nations will follow you. Asoka's council was a council of the Buddhist faith. Akbar's, though more to the purpose, was only a parlour-meeting. **It was reserved for America to proclaim to all quarters of the globe that the Lord is in every religion.**

May He who is the Brahman of the Hindus, the Ahura-Mazda of the Zoroastrians, the Buddha of the Buddhists, the Jehovah of the Jews, the Father in Heaven of the Christians, give strength to you to carry out your noble idea! The star arose in the East; it travelled steadily towards the West, sometimes dimmed and sometimes effulgent, till it made a circuit of the world; and now it is again rising on the very horizon of the East, the borders of the Sanpo, a thousandfold more effulgent than it ever was before.

Hail, Columbia, motherland of liberty! It has been given to thee, who never dipped her hand in her neighbour's blood, who never found out that the shortest way of becoming rich was by robbing one's neighbours, it has been given to thee to march at the vanguard of civilisation with the flag af harmony.

Religion not the Crying Need of India

20th September, 1893

Christians must always be ready for good criticism, and I hardly think that you will mind if I make a little criticism. You Christians, who are so fond of sending out missionaries to save the soul of the heathen—why do you not try to save their bodies from starvation? In India, during the terrible famines, thousands died from hunger, yet you Christians did nothing. You erect churches all through India, but the crying evil in the East is not religion—they have religion enough—but it is bread that the suffering millions of burning India cry out for with parched throats. They ask us for bread, but we give them stone.

It is an insult to a starving people to offer them religion; it is an insult to a starving man to teach him metaphysics. In India a priest that preached for money would lose caste and be spat upon by the people. I can be here to seek aid for my impoverished people, and I fully realised how difficult it was to get help for heathens from Christians in a Christian land.

Buddhism, the Fulfilment of Hindusim

26th September, 1893

I am not a Buddhist, as you have heard, and yet I am. If China, or Japan, or Ceylon follow the teachings of the Great Master, India worships him as God incarnate on earth. You have just now heard that I am going to criticise Buddhism, but by that I wish you to understand only this. Far be it from me to criticise him whom I worship as God incarnate on earth. But our views about Buddha are that he was not understood properly by his disciples. The relation between Hinduism and Hinduism, I mean the religion of the Vedas and what is called Buddhism at the present day is nearly the same as between Judaism and Christianity.

Jesus Christ was a Jew, and Shakya Muni was a Hindu. The Jews rejected Jesus Christ, nay, crucified him, and the Hindus have accepted Shakya Muni as God and worship him. But the real difference that we Hindus want to show between modern Buddhism and what we should understand as the teachings of Lord Buddha lies principally in this: Shakya Muni came to preach nothing new. He also, like Jesus, came to fulfil and not to destroy. Only, in the case of Jesus, it was the old people, the Jews, who did not understand him, while in the case of Buddha, it was his own followers who did not realise the import of his teachings. As the Jew did not understand the fulfilment of the Old Testament, so the Buddhist did not understand the fulfilment of the truths of the Hindu religion. Again, I repeat,

Shakya Muni came not to destroy, but he was the fulfilment, the logical conclusion, the logical development of the religion of the Hindus.

The religion of the Hindus is divided into two parts: the ceremonial and the spiritual. The spiritual portion is specially studied by the monks. In that there is no caste. A man from the highest caste and a man from the lowest may become a monk in India, and the two castes become equal. In religion there is no caste; caste is simply a social institution. Shakya Muni himself was a monk, and it was his glory that he had the large-heartedness to bring out the truths from the hidden Vedas and threw them to broadcast all over the world. **He was the first being in the world who brought missionarising into practice—nay, he was the first to conceive the idea of proselytising.**

The great glory of the Master lay in his wonderful sympathy for everybody, especially for the ignorant and the poor. Some of his disciples were Brahmins. When Buddha was teaching, Sanskrit was no more the spoken language in India. It was then only in the books of the learned. Some of Buddha's Brahmin disciples wanted to translate his teachings into Sanskrit, but he distinctly told them, "I am for the poor, for the people; let me speak in the tongue of the people." And so to this day the great bulk of his teachings are in the vernacular of that day in India.

Whatever may be the position of philosophy, whatever may be the position of metaphysics, so long as there is such a thing as death in the world, so long as there is such a thing as weakness in the human heart, so long as there is a cry going out of the heart of man in his very weakness, there shall be a faith in God.

On the philosophic side the disciples of the Great Master dashed themselves against the eternal rocks of the Vedas and could not crush them, and on the other side, they took away from the nation that eternal God to which every one, man or woman, clings so fondly. And the result was that Buddhism had to die a natural death in India. At the present day there is not one who calls oneself a Buddhist in India, the land of its birth.

But at the same time, Brahminism lost something—that reforming zeal, that wonderful sympathy and charity for everybody, that wonderful leaven which Buddhism had brought to the masses and which had rendered Indian society so great that a Greek historian who wrote about India of that time was led to say that no Hindu was known to tell an untruth and no Hindu woman was known to be unchaste.

Hinduism cannot live without Buddhism, nor Buddhism without Hinduism. Then realise what the separation has shown to us, that **the Buddhists cannot stand without the brain and philosophy of the Brahmins, nor the Brahmin without the heart of the Buddhist. This separation between the Buddhists and the Brahmins is the cause of the downfall of India.** That is why India is populated by three hundred millions of beggars, and that is why India has been the slave of conquerors for the last thousand years. Let us then join the wonderful intellect of the Brahmins with the heart, the noble soul, the wonderful humanising power of the Great Master.

Address at the Final Session

27th September, 1893

The World's Parliament of Religions has become an accomplished fact, and the merciful Father has helped those who laboured to bring it into existence, and crowned with success their most unselfish labour.

My thanks to those noble souls whose large hearts and love of truth first dreamed this wonderful dream and then realised it. My thanks to the shower of liberal sentiments that has overflowed this platform. My thanks to this enlightened audience for their uniform kindness to me and for their appreciation of every thought that tends to smooth the friction of religions. A few jarring notes were heard from time to time in this harmony. My special thanks to them, for they have, by their striking contrast, made general harmony the sweeter.

Much has been said of the common ground of religious unity. I am not going just now to venture my own theory. But if anyone here hopes that this unity will come by the triumph of anyone of the religions and the destruction of the others, to him I say, "Brother, yours is an impossible hope." Do I wish that the Christian would become Hindu? God forbid. Do I wish that the Hindu or Buddhist would become Christian? God forbid.

The seed is put in the ground, and earth and air and water are placed around it. Does the seed become the earth, or the air, or the water? No. It becomes a plant, it develops after the law of its own growth, assimilates the air, the earth, and the water, converts them into plant substance, and grows into a plant.

Similar is the case with religion. The Christian is not to become a Hindu or a Buddhist, nor a Hindu or a Buddhist to become a Christian. But each must assimilate the spirit of the others and yet preserve his individuality and grow according to his own law of growth.

If the Parliament of Religions has shown anything to the world it is this: It has proved to the world that holiness, purity and charity are not the exclusive possessions of any church in the world, and that every system has produced men and women of the most exalted character. In the face of this evidence, if anybody dreams of the exclusive survival of his own religion and the destruction of the others, I pity him from the bottom of my heart, and point out to him that **upon the banner of every religion will soon be written, in spite of resistance: "Help and not Fight," "Assimilation and not Destruction," "Harmony and Peace and not Dissension."**

❑❑❑

In Chicago, 1893

Reports in American Newspapers

An Orator by Divine Right

Presented here are the reports that appeared in the first year, 1893, only. Divided into two parts, the first one gives the reports that appeared during and after the Parliament meeting, and in the second, some of those that appeared before the Parliament. No changes have been made in the originals, the wrong spellings, punctuation, etc., have all been retained. Of course, the stress expressed by printing portions in bold letters is by the editor, to underline their significance.

Please note the various spellings of the Swami's name, a difficult one indeed used in the papers, and make sure that these do not confuse you.

1

After the Parliament

-.-

RESPONSE TO WELCOME

[Editorial synthesis of four Chicago newspaper reports from: *Herald, Inter Ocean, Tribune*, and *Record*, September 11, 1893]

[Sisters and Brothers of America,]

It fills my heart with joy unspeakable to rise in response to the grand words of welcome given to us by you. I thank you in the name of the most ancient order of monks the world has ever seen, of which Gautama was only a member. I thank you in the name of the Mother of religions, of which Buddhism and Jainism are but branches; and I thank you, finally, in the name of the millions and millions of Hindoo people of all castes and sects. My thanks also to some of the speakers on the platform who have told you that these different men from far-off nations will bear to the different lands the idea of toleration which they may see here. My thanks to them for this idea.

I am proud to belong to a religion which has taught the world both tolerance and universal acceptance. We believe not only in universal tolerance but we accept all religions to be true. I am proud to tell you that I belong to a religion in whose sacred language, the Sanskrit, the word exclusion is untranslatable. (**Applause**) I am proud to belong to a nation which has sheltered the persecuted and the refugees of all religions and all nations of the earth. I am proud to tell you that we have gathered in our bosom the purest remnant of the Israelites, a remnant of which came to southern India and took refuge with us in the very years in which their holy temple was shattered to pieces by Roman tyranny. I am proud to belong to the religion which has sheltered and is still fostering the remnant of the grand Zoroastrian nation.

I will quote to you, brothers, a few lines from a hymn which every Hindoo child repeats every day. I feel that the very spirit of this hymn, which I remember to have repeated from my earliest boyhood, which is every day repeated by millions and millions of men in India, has at last come to be realized. "As the different streams, having their sources in different places, all mingle their water in the sea; O Lord, so the different paths which men take through different tendencies, various though they appear, crooked or straight, all lead to Thee."

The present convention, which is one of the most august assemblies ever held, is in itself an indication, a declaration to the world of the wonderful doctrine preached in the *Gita:* "Whosoever comes to Me, through whatsoever form I reach him, all are struggling through paths that in the end always lead to me." **Sectarianism, bigotry and its horrible descendant fanaticism, have possessed long this beautiful earth. It has filled the earth with violence, drenched it often and often with human gore, destroyed civilization and sent whole nations into despair. But its time has come, and I fervently believe that the bell that tolled this morning in honor of the representatives of the different religions of the earth, in this parliament assembled, is the death-knell to all fanaticism** (**Applause**), that it is the death-knell to all persecution with the sword or the pen, and to all uncharitable feelings between brethren wending their way to the same goal, but through different ways.

Parlor Talk

[*Chicago Record*, September 11, 1893]

Four leaders of religious thought were sitting in Dr. Barrow's [Barrows's] parlor—the Jain, George Condin [Candlin], the missionary who has passed sixteen years in China, Swami Vivekananda, the learned Brahman Hindoo, and Dr. John H. Barrows, the Chicago Presbyterian. These four talked as if they were brothers of one faith.

The Hindoo is of smooth countenance. His rather fleshy face is bright and intelligent. He wears an orange turban and a robe of the same color. **His English is very good**. "I have no home," said he.

"I travel about from one college to another in India, lecturing to the students. Before starting for America I had been for some time in Madras. Since arriving in this country I have been treated with utmost courtesy and kindness. It is very gratifying to us to be recognized in this Parliament, which may have such an important bearing on the religious history of the world. We expect to learn and take back some great truths to our 15,000,000 faithful Brahmins."

Religion not the Crying Need of India

[*Chicago Inter Ocean*, September 21, 1893]

[A verbatim transcript of the address, delivered at the Parliament of Religions, September 20, 1893]

SWAMI VIVEKANANDA

At the close of the reading of Mr. Headland's paper on "Religion in Peking" Dr. Momerie announced that the other speakers bulletined for the evening had failed to appear. It was but 9 o'clock, and the main auditorium and galleries were well filled. There was an outburst of applause as they caught sight of the Hindoo monk, Vivekananda, sitting in his orange robe and scarlet turban upon the platform.

This popular Hindoo responded to the generous applause by saying that he did not come to speak tonight. He took occasion, however, to criticise many of the statements made in the paper by Mr. Headland. **Referring to the poverty which prevails in China, he said that the missionaries would do better to work in appeasing hunger than in endeavoring to persuade the Chinese to renounce their faith of centuries and embrace Christianity at [as] the price of food.** And then the Hindoo stepped back on the platform and whispered to Bishop Keane, of the Catholic church, a moment.

He then resumed his address by saying that Bishop Keane had told him that Americans would not be offended at honest criticism. He said he had heard of all the terrible things and horrible conditions which prevail in China but he had not heard that any asylums had been erected by Christians for remedying all these difficulties. He said:

Christian brethren of America, you are so fond of sending out missionaries to save the souls of heathens. I ask you what have you done and are doing to save their bodies from starvation? (**Applause**). In India, there are 300,000,000 men and women living on an average of a little more than 50 cents a month. I have seen them living for years upon wild flowers. Whenever there was a little famine hundreds of thousands died of starvation. **Christian missionaries come and offer life but only on condition that the Hindoos become Christians, abandoning the faith of their fathers and forefathers.** Is it right? There are hundreds of asylums, but if the Mohammedans or the Hindoos go there they would be kicked out. There are thousands of asylums erected by Hindoos where anybody would be received. There are hundreds of churches that have been erected with the assistance of the Hindoos, but no Hindoo temples for which a Christian has given a penny.

What the East Needs

Brethren of America, the crying evil of the East is not religion. We have more than enough religion; what they want is bread, but they are given a stone. (**Applause**). It is an insult to a suffering man dying of hunger to preach to him metaphysics. Therefore, if you wish to illustrate the meaning of "brotherhood" treat the Hindoo more kindly, even though he be a Hindoo and is faithful to his religion. Send missionaries to them to teach them how better to earn a better piece of bread and not to teach them metaphysical nonsense. (**Great applause**).

And then the monk said he was in ill health today and wished to be excused. **But there were thunders of applause and cries of "Go on" and Mr. Vivekananda continued.**

The paper just read says something about the miserable and ignorant priest. The same may be said of India. I am one of those monks who have been described as beggarly. That is the pride of my life. (**Applause**). I am proud in that sense to be Christ-like. I eat what I have today and think not of tomorrow. "Behold the lilies of the field; they toil not, neither do they spin." The Hindoo carries that out literally. Many gentlemen present in Chicago sitting on this platform can testify that for the last twelve years I never knew whence my next meal was coming. I am proud to be a beggar for the sake of the Lord. The idea in the east is [that] to preach or teach anything for the sake of money is low and voltage, but to teach the name of the Lord for pay is such a degradation as would cause the priest to lose caste and be spat upon. There is one suggestion in the paper that is true: **If the priests of China and India were organized there is an enormous amount of potential energy which could be used for regeneration of society and humanity.** I endeavored to organize it in India, but failed for lack of money. It may be I shall get the help I want in America.

But we know it is very hard for a heathen to get any help from "Christian people". (**Great applause**). I have heard so much of this land of freedom, of liberty and freedom of thought that I am not discouraged. I thank you, ladies and gentlemen.

And then the popular visitor bowed gracefully and sought to retire with a graceful smile, **but the audience cried to him to proceed.** Mr. Vivekananda, fairly bubbling with an expression of good nature, then explained the Hindoo theory of [re]incarnation. At the close of the address Dr. Momerie [a delegate from England] said that he now understood why the newspapers had well called this parliament an approach to the millennium. . . .

The Chicago Letter

[*New York Critic*, November 11, 1893]

. . . It was an outgrowth of the Parliament of Religions, which opened our eyes to the fact that the philosophy of the ancient creeds contains much beauty for the moderns. When we had once clearly perceived this, our interest in their exponents quickened, and with characteristic eagerness we set out in pursuit of knowledge. The most available means of obtaining it, after the close of the Parliament, was through the addresses and lectures of Suami Vivekananda, who is still in this city. His original purpose in coming to this country was to interest Americans in the starting of new industries among the Hindoos, but he has abandoned this for the present, because he finds that, as "the Americans are the most charitable people in the world," every man with a purpose comes here for assistance in carrying it out. When asked about the relative condition of the poor here and in India, he replied that your poor would be princes there, and that he had been taken through the worst quarter of the city only to find it, from the standpoint of his knowledge, comfortable and even pleasant.

A Brahmin of the Brahmins, Vivekananda gave up his rank to join the brotherhood of monks, where all pride of caste is voluntarily relinquished. And yet he bears the mark of race upon his person. **His culture, his eloquence, and his fascinating personality have given us a new idea of Hindoo civilization. He is an interesting figure, his fine, intelligent, mobile face in its setting of yellows, and his deep, musical voice prepossessing one at once in his favor. So it is not strange that he has been taken up by the literary clubs, has preached and lectured in churches, until the life of Buddha and the doctrines of his faith have grown familiar to us. He speaks without notes, presenting his facts and his conclusions with the greatest art, the most convincing sincerity; and rising at times to a rich, inspiring eloquence.** As learned and cultivated, apparently, as the most accomplished Jesuit, he has also something Jesuitical in the character of his mind; but **though the little sarcasms thrown into his discourses are as keen as a rapier, they are so delicate as to be lost on many of his hearers.** Nevertheless his courtesy is unfailing, for these thrusts are never pointed so directly at our customs as to be rude. At present he contents himself with enlightening us in regard to his religion and the words of its philosophers. He looks forward to the time when we shall pass beyond idolatry—now necessary in his opinion to the ignorant classes,—beyond worship, even, to a knowledge of the presence of God in nature, of the divinity and responsibility of man. "Work out your own salvation," he says with the dying Buddha; "I cannot help you. No man can help you. Help yourself."

Religions of India

Viva Kananda, the Hindoo Orator Delivers an Interesting Lecture

[*Daily Cardinal*, University of Wisconsin at Madison, November 21, 1893]

A crowded house greeted Viva Kananda at the Congregational Church last evening. The speaker was attired in native costume, which consisted of a cream turban, with yellow gown and cardinal sash.

The first part of the lecture was devoted to illustrating the many resemblances of Sanscrit, the language of the Hindoos, to that of English. They have no word in their language which means salvation; to them it is freedom from bondage. They believe that man's real nature is perfect, and that cause and effect controls all except God. Religion was aptly illustrated by the story of the blind men who each felt of a portion of a huge elephant, and each thought the animal like the particular part he felt of it; so with religion each of the various sects have a part of the whole truth, while truth itself is infinite and no man can say "I have seen it all."

The Hindoo belief was shown to be one of the most charitable of beliefs. **Persecution is something unknown in India**; there is no such word in their language. **The lecturer challenged the world to show an instance in Hindoo progress, of a Christian missionary being persecuted.** A Greek historian, writing of them said: "No Hindoo man is dishonest, no Hindoo woman unchaste."

Viva Kananda came to this country from India in the interest of the world's congress of religions, and his lecture last evening on the "Religions of India," was an inspiration to all who heard him. **He has a pleasant, clear-cut, dusky face, and a decidedly impressive manner and bearing. His voice is low and pleasant with a secret something which rivets your attention at the start.**

All Religions are True, Such is the Message Brought from India

BY A HINDU MONK

[*Daily Iowa Capitol*, November 28, 1893]

Swami Vivekananda Tells of Ancient Faith, Speaks Again Tonight

It was a rare as well as an odd treat which the people of Des Moines enjoyed last evening at the Central Church of Christ. A monk, of the ancient faith of Brahma, made a happy presentation of that faith, not so much of its peculiarities as of its underlying principles. The audience was a good sized one, perhaps 500 or 600 persons being present. The main floor being well filled and there were perhaps a couple of hundred in the gallery.

The speaker opened by saying that all religious systems were an attempt to answer the question What am I? This and the kindred ones, Whence Come I? and Whither Am I Going? are constantly recurring. Without following the speaker throughout the entire lecture, suffice it to say, that underlying the Hindu religion according to the speaker is the belief that "We are all divine." In each is a conscious spirit that survives the body and the mind and is a part of the absolute. **The speaker very ably defended religion against the attacks of science.** The latter can use only the five senses, and unless a thing can be proven to be by these senses [it] is disposed to doubt its existence. But does science know that there are only five senses? **The speaker contended for the existence of a supersensuous sense; through which man obtains revelations of spiritual truths.** The Hindu word for revelation is "Veda". Hence the "Vedas" are the revelations. These writings are not confined to those of the Hindus but include those of all peoples; because, said the speaker, all religions are true.

When "revelations" undertake to tell of material things they enter upon a domain which belongs to science and are not to be accepted. There was an ancient superstition that because Moses gave a revelation of the will of God, therefore everything Moses wrote must be true. There is a modern superstition that, because there are mistakes in the writings of Moses, therefore nothing Moses wrote is true. When Moses wrote the tables of the law he was inspired. When he told of the creation what he said was merely the speculations of Moses the Jew.

The speaker was not favorably impressed with the efforts to make Hindu converts—perverts he calls them—to Christianity, nor the converse. All religions being true, such

perversions serve no good end. The Hindu religion the speaker claimed is not disposed to antagonize any belief; it absorbs them. As for tolerating different beliefs, **the language of the Hindu has no word corresponding with the English word "intolerance".** That language had a word for religion and one for sect. The former embraced all beliefs. The conception of the latter the speaker illustrated by telling the story of the frog, who had no idea there was any world outside the well in which he had always lived.

The speaker urged his hearers to cultivate the divine within them and to discard the "nonsense" of sects.

The lecturer is an able, dignified and forcible speaker. His mastery of English is perfect, there being only the faintest indications of a foreign accent. The lecturer was followed with closest attention by the audience. After the lecture, the speaker consented to answer questions to a portion of the audience that remained for that purpose. In the course of the answers he said that the Hindus were altogether opposed to the destruction of the life of any animal. He admitted the worship of the sacred cow. He said further that **the Hindus had nothing answering to our church organizations. He was his own priest, bishop and pope. . . .**

A Message from India

Vive Kananda, the Famous Hindoo Monk and Scholar, Appears in Des Moines

[*Iowa State Register*, November 28, 1893]

A Young Man of Thirty Years and a Big, Active Brain and True Heart

The people of Des Moines had a glimpse of Oriental life and thought at its best yesterday, from the lips of the famous Hindoo monk, Swami Vive Kananda. A central figure in the great Parliament of Religions at Chicago this summer, **where he coped with some of the greatest minds of the country with honor to**

himself and his people, he gave those who heard him, and especially those who met him at Dr. Breeden's, something new to think about. It was a message from over the sea, from another people of wholly different surroundings, training, customs and traditions, but as the monk says, the basic principles are the same in all religions. **It is his doctrine that there is good in all religions and he preaches it with great power. . . .**

Yesterday afternoon he met a large number of the brightest women in Des Moines, members of the various literary clubs, at the invitation of Mrs. H. O. Breeden, at her home, 1318 Woodland Avenue, and he talked to them for two or three hours about his religion, his view of Christianity, in which he heartily concurs, and of the manners and customs of his people. The thing which Vive Kananda most strongly insists upon is that the Hindoo religion is not to be blamed for all that is bad in India any more than Christianity is to be blamed for all that is bad in America. And he insists that it is absurd to give Christianity credit for all the marvelous undertakings and achievements of the people who cherish it. He joins in the praise of the sublime things in the bible, but says that when Moses undertook to speak of the creation of the world, he was merely Moses, the Jew and nothing more.

This view from the other side, and a sympathetic side at that, is a most helpful and instructive and intensely interesting one. **Vive Kananda uses the purest English, for he was well educated in the English university, Calcutta.**

He praises the American women most enthusiastically.

I do not know what would have become of me if it had not been for your women, he said to a reporter for *The Register* last night.

They took me up and took care of me and made all necessary arrangements for me. They are the best women in the world. They have been so kind to me, [the Swami said] with a grateful smile.

Reincarnation

[*Daily Iowa Capitol*, November 29, 1893]

Swami Vivekananda last night talked of reincarnation. It is based, he contended, on the fact that there never has been a new creation; that creation has existed coevally with God from all eternity. Departed souls find bodies to inhabit either better or worse than their former tenement, according as they made them fit for one or the other. The lecturer will speak again on Thanksgiving evening at the same place on the manners and customs of India.

An Intellectual Feast

[*Iowa State Register*, November 30, 1893]

The remarkable discussions started by the famous Hindu monk, Vive Kananda, were the topic of interest in intellectual circles yesterday. Especially so was his comment on the work of American missionaries in India, and his strong defense of his own people and morals and religion. His position is that the people of India do not need any more religion, but training in the practical things of life that will enable them to cope with English who have occupied India. Vive Kananda was the guest of Mr. F.W. Lehman and Mr. O.H. Perkins yesterday and in their company visited the state house, which he very much admired. He took a special interest in the portraits of the American Indians that he saw there. . . .

A Prayer Meeting

[*Des Moines Daily News*, November 30, 1893]

Vive Kananda attended a prayer meeting Wednesday evening and witnessed the baptism of two young women. The service impressed him very much. He said:

I see. The sentiment is ennobling and the ceremony beautiful. It is more impressive that the minister is honest, earnest and believes what he says.

On American Women

[*Daily Iowa Capitol*, November 30, 1893]

The now celebrated Hindu monk, Swami Vivekananda will lecture for the last time in Des Moines tonight. He will speak on "Life in India" ["Manners and Customs of India"] a most interesting theme. The renowned Hindu is a brilliant man about 30 years old. He says American women are lovely, but American men are entirely too practical.

On the Brahmo Samaj

[*Iowa State Register*, December 1, 1893]

Before he left the city [Des Moines, Iowa], Vive Kananda took occasion to say a warm word of praise for the Bramo Somaj the work it is doing in India, especially for the women, and of its representative in this country. The visit of Vive Kananda, **stirring as it did the intellectual centers of the city of their depths and starting a lively religious discussion,** prepared the way for the present visitor [Nagarkar] from the Orient and heightened public interest in whatever he might have to say.

A Witty Hindu

[*Minneapolis Journal*, December 15, 1893]

Swami Vivekananda

Entertains Another Large Audience

A large number of people assembled at the Unitarian Church last evening for the purpose of listening to Swami Vivekananda of India. The customs and manners of the people of that country were described, and **during his lecture the Brahmin took occasion to show up some of the rough points of America. He is of the humorist order and his quick replies and witty sallies rarely failed to evoke applause.** He would not admit that his people were wrong in everything, but there were a great many things peculiar to India which the Americans did not approve of and yet which might be all right. He had never seen husband and wife go before a magistrate to tell their troubles. They grew up with the idea that they were to be married and they loved each other as brothers and sisters.

He described the customs of his country, the temples, the art of the juggler and all of the other peculiarities of oriental countries in a manner that was charming. Following the address a number of questions were asked by persons in the audience.

The Manners and Customs of India

[*Minneapolis Tribune*, December 15, 1893]

Swami Vive Kananda, the Brahmin priest, was greeted by a packed house last evening at the First Unitarian Church, when he appeared before his second Minneapolis audience. **Vive Kananda is a bright, quick witted talker, ready at all points to attack or defend, and inserts a humor into his speeches that is not lost upon his auditors.** He spoke last evening under the auspices of the Kappa Kappa Gammas of the University, and the audience embraced a large number of earnest thinking men and women, pleased to be enlightened upon the "Manners and Customs of India," which was his chosen subject.

Robed in his native garb, with his hands for the most part clasped behind his back, Kananda paces back and forth the narrow platform, talking as he paces, with long pauses between his sentences, as if willing that his words should sink into the deepest soil. His talk is not so weighty that the frivolous mind may not appreciate some of his sayings, but he also speaks a philosophy that carries gravest truth. He tells of the manners and customs of India, of the divided life between the male and female, of the reverence for and holiness of women, and again of their degeneracy; of the calm and peaceful life, that yet is not true life because it is not liberty; he speaks of the Mohammedans, who form one-fifth of the Indian population, and that 65,000,000 equal to the entire population of the United States. He describes the magnificence of the temples, the art of the jugglers, who are the gypsies of the Indian race, and he touches upon the superstitions of the people, of how they fill the water jars and stand them in the doorway before starting on a journey; he speaks of the metaphysical knowledge of the plowman, who yet only knows that he "pays taxes to the government"; he admits the reverence of the Hindu for the river Ganges, and his ever lingering wish that he shall die on its banks; **he tells all these things in a quiet, half supercilious voice that presently leads to some remark on the American way of doing things, and then his audience is in a ripple of laughter, and a tremor of clapping expresses amused acknowledgment of his sarcasm. . . .**

When someone at the close of his lecture asked him "What class of people are reached and converted by the missionaries?" he quickly replied, "You know as much about that, the American sees the reports, we never do," he has turned the query into a cause for smiling, and while the house regains its composure he paces quietly to and fro. The address was followed with the closest attention and was supplemented by several questions and answers among the audience, from whom he invited interrogation.

Hindus at the Fair

(*Boston Evening Transcript*, September 30, 1893)

Chicago, Sept. 23: There is a room at the left of the entrance to the Art Palace marked "No. I—keep out." To this the speakers at the Congress of Religions all repair sooner or later, either to talk with one another or with President Bonney, whose private office is in one corner of the apartment. The folding doors are jealously guarded from the general public, usually standing far enough apart to allow peeping in. Only delegates are supposed to penetrate the sacred precincts, but it is not impossible to obtain an "open sesame", and thus to enjoy a brief opportunity of closer relations with the distinguished guests than the platforms in the Hall of Columbus affords.

The most striking figure one meets in this anteroom is Swami Vivekananda, the Brahmin monk. He is a large, well-built man, with the superb carnage of the Hindustanis, his face clean-shaven, squarely moulded regular features, white teeth, and with well-chiselled lips that are usually parted in a

benevolent smile while he is conversing. His finely poised head is crowned with either a lemon colored or a red turban, and his cassock (not the technical name for this garment), belted in at the waist and falling below the knees, alternates in a bright orange and rich crimson. **He speaks excellent English and replied readily to any questions asked in sincerity.**

Along with his simplicity of manner there is a touch of personal reserve when speaking to ladies, which suggests his chosen vocation. When questioned about the laws of his order, he has said, "I can do as I please, I am independent. Sometimes I live in the Himalaya mountains, and sometimes in the streets of cities. I never know where I will get my next meal, I never keep money with me. I came here by subscription." Then looking round at one or two of his fellow-countrymen who chanced to be standing near, he added, "They will take care of me," giving the inference that his board bill in Chicago is attended to by others. When asked if he was wearing his usual monk's costume, he said, "This is a good dress; when I am home I am in rags, and I go barefooted. Do I believe in caste? **Caste is a social custom; religion has nothing to do with it;** all castes will associate with me."

It is quite apparent, however, from the deportment, the general appearance of Mr. Vivekananda that he was born among high castes—years of voluntary poverty and homeless wanderings have not robbed him of his birthright of gentleman; even his family name is unknown; he took that of Vivekananda in embracing a religious career and "Swami" is merely the title of reverend accorded to him. **He cannot be far along in the thirties, and looks as if made for this life and its fruition, as well as for meditation on the life beyond.** One cannot help wondering what could have been the turning point with him.

"Why should I marry," was his abrupt response to a comment on all he had renounced in becoming a monk, "when I see in every woman only the divine Mother? Why do I make all these sacrifices? To emancipate myself from earthly ties and attachments so that there will be no rebirth for me. When I die I want to become at once absorbed in the divine, one with God. I would be a Buddha."

Vivekananda does not mean by this that he is a Buddhist. No name or sect can label him. He is an outcome of the higher Brahminism, a product of the Hindu spirit, which is vast, dreamy, self-extinguishing, a Sanyasi or holy man.

He has some pamphlets that he distributes, relating to his master, Paramhansa Ramakrishna, a Hindu devotee, who so impressed his hearers and pupils that many of them became ascetics after his death. Mozoomdar also looked upon this saint as his master, but Mozoomdar works for holiness in the world, in it but not of it, as Jesus taught.

Vivekananda's address before the parliament was broad as the heavens above us, embracing the best in all religions, as the ultimate universal religion—charity to all mankind, good works for the love of God, not for fear of punishment or hope of reward. He is a great favorite at the parliament, from the grandeur of his sentiments and his appearance as well. If he merely crosses the platform he is applauded, and this marked approval of thousands he accepts in a childlike spirit of gratification, without a trace of conceit. It must be a strange experience too for this humble young Brahmin monk, this sudden transition from poverty and self-effacement to affluence and aggrandize-ment. When asked if he knew anything of those brothers in the Himalayas so firmly believed in by the Theosophists, he answered with the simple statement, "I have never met one of them," as much as to imply, "There may be such persons, but though I am at home in the Himalayas, I have yet to come across them."

At the Parliament of Religions

(*The Dubuque, Iowa Times*, September 29, 1893)

WORLD'S FAIR, Sept. 28. (Special)—The Parliament of Religions reached a point where sharp acerbities develop. The thin veil of courtesy was maintained, of course, but behind it was ill feeling. **Rev. Joseph Cook criticised the Hindoos sharply and was more sharply criticised in turn. He said that to speak of a universe that was not created is almost unpardonable nonsense, and the Asiatics retorted that a universe which had a beginning is a self-evident absurdity. Bishop J. P. Newman, firing at long range from the banks of the Ohio, declared that the orientals have insulted all the Christians of the United States by their misrepresentations of the missionaries, and the orientals, with their provokingly calm and supercilious smile, replied that this was simply the bishop's ignorance.**

Buddhist Philosophy

In response to the question direct, three learned Buddhists gave us in remarkably plain and beautiful language their bedrock belief about God, man and matter.

[Following this is a summary of Dharmapala's paper on "The World's Debt to Buddha", which he prefaced, as we learn from another source, by singing a Singhalese song of benediction. The article then continues:]

His [Dharmapala's] peroration was as pretty a thing as a Chicago audience ever heard. Demosthenes never exceeded it.

Cantankerous Remarks

Swami Vivekananda, the Hindoo monk, was not so fortunate. He was out of humor, or soon became so, apparently. He wore an orange robe and a pale yellow turban and **dashed at once into a savage attack on Christian nations in these words: "We who have come from the east have sat here day after day and have been told in a patronising way that we ought to accept Christianity because Christian nations are the most prosperous. We look about us and we see England the most prosperous Christian nation in the world, with her foot on the neck of 250,000,000 Asiatics. We look back into history and see that the prosperity of Christian Europe began with Spain. Spain's**

prosperity began with the invasion of Mexico. Christianity wins its prosperity by cutting the throats of its fellow men. At such a price the Hindoo will not have prosperity."

And so they went on, each succeeding speaker getting more cantankerous, as it were.

• • •

(*Outlook*, October 7, 1893)

. . . The subject of Christian work in India calls Vivekananda, in his brilliant priestly orange, to his feet. He criticises the work of Christian missions. It is evident that he has not tried to understand Christianity, but neither, as he claims, have its priests made any effort to understand his religion, with its ingrained faiths and race prejudices of thousands of years standing. They have simply come, in his view, to throw scorn on his most sacred beliefs, and to undermine the morals and spirituality of the people he has been set to teach.

• • •

(*Critic*, October 7, 1893)

But the most impressive figures of the Parliament were the Buddhist priest, H. Dharmapala of Ceylon, and the Hindoo monk, Suami Vivekananda. "If theology and dogma stand in your way in search of truth," said the former incisively, "put them aside. Learn to think without prejudice, to love all beings for love's sake, to express your convictions fearlessly, to lead a life of purity. and the sunlight of truth will illuminate you." But eloquent as were many of the brief speeches at this meeting, whose triumphant enthusiasm rightly culminated in the superb rendering by the Apollo Club of the Hallelujah chorus, no one expressed so well the spirit of the Parliament, its limitations and its finest influence, as did the Hindoo monk. I copy his address in full, but I can only suggest its effect upon the audience, for **he is an orator by divine right, and his strong intelligent face in its picturesque setting of yellow and orange was hardly less**

interesting than these earnest words and the rich, rhythmical utterance he gave them. . . . [After quoting the greater part of Swamiji's Final Address, the article continues:]

Perhaps the most tangible result of the congress was the feeling it aroused in regard to foreign missions. **The impertinence of sending half-educated theological students to instruct the wise and erudite Orientals was never brought home to an English-speaking audience more forcibly.** It is only in the spirit of tolerance and sympathy that we are at liberty to touch their faith, and the exhorters who possess these qualities are rare. It is necessary to realize that we have quite as much to learn from the Buddhists as they from us, and that only through harmony can the highest influence be exerted.

Chicago, 3 Oct., 1893. —*Lucy Monroe*

• • •

[To a request of the *New York World* of October 1, 1893, for "a sentiment or expression regarding the significance of the great meeting" from each representative, Swamiji replied with a quotation from the Gita and one from Vyasa:]

"I am He that am in every religion—like the thread that passes through a string of pearls."

"Holy, perfect and pure men are seen in all creeds, therefore they all lead to the same truth—for how can nectar be the outcome of poison?"

Reincarnation

(*Evanston Index*, October 7, 1893)

At the Congregational Church, during the past week, there have been given a course of lectures which in nature much resembled the Religious Parliament which has just been completed. The lecturers were Dr. Carlvon Bergen of Sweden, and Suami Vivekananda, the Hindu monk. . . . Suami Vivekananda is a representative from India to the Parliament of Religions. He has attracted a great deal of attention on account of his unique attire in Mandarin colors, by his magnetic presence and by his brilliant oratory and wonderful exposition of Hindu philosophy. **His stay in Chicago has been a continual ovation.** The course of lectures was arranged to cover three evenings.

[The lectures of Saturday and Tuesday evenings are listed without comment; then the article continues:]

On Thursday evening Oct. 5, Dr. Carlvon Bergen spoke on "Huldine Beamish, the Founder of the King's Daughters of Sweden," and "Reincarnation" was the subject treated by the Hindu monk. The latter was very interesting; the views being those that are not often heard in this part of the world. **The doctrine of reincarnation of the soul, while comparatively new and little understood in this country, is well-known in the east, being the foundation of nearly all the religions of those people.** Those that do not use it as dogma, do not say anything against it. The main point to be decided in regard to the doctrine is, as to whether we have had a past. We know that we have a present and feel sure of a future. Yet how can there be a present without a past? Modern science has proved that matter exists and continues to exist. Creation is merely a change in appearance. We are not sprung out of nothing. Some regard God as the common cause of everything and judge this a sufficient reason for existence. But in everything we must consider the phenomena; whence and from what matter springs. **The same arguments that prove there is a future prove that there is a past. It is necessary that there should be causes other than God's will. Heredity is not able to give sufficient cause.** Some say that we are not conscious of a former existence. Many cases have been found where there are distinct reminiscences of a past. And here lies the germ of the theory. Because the Hindu is kind to dumb animals many believe that we believe in the reincarnation of souls in lower orders. They are not able to conceive of kindness to dumb animals being other than the result of superstition. An ancient Hindu priest **defines religion as anything that lifts one up. Brutality is driven out, humanity gives way to divinity.** The theory of incarnation does not confine man to this small earth. His soul can go to other, higher earths where he will be a loftier being, possessing, instead of five senses, eight, and continuing in this way he will at length approach the acme of perfection, divinity, and will be allowed to drink deep of oblivion in the "Islands of the Blest".

Hindu Civilisation

[Although the lecture at Streator on October 9 was well attended, the *Streator Daily Free Press* of October 9 ran the following somewhat dreary review:]

The lecture of this celebrated Hindoo at the Opera House, Saturday night, was very interesting. By comparative philology, he sought to establish the long admitted relationship between the Aryan races and their descendants in the new world. He mildly defended the caste system of India which keeps three fourths of the people in utter and humiliating subjection, and boasted that the India of today was the same India that had watched for centuries the meteoric nations of the world flash across the horizon and sink into oblivion. In common with the people, he loves the past. He lives not for self, but for God. In his country a premium is placed on beggary and tramps, though not so distinguished in his lecture. When the meal is prepared, they wait for some man to come along who is first served, then the animals, the servants, the man of the house and lastly, the women of the household. Boys are taken at 10 years of age and are kept by professors for a period of ten to twenty years, educated and sent forth to resume their former occupations or to engage in a life of endless wandering, preaching, and praying, taking along only that which is given them to eat and wear, but never touching money. Vivekananda is of the latter class. Men approaching old age withdraw from the world, and after a period of study and prayer, when they feel themselves sanctified, they also go forward spreading the gospel. He observed that leisure was necessary for intellectual development and sconed Americans for not educating the Indians whom Columbus found in a state of savagery. In this he exhibited a lack of knowledge of conditions.

His talk was lamentably short and much was left unsaid of seeming greater importance than much that was said.

An Interesting Lecture

(*Wisconsin State Journal*, November 21, 1893)

The lecture at the Congregational Church [Madison] last night by the celebrated Hindoo monk, Vivekananda, **was an extremely interesting one, and contained much of sound philosophy and good religion.** Pagan though he be, **Christianity may well follow many of his teachings.** His creed is as wide as the universe, taking in all religions, and accepting truth wherever it may be found. Bigotry and superstition and idle ceremony, he declared, have no place in "the religions of India".

The Hindoo Religion

(*Minneapolis Star*, November 25, 1893)

"Brahminism" in all its subtle attraction, because of its embodiment of ancient and truthful principles, was the subject which held an audience in closest attention last evening at the First Unitarian Church [Minneapolis], while Swami Vive Kananda expounded the Hindoo faith. It was an audience which included thoughtful women and men, for the lecturer had been invited by the "Peripatetics," and among the friends who shared the privilege with them were ministers of varied denominations, as well as students and scholars. Vive Kananda is a Brahmin priest, and he occupied the platform in his native garb, with caftan on head, orange-colored coat confined at the waist with a red sash, and red nether garments.

He presented his faith in all sincerity, speaking slowly and clearly, convincing his hearers by quietness of speech rather than by rapid action. His words were carefully weighed, and each carried its meaning direct. He offered the simplest truths of the Hindoo religion, and while he said nothing harsh about Christianity, he touched upon it in such a manner as to place the faith of Brahma before all. The all-pervading thought and **leading principle of the Hindoo religion is the inherent divinity of the soul; the soul is perfect, and religion is the manifestation of divinity already existing in man.** The present is merely a line of demarkation between the past and future, and of the two tendencies in man, if the good preponderates he will move to a higher sphere, if the evil has power, he degenerates. These two are continually at work within him; what elevates him is virtue, that which degenerates is evil.

Kananda will speak at the First Unitarian Church tomorrow morning.

• • •

(*Des Moines News*, November 28, 1893)

Swami Vivekananda, the talented scholar from far-off India, spoke at the Central Church last night [November 27]. He was a representative of his country and creed at the recent parliament of religions assembled in Chicago during the world's fair. Rev. H. O. Breeden introduced the speaker to the audience. He arose and after bowing to his audience, commenced his lecture, the subject of which was "Hindoo Religion". His lecture was not confined to any line of thought but consisted more of some of his own philosophical views relative to his religion and others. He holds that one must embrace all the religions to become the perfect Christian. What is not found in one religion is supplied by another. They are all right and necessary for the true Christian. When you send a missionary to our country he becomes a Hindoo Christian and I a Christian Hindoo. **I have often been asked in this country if I am going to try to convert the people here. I take this for an insult. I do not believe in this idea of conversion.** Today we have a sinful man; tomorrow according to your idea he is converted and by and by attains unto holiness. Whence comes this change? How do you explain it? The man has not a new soul for the soul must die. You say he is changed by God. God is perfect, all powerful and is purity itself. Then after this man is converted he is that same God minus the purity he gave that man to become holy. **There are in our country two words which have an altogether different meaning than they do in this country. They are "religion" and "sect". We hold that religion embraces all religions. We tolerate everything but intoleration. Then there is that word "sect". Here it embraces those sweet people who wrap themselves up in their mantle of charity and say, "We are right; you are wrong."** It reminds me of the story of the two frogs. A frog was born in a well and lived its whole life in that well. One day a frog from the sea fell in that well and they commenced to talk about the sea. The frog whose home was in the well asked the visitor how large the sea was, but was unable to get an intelligent answer. Then the at home frog jumped from one corner of the well to another and asked his visitor if the sea was that large. He said yes. The frog jumped again and said, "Is the sea that large?" and receiving an affirmative reply, he said to himself, "This frog must be a liar; I will put him out of my well." That is the way with these sects. They seek to eject and trample those who do not believe as they do.

❑❑❑

2

Before the Parliament

INDIA: HER RELIGION AND CUSTOMS

[*Salem Evening News*, August 29, 1893]

In spite of the warm weather of yesterday afternoon, a goodly number of members of the Thought and Work Club, with guests, gathered in Wesley Chapel to meet Swami Vive Kanonda, a Hindoo monk, now travelling in this country, and to listen to an informal address from that gentleman, principally upon the religion of the Hindoos as taught by their Vedas or sacred books. He also spoke of caste, as simply a social division and in no way dependent upon their religion.

The poverty of the majority of the masses was strongly dwelt upon. India with an area much smaller than the United States, contains twenty three hundred millions of people, and of these, three hundred millions [sic] earn wages, averaging less than fifty cents per month. In some instances the people in whole districts of the country subsist for months and even years, wholly upon flowers, produced by a certain tree which when boiled are edible.

In other districts the men eat rice only, the women and children must satisfy their hunger with the water in which the rice is cooked. A failure of the rice crop means famine. Half the people live upon one meal a day, the other half know not whence the next meal will come. According to Swami Vive

Kanonda, the need of the people of India is not more religion, or a better one, but as he expresses it, "practicality," and it is with the hope of interesting the American people in this great need of the suffering, starving millions that he has come to this country.

He spoke at some length of the condition of his people and their religion. In course of his speech he was frequently and closely questioned by Dr. F. A. Gardner and Rev. S. F. Nobbs of the Central Baptist Church. He said the missionaries had fine theories there and started in with good ideas, but had done nothing for the industrial condition of the people. **He said Americans, instead of sending out missionaries to train them in religion, would better sendsome one out to give them industrial education.**

Asked whether it was not a fact that Christians assisted the people of India in times of distress, and whether they did not assist in a practical way by training schools, the speaker replied that they did it sometimes, but really it was not to their credit for the law did not allow them to attempt to influence people at such times.

He explained the bad condition of women in India on the ground that Hindoo men had such respect for woman that it was thought best not to allow her out. The Hindoo women were held in such high esteem that they were kept in seclusion. He explained the old custom of women being burned on the death of their husbands, on the ground that they loved them so that they could not live without the husband. They were one in marriage and must be one in death.

He was asked about the worship of idols and the throwing themselves in front of the juggernaut car, and said one must not blame the Hindoo people for the car business, for it was the act of fanatics and mostly of lepers.

The speaker explained his mission in his country to be to organize monks for industrial purposes, that they might give

the people the benefit of this industrial education and thus elevate them and improve their condition.

This afternoon Vive Kanonda will speak on the children of India to any children or young people who may be pleased to listen to him at 166 North Street, Mrs. Woods kindly offering her garden for that purpose. In person he is a fine looking man, dark but comely, dressed in a long robe of a yellowish red colour confined at the waist with a cord, and wearing on his head a yellow turban. Being a monk he has no caste, and may eat and drink with anyone.

• • •

(*Daily Gazette*, August 29, 1893)

Rajah Swami Vivi Kananda of India was the guest of the Thought and Work Club of Salem yesterday afternoon in the Wesley Church.

A large number of ladies and gentlemen were present and shook hands, American fashion, with the distinguished monk. He wore an orange-colored gown, with red sash, yellow turban, with the end hanging down on one side, which he used for a handkerchief, and congress shoes.

He spoke at some length of the condition of his people and their religion. In course of his speech he was frequently and closely questioned by Dr. F. A. Gardner and Rev. S. F. Nobbs of the Central Baptist church. He said the missionaries had fine theories there and started in with good ideas, but had done nothing for the industrial condition of the people. He said Americans, instead of sending out missionaries to train them in religion, would better send someone out to give them industrial education.

Speaking at some length of the relations of men and women, he said the husbands of India never lied and never persecuted, and named several other sins they never committed.

Asked whether it was not a fact that Christians assisted the people of India in times of distress, and whether they did not assist in a practical way by training schools, the speaker replied that they did it sometimes, but really it was not to their credit, for the law did not allow them to attempt to influence people at such times.

He explained the bad condition of women in India on the ground that Hindoo men had such respect for woman that it was thought best not to allow her out. The Hindoo women were held in such high esteem that they were kept in seclusion. He explained the old custom of women being burned on the death of their husbands, on the ground that they loved them so that they could not live without the husband. They were one in marriage and must be one in death.

He was asked about the worship of idols and the throwing themselves in front of the juggernaut car, and said one must not blame the Hindoo people for the car business, for it was the act of fanatics and mostly of lepers.

As for the worship of idols he said he had asked Christians what they thought of when they prayed, and some said they thought of the church, others of G-O-D. Now his people thought of the images. For the poor people idols were necessary. He said that in ancient times, when their religion first began, women were distinguished for spiritual genius and great strength of mind. Inspite of this, as he seemed to acknowledge, the women of the present day had degenerated. They thought of nothing but eating and drinking, gossip and scandal.

The speaker explained his mission in his country to be to organize monks for industrial purposes, that they might give the people the benefit of this industrial education and thus to elevate them and improve their condition.

• • •

(*Salem Evening News*, September 1, 1893)

The learned Monk from India who is spending a few days in this city, will speak in the East Church Sunday evening at 7-30. Swami (Rev.) Viva Kananda preached in the Episcopal

Church at Annisquam last Sunday evening, by invitation of the pastor and Professor Wright of Harvard, who has shown him great kindness.

On Monday night he leaves for Saratoga, where he will address the Social Science Association. Later on he will speak before the Congress in Chicago. Like all men who are educated in the higher Universities of India, Viva Kananda speaks English easily and correctly. His simple talk to the children on Tuesday last concerning the games, schools, customs and manners of children in India was valuable and most interesting. His kind heart was touched by the statement of a little miss that her teacher had "licked her so hard that she almost broke her finger". . . . As Viva Kananda, like all monks, must travel over his land preaching the religion of truth, chastity and the brotherhood of man, no great good could pass unnoticed, or terrible wrong escape his eyes. **He is extremely generous to all persons of other faiths,** and has only kind words for those who differ from him.

• • •

(*Daily Gazette*, September 5, 1893)

Rajah Swami Vivi Kananda of India spoke at the East Church Sunday evening, on the religion of India and the poor of his native land. A good audience assembled, but it was not so large as the importance of the subject or the interesting speaker deserved. The monk was dressed in his native costume, and spoke about forty minutes. The great need of India today, which is not the India of fifty years ago, is, he said, missionaries to educate the people industrially and socially and not religiously. The Hindoos have all the religion they want, and the Hindoo religion is the most ancient in the world. **The monk is a very pleasant speaker and held the close attention of his audience.**

• • •

(*Daily Saratogian*, September 6, 1893)

. . . The platform was next occupied by Vive Kananda, a monk of Madras, Hindoostan, who preached throughout India. He is interested in social science and is an intelligent and interesting speaker. He spoke on Mohammedan rule in India.

The program for today embraces some very interesting topics, especially the paper on "Bimetallism", by Col. Jacob Greene of Hartford. Vive Kananda will again speak, this time on the Use of Silver in India.

❑❑❑

The Swami Who Shook America (and Europe)

Life-Sketch by
Romain Rolland
French Nobel Laureate and Author
of the all-time classic JEAN CHRISTOPHE

India's Warrior-Saint

A King among Men

The great disciple whose task it was to take up the spiritual heritage of Ramakrishna and disseminate the grain of his thought throughout the world, was both physically and morally his direct antithesis.

The Seraphic Master had spent his whole life at the feet of the Divine Beloved, the Mother—the Living God. It was not given to his proudest disciples to emulate him. The greatest of them, the spirit with the widest wings—Vivekananda—could only attain his heights by sudden flights amid tempests, which remind me over and over again of Beethoven. Even in moments of rest upon its bosom the sails of his ship were filled with every wind that blew. Earthly cries, the sufferings of the ages fluttered round him life a flight of burnished gulls. The passions of strength never of weakness were striving within his lion's heart. He was energy personified, and action was his message to men. For him, it was the root of all the virtues. He went so far in his aversion to passivity, as to say, 'Above all, be strong, be manly! I have a respect even for one who is wicked, so long as he is manly and strong, for his strength will make him some day give up his wickedness, or even give up all work for selfish ends, and will then eventually bring him into the Truth.'

He was tall five feet eight and a half inches, square-shouldered, broad-chested, stout, rather heavily built; his arms were muscular and trained to all kinds of sports. He had an olive complexion, a full face, vast forehead, strong jaw, a pair of magnificent eyes, large, dark and rather prominent, with heavy lids, whose shape recalled the classic comparison to a lotus petal. Nothing escaped the magic of his glance, capable equally of embracing in its irresistible charm, or of sparkling with wit, irony, or kindness, of losing itself in ecstasy, or of plunging imperiously to the very depths of consciousness and of withering with its fury. But his pre-eminent characteristic was kingliness. **He was a born king and nobody ever came near him either in India or America without paying homage to his majesty.**

When this quite unknown young man of thirty appeared in Chicago at the inaugural meeting of the Parliament of Religions, opened in September 1893, by Cardinal Gibbons, all his fellow-members were forgotten in his commanding presence. His strength and beauty, the grace and dignity of his bearing, the dark light of his eyes, his imposing appearance, and from the moment he began to speak, the splendid music of his rich deep voice enthralled the vast audience of American Anglo-Saxons, previously prejudiced against him on account of his colour. The thought of **this warrior-prophet of India** left a deep mark upon the United States.

He was a member of a great aristocratic Kayastha family which he regarded as Kshatriya; and his whole life showed the stamp of that warrior caste. He was born on January 12, 1863, at Calcutta. His mother was a highly educated woman of regal majesty, whose heroic spirit had been nurtured on the great Hindu epics. His father, who led an ostentatious and restless life, showed an independence of spirit almost Voltairean in quality, and an indifference to caste, due at once to his large sentiment of humanity and to the smiling consciousness of his own superiority.

His childhood and boyhood were those of a young artist Prince of the Renaissance. He was gifted with a multiplicity of talents, and cultivated them all. The possessor of physical courage and the build of an athlete, he was a past master in all physical exercises. He could box, swim, row and had a passion for horses. He studied vocal and instrumental music for four or five years under famous Hindu and Muslim professors. He wrote tunes and published a documented essay on the science and philosophy of Indian music.

At college he was distinguished for his brilliant intellect, embracing with equal zest the sciences, astronomy, mathematics, philosophy and Indian and Western languages. At night he used to pore over *The Imitation of Jesus Christ* and the Vedanta. He loved philosophic discussions. It was this mania for argument, criticism, discrimination, that later won for him the name of Vivekananda.

He was first moved by reading Stuart Mill's *Essays on Religion*. He imposed upon himself the life of an ascetic, living in a dark, damp room, lying on the ground upon a quilt with books everywhere, making tea on the floor, reading and meditating day and night. He suffered excruciating and stabbing pains in his head, but he did not achieve the reconciliation of the conflicting passions of his nature.

Such was he at the moment when he went to meet the Master, who was to govern the rest of his life. In the great city Calcutta, he had made the round of the great religious individualities, but he had returned unsatisfied.

At the beginning of 1884 his careless and prodigal father died, suddenly carried off by a heart attack, and the family found itself faced with ruin. From that day onwards Naren tasted misery, knew the vain search for employment and the denial of friends. All judged him lost except Ramakrishna in his retreat at Dakshineswar, and he kept his confidence in Naren. He knew that Naren's salvation could only come from him.

One evening when he had eaten nothing, he sank down, exhausted and went through, by the side of the road in front of a house. The delirium of fever raged in his prostrate body. Suddenly it seemed as if the folds enveloping his soul were rent asunder, and there was light. All his past doubts were automatically solved. He could say truly, 'I see, I know, I believe, I am undeceived...' From that day a new life began for him.

One sublime cry proclaimed his faith to the world. 'The only God in whom I believe is the sum total of all souls, and above all I believe in my God the wicked, my God the miserable, my God the poor of all races....'

•

After Christmas Night, 1886, the mystic vigil of Antpore where the New Communion of Apostles was founded amid tears of love in memory of the lost Master—many months and years elapsed before the work was begun that translated Ramakrishna's thought into living action.

His meeting with suffering and human misery—not only vague and general—but definite misery, misery close at hand, the misery of his people, the misery of India—was to be the flint upon the steel, whence a spark would fly to set the whole soul on fire. And with this as its foundation-stone, all his powers and all his desires were thrown into the mission of human service and united into one single flame: 'A religion which will give us faith in ourselves, a national self-respect, and the power to feed and educate the poor and relieve the misery around me..... If you want to find God, serve man!'

Naren had no doubt that a mission awaited him. He left Calcutta in 1888 and went through Varanasi, Ayodhya, Lucknow, Agra, Vrindaban, Hathras, and the Himalayas. The journeys brought ancient India vividly before his eyes, eternal India, the India of the Vedas, with its race of heroes and gods, clothed in the glory of legend and history, Aryans, Moguls and Dravidians—all one. In the retreats of the Himalayas he meditated on the Vedas.

In 1890, it was the misery under his eyes, the misery of India, that filled his mind to the exclusion of every other thought. At Cape Comorin it caught and held him in its jaws. He dedicated his life to the unhappy masses.

But how could he help them? He had no money, and time was pressing, and the princely gifts of one or two Maharajas or the offerings of several groups of well-wishers could only nourish a thousandth part of the most urgent needs. He must appeal to the whole world. The whole world had need of India. The health of India, the death of India, was its concern as well. Could her immense spiritual reserves be allowed to be destroyed as so many others had been—Egypt and Chaldea—which long afterwards men struggled to exhume, when nothing was left but debris, their soul being dead for ever?... An appeal from India to Europe and America began to take shape in the mind of the solitary thinker.

It was at the end of 1891 between Junagadh and Porbander that he appears to have thought of it for the first time. At Porbander, where he began to learn French, a pandit advised him to go to the West, where his thought would be better understood than in his own country: 'Go and take it by storm and then return!' At Khandwa in the early autumn of 1892 he heard of a Parliament of Religions to be held during the following year at Chicago, and his first thought was how he might take part in it.

Nabobs and bankers offered him money for his journey overseas, but he refused it. He asked the disciples, who were collecting subscriptions, to appeal rather to the middle classes. He went to Khetri, where his friend the Maharaja gave him his Dewan to escort him to Bombay, where he embarked. At the moment of departure he put on, with the robe of silk and ochre turban, the name of Vivekananda, which he was about to impose upon the world.

•

He left Bombay on May 31, 1893, and went by way of Ceylon, Penang, Singapore, Hongkong, and then visited Canton and Nagasaki. Thence he went by land to Yokohama, seeing Osaka, Kyoto, and Tokyo.

He went from Yokohama to Vancouver; thence by train he found himself towards the middle of July in a state of bewilderment at Chicago. Everything was new to him and both surprised and stupefied him. He had never imagined the power, the riches, the inventive genius of this Western world.

For twelve days he filled his eager eyes with this new world. A few days after his arrival in Chicago he bethought himself to go to the Information Bureau of the Exposition. What a shock! He discovered that the Parliament did not open until after the first week of September—and that it was too late for the registration of delegates—moreover, that no registration would be accepted without official references.

Fate helped him. Vivekananda never passed anywhere unnoticed, but fascinated even while he was unknown. In the Boston train his appearance and conversation struck a fellow traveller, a rich Massachusetts lady, who questioned him and then interested herself in him, invited him to her house, and introduced him to the Hellenist, J. H. Wright, a professor at Harvard; the latter was at once struck by the genius of this young Hindu and put himself entirely at his disposal; he insisted that Vivekananda should represent Hinduism at the Parliament of Religions, and wrote to the President of the Committee. All his difficulties were removed.

On Monday, September 11, 1893, the first session of the Parliament was opened. In the centre sat Cardinal Gibbons. Round him to left and right were grouped the oriental delegates Pratap Chunder Mozoomdar, the chief of the Brahmo Samaj, an old friend of Vivekananda, representing the Indian theists together with Nagarkar of Bombay; Dharmapala, representing the Buddhists of Ceylon; one Gandhi representing the Jains; Chakravarti representing with Annie Besant the Theosophical Society. But amongst them all it was the young man who represented nothing—and everything—the man belonging to no sect, but rather to India as a whole, who drew the glance of the assembled thousands. It was the first time that he had had to speak before such an assembly and as the delegates, presented one by one, had to announce themselves in public in a brief harangue, Vivekananda let his turn go by hour after hour until the end of the day. The improvident one had prepared nothing while the others all read from a written text.

But then **his speech was like a tongue of flame. Among the grey wastes of cold dissertation it fired the souls of the listening throng. Hardly had he pronounced the very simple opening words—'Sisters and brothers of America!' than hundreds arose in their seats and applauded.** He greeted the youngest of the nations in the name of the most ancient monastic order in the world—the Vedic order of Sannyasins. He presented Hinduism as the mother of religions, who had taught them the double precept 'Accept and understand one another!'

Each of the other orators had spoken of his God, of the God of his sect. He—he alone—spoke of all their Gods and embraced them all in the Universal Being. It was the breath of Ramakrishna, breaking down the barriers through the mouth of his great disciple. The Parliament of Religions gave the young orator an ovation.

During the ensuing days he spoke again ten or twelve times. Each time he repeated with new arguments but with the same force of conviction **his thesis of a universal religion without limit of time or space, uniting the whole Credo of the human spirit, from the enslaved fetishism of the savage to the most liberal creative affirmations of modern science.**

The effect of these mighty words was immense. Over the heads of the official representatives of the Parliament they were addressed to all and appealed to outside thought. Vivekananda's fame at once spread abroad, and India as a whole benefited. The American Press recognized him as "Undoubtedly the greatest figure in the Parliament of Religions. **After hearing him we feel how foolish it is to send missionaries to this learned nation.**"

Vivekananda became the man of the hour. In order to serve the cause of his unfortunate India and to free himself from the tutelage of his rich protectors, he accepted the offer of a Lecture Bureau for a tour of the United States: the East and the Middle

West, Chicago, Iowa, Des Moines, Minneapolis, Detroit, Boston, Cambridge, Baltimore, Washington, New York, etc.

His first feeling of attraction and admiration for the formidable power of the young republic had faded. Vivekananda almost at once fell foul of the brutality, the inhumanity, the littleness of spirit, the narrow fanaticism, the monumental ignorance, the crushing incomprehens-ion, so frank and sure of itself with regard to all who thought, who believed, who regarded life differently from the paragon nation of the human race.... And so he had no patience. He hid nothing. He stigmatized the vices and crimes of the Western civilisation with its characteristics of violence, pillage, and destruction.

He was especially bitter against false Christianity and religious hypocrisy: 'With all your brag and boasting, **where has your Christianity succeeded without the sword?** Yours is a religion preached in the name of luxury. It is all hypocrisy that I have heard in this country. All this prosperity, all this from Christ? Those who call upon Christ care for nothing but to amass riches? Christ would not find a stone on which to lay his head among you.... **You are not Christians. Return to Christ!'**

An explosion of anger was the answer to this scornful lesson, and from that moment he had always at his heels a band of clergymen, who followed him with invective and accusation, even going so far as to spread infamous calumnies of his life and behaviour in America and India. No less shameful was the action of certain Hindu representatives of rival societies, who were offended by Vivekananda's glory, and did not scruple to spread the base charges started by malevolent missionaries.

For the honour of America it must be said here and now that his moral intransigence, his virile idealism, his dauntless loyalty attracted to him from all sides a chosen band of defenders and admirers, a group of whom were to form his first Western disciples and the most active agents in his work for human regeneration.

The whole of the spiritual manifestations that I have just explained in brief—I delegate their deep study to the future historian of the new Soul of the West—will have made it clear that the thought of the United States, thus fermenting and working for half a century, was more ready than any in the West to receive Vivekananda.

Hardly had he begun to preach than men and women athirst for his message came flocking to him. They came from all parts: from salons and universities, sincere and pure Christians and sincere free-thinkers and agnostics. Despite sudden outbreaks of passion, to which his hot-headed character was prone, Vivekananda was great enough to keep the balance between sympathy and antipathy; he always recognized the virtues and the real energy of Anglo-Saxon America.

It was not only the material goods of the West that he counted, but social and moral goods as well. He was filled with admiration and emotion by the apparent democratic equality inherent in the spectacle of a millionaire and a working woman elbowing each other in the same tramway, and he gave it a greater significance than it deserved; for he did not realize the remorselessness of the machine grinding down all who fell. He therefore felt more poignantly the murderous inequality of the castes and the outcasts of India.

He preached the primordial necessity of an organization that will teach Hindus mutual help and appreciation after the pattern of Western democracies.

In America, he undertook a series of apostolic campaigns with the object of spreading over this immense spiritual stretch of fallow land the Vedantic seed, and watering it with Ramakrishna's rain of love. From the former he himself was to select such parts as were appropriate to the American public on account of their logical reasoning. He had avoided all mention of the latter, his Master, although he had preached his word.

His first course lasted from February to June 1895, and in it he explained the Upanishads. Everyday he instructed several chosen disciples in the exercise of the double method of Raja

Yoga and Jnana Yoga—the first more especially psycho-physiological, aiming at concentration through control of the vital energies by the subordination of the organism to the mind, by silence imposed on the agitation of inner currents so that nothing but the clear voice of the Beings might make itself heard—the second, purely intellectual, and akin to scientific reason, **seeking the unification of the spirit with the Universal Law, the Absolute Reality: the Science-Religion.**

His stay in the United States was broken from August to December 1895, by a visit to England. It was resumed in the winter and lasted until the middle of April 1896.

He spoke in all kinds of places in New York, Boston, and Detroit, before popular audiences, before the Metaphysical Society of Hartford, before the Ethical Society of Brooklyn, and before students and professors of philosophy at Harvard. At **Harvard he was offered the Chair of Oriental Philosophy, at Columbia the Chair of Sanskrit.** At New York under the presidency of Mr. Francis Leggett he organized the Vedanta Society, which was to become the centre of the Vedantist movement in America.

•

It was thought that a journey to Europe would distract him, but wherever he went he always spent himself. He stayed three times in England, from September to the end of November 1895, from April to the end of July 1896, from October to December 16, 1896. He came through Paris in August 1895, before going to London. But he only gave it a brief glance this first time visiting museums, cathedrals, the tomb of Napoleon, and his dominant impression was of an artistic people, highly gifted.

In Europe Vivekananda was to measure himself against the masters of Indology, such as Max Muller and Paul Deussen. The greatness of philosophical and philological science in the West was revealed to him in all its patient genius and scrupulous honesty.

But the discovery of England had reserved for him an emotion of quite a different order. He came as an enemy, and he was conquered. On his return to India he was to proclaim it with superb loyalty, **'No one ever landed on English soil with more hatred in his heart for a race than I did for the English.... There is none among you...who loves the English people more than I do now....'**

He discovered 'a nation of heroes: the true Kshatriyas... brave and steady.... Their education is to hide their feelings and never to show them. They have solved the secret of obedience without slavish cringing—great freedom with great law-abidingness.'

During his second visit he opened regular classes in Vedantic instruction; and, certain of an intelligent public, he started with the Yoga of the mind: the Jnana Yoga. Five classes a week, and on Friday evenings in addition a class for open discussion. In addition he gave several courses of lectures in a Piccadilly Picture Gallery, at Princes' Hall, in clubs, to educational societies, at Annie Besant's lodge, and to private circles. He felt the seriousness of his English hearers, in contrast to the superficial infatuation of the American public. Vivekananda felt more at his ease and trusted them more.

It was Ramakrishna who brought him into contact with Max Muller. The old Indianist, whose young regard followed with ever fresh curiosity all the palpitations of the Hindu religious soul, had already perceived, like the Magi of old, in the East the rising star of Ramakrishna. He was invited to his house on May 28, 1896; and the young Swami of India bowed before the old sage of Europe and hailed him as a spirit of his race, the reincarnation of an ancient Rishi, recalling his first births in the ancient days of Vedic India—'a soul that is every day realizing its oneness with Brahman....'

And England was to give him still more in the shape of perhaps the most beautiful friendships of his life: J.J. Godwin, Margaret Noble, Mr. and Mrs. Sevier.

Margaret Noble made a complete gift of herself. The future will always unite her name of initiation, Sister Nivedita, to that of her beloved Master. She always argued and resisted, being one of those English souls who are hard to overcome, but once conquered, faithful for ever, Vivekananda said to himself, 'There are no more trustworthy souls!' She was twenty-eight when she made up her mind to place her fate in the Swami's hands. He made her come to India in Jan. 1898, to devote herself of the education of Hindu women.

The terrible fatigue began to weigh upon him at times. He was tired of the world and the bondage of works. He longed for rest. The evil that consumed the walls of his body in secret, made him for long periods quite detached from existence. At such times he refused to construct anything new. He wrote on August 23, 1896: 'I have begun the work; let others work it out! Now I am sure my part of the work is done, and I have no more interest in Vedanta, or in any philosophy in the world, or in the work itself.... I am getting ready to depart to return no more to this hell, this world.'

A pathetic cry, whose poignancy will be felt by all who know the terrible exhaustion of the disease that was wasting him.

The affectionate friends, who were watching over him, took him again for a rest to Switzerland. He spent most of the summer of 1896 there, at Geneva, Montreux, Chillon, Chamounix, the St. Bernard, Lucerne, the Rigi, Zermatt, Schaffhausen. And he seems to have benefited greatly in enjoyment of the air from the snows, the torrents, and mountains, which reminded him of the Himalayas, It was there in a village at the foot of the Alps, between Mont Blanc and the Little St. Bernard, that he first conceived the plan of founding in the Himalayas a monastery where his Western and Eastern disciples might be united. And the Seviers, who were with him, never let the idea lapse: it became their life-work.

To his mountain retreat there came a letter from Professor Deussen, inviting him to visit him at Kiel. He visited in Kiel the Schopenhauer Society. His reception was as cordial, and their relations as animated as might have been expected from such an ardent vedantist as Paul Deussen who saw in the Vedanta not only 'one of the most majestic structures and valuable products of the genius of man in his search for truth, but the strongest support of pure morality, and the greatest consolation in the sufferings of life and death.'

Deussen rejoined Vivekananda at Hamburg, they travelled together in Holland, spent three days at Amsterdam, then went to London, where for two weeks they met every day. During the same time Vivekananda saw Max Muller again at Oxford.

Two years later in 1899, he still had bouts of despair because all his success, all **his glory, had not brought him the three hundred million rupees necessary for his dream of his material regeneration of India.** But he had learnt by this time that we are not born to see success.

•

The news of Vivekananda's success at the Parliament of Religions was slow in reaching India, but once it became known, it created an outburst of joy and national pride. Rajas, pandits, and peoples rejoiced. India celebrated its conquering champion. Enthusiasm reached its height in Madras and Bengal, their tropic imaginations afire. On September, 5, 1894, a year after the Congress at Chicago, a meeting was held in the Town Hall of Calcutta: all classes of the population, all sections of Hinduism, were represented; and they had come together to celebrate Vivekananda and to thank the American people.

He announced his intention of founding two general headquarters at Madras and Calcutta, and later two more in Bombay and Allahabad.

Vivekananda once again recrossed the land of India from the South to the North, as he had done formerly as a beggar along its roads. By Colombo, Kandy, Anuradhapura, Jaffna, Pamban, Rameshwaram, Ramnad, Madura, Kumbakonam, a small railway station—where **hundreds of people in the open country laid themselves on the rails so as to stop his train—**

Madras, and from thence by sea to Calcutta. But today his was a triumphal progress with an escort of delirious people. **Rajas prostrated themselves before him or drew his carriage. The cannon boomed**, and in the exotic processions wherein elephants and camels rode, choirs chanted the victory of *Judas Maccabeus* Choruses from Handel.

He set out upon a second journey to the West in order to inspect the works he had founded and to fan the flame. This time he took with him one of the most learned of his brethren, Turiyananda, a man of high caste and noble life, and learned in Sanskrit studies. Nivedita went with them.

On June 20, 1899 he travelled from Calcutta via Madras, Colombo, Aden, Naples, Marseilles. On July 31, he was in London. On August 16, he left Glasgow for New York. He stayed in the United States until 20, 1900, chiefly in California. From August 1 to October 24, he visited France, and went to Paris and Brittany. Then via Vienna, the Balkans, Constantinople, Greece, and Egypt he returned to India and arrived at the beginning of December 1900.

The older he grew, the deeper was his conviction that the East and the West must espouse each other. **He saw in India and Europe 'two organisms in full youth... two great experiments neither of which is yet complete.'**

•

In October 1901, the great festival of Durga Puja—the adoration of the Mother—the national festival of Bengal, corresponding to Christmas, celebrated with great magnificence the joys of the scented autumn, when men are reconciled to each other and exchange gifts, and the monastery feeds hundreds of poor for three days. In February 1902, the festival of Ramakrishna brought together more than thirty thousand pilgrims to Belur. But the Swami was feverish and confined to his room by the swelling of his legs. From his window he watched the dances of the Sankirtanas, and sought to comfort the tears of the disciple who was nursing him; alone with his memories he lived, again the days he had spent in the past at the feet of the Master at Dakshineswar.

On the supreme day, Friday, July 4, 1902, he was more vigorous and joyous than he had been for years. He rose very early. Going to the chapel, contrary to his wont of opening everything, he shut the windows and bolted the doors. There he meditated alone from eight to eleven o' clock in the morning, and sang a beautiful hymn to Kali. When he went out into the court he was transfigured. He ate his meal with an appetite in the midst of his disciples. Immediately afterwards he gave the novices a Sanskrit lesson for three hours and was full of life and humour. Then he walked with Premananda along the Belur road for nearly two miles; he spoke of his plan of Vedic College and talked of Vedic study: 'It will kill superstition,' he said.

Seven o'clock.... the convent bell sounded for Arati. He went into his room and looked out over the Ganga. Then he sent away the novice who was with him, desiring that his meditation should not be disturbed. Forty-five minutes later he called in the monk, had all the windows opened, lay down quietly on the floor on his left side and remained motionless. He seemed to be meditating. At the end of an hour he turned round, gave a deep sigh—there was silence for several seconds—his eyes were fixed in the middle of his eyelids—a second deep sigh...and eternal silence fell.

He was thirty-nine. He had said, 'I shall not live to be forty years old.'

❑❑❑

Vivekananda's Contribution to World Culture

Of a truth, religion, as Vivekananda understood it, had such vast wings that when it was at rest it could brood over all the eggs of the liberated Spirit. He repudiated no past of sincere and sane forms of Knowledge. To him religion was the fellow citizen of every thinking man, and its only enemy was intolerance.

'Religion,' for Vivekananda, is synonymous with 'Universalism' of the spirit. And it is not until 'religious' conceptions have attained to this universalism, that religion is fully realised. For, contrary to the belief of all who know it not, religion is a matter for the future far more than for the past. It has only just begun.

'...It is said sometimes that religions are dying out, that spiritual ideas are dying out of the world. To me it seems that they have just begun to grow.... So long as religion was in the hands of a chosen few, or of a body of priests, it was in temples, churches, books, dogmas, ceremonials, forms and rituals. But when we come to the real, spiritual, universal concept, then and then alone religion will become real, and living; it will come into our very nature, live in our every moment, penetrate every pore of our society, and be infinitely more a power for good than it has ever been before.'

And such a religion exsits; it is the Advaita of India, Non-Dualism, Unity, the idea of the Absolute, of the Impersonal God, the only religion that can have any hold on intellectual people.

'The Advaita has twice saved India from materialism. By the coming of Buddha, who appeared in a time of most hideous and widespread materialism.... By the coming of Shankara, who when materialism had reconquered India in the form of the demoralisation of the governing classes and of superstition in the lower orders, put fresh life into Vedanta, by making a rational philosophy emerge from it.'

'We want today that bright sun of intellectuality, joined with the heart of Buddha, the wonderful, infininte heart of love and mercy. This union will give us the highest philosophy. Science and religion will meet and shake hands. Poetry and philosophy will become friends.

At bottom, although its Mission is to unite, the stumbling block to mutual understanding, the great obstacle to the coincidence of mankind is the word 'God', for that word embraces all possible ambiguities of thought, and is used oppressively to bandage the clear eyes of Freedom. Vivekananda was fully aware of this fact: '...I have been asked many times, "Why do you use that old word God?" Because it is the best word for our purpose, ...because all the hopes, aspirations, and happiness of humanity have been centred in that word. The word God has been used from time immemorial, and the idea of this cosmic intelligence, and all that is great and holy associated with it.

This 'cosmic intelligence' is tacitly implied in scientific reasoning. The chief difference is that with science it remains a piece of mechanism, while Vivekananda breathes life into it.

But it is a matter of indifference to the calm pride of him who deems himself the stronger whether science accepts free religion, in Vivekananda's sense of the term, or not: for **his religion accepts science**. It is vast enough to find a place at its table for all loyal seekers after truth.

No single great religion, said Vivekananda, throughout the course of twenty centuries, had died. Buddhism, Hinduism, Islam, Christianity, continue to grow in numbers and quality.

(Further, the religion of science, of liberty, and of human solidarity is also growing.)

Each great system of faith, whether 'religion' or 'lay', represents one portion of Universal Truth and spends its force in converting that into a type. Each, therefore, should unite with the others, instead of being mutually exclusive.

Each group had a living, beating heart, its own mission, and its own note in the complete harmony of sound; each one has conceived its own splendid but incomplete ideal; Christianity, its dream of moral purity; Hinduism, spirituality; Islam, social equality; ...etc. And each group is divided into families each with a different temperament: rationalism, puritanism, scepticism, worship of the senses or of the mind... They are all of diverse and graded powers in the divine economy of the Being, as it ceaselessly advances. Vivekananda uttered this profound saying, which we should do well to read, mark, learn, and inwardly digest.

By what practical means can silence and peace be secured among the drawing throng squabbling round the well? Let each one drink his own water and allow the rest to drink theirs! And it is stupid to want everyone to drink God out of the same pitcher. Vivekananda breaks in the midst of the hubbub and tries to make the disputants listen to at least two maxims of conduct, two provisional rules.

The first: 'Do not destroy!'—Build, if you can help to build. But if you cannot, do not interfere! It is better to do nothing than to do ill. Never speak a word against any sincere conviction.

The second: 'Take man as he stands, and from thence give him a lift' along his own road. You need not fear that road will take you out of your way. God is the centre of all the radii, and each one of us is converging towards Him along one of them.

With him it was true that 'the knowledge of Brahman is the ultimate purpose, the highest destiny of man. But man cannot remain absorbed in Brahman all the time.' Such absorption is only for exceptional moments.

Hence, by a perpetual coming and going between the infinite Self of perfect knowledge and the ego implied in the Game of Maya, we maintain the union of all the forces of life. In the bosom of contemplation we receive the necessary energy for love and work, for faith and joy in action, for the framework of our days. But each deed is transposed into the key of Eternity. At the heart of intense action reigns eternal calm, and the Spirit at the same time partakes of the struggles of life, and yet floats above the strife.

❑❑❑

A WREATH OF POEMS

The Hymn of Creation

Two translations of the *Nasadiya-Sukta*

Existence was not then, nor non-existence,
The world was not, the sky beyond was neither.
What covered the mist? Of whom was that?
What was in the depths of darkness thick?

Death was not then, nor immortality,
The night was neither separate from day,
But motionless did *That* vibrate
Alone, with Its own glory one—
Beyond *That* nothing did exist.

At first in darkness hidden darkness lay,
Undistinguished as one mass of water,
Then *That* which lay in void thus covered
A glory did put forth by *Tapah!*

First desire rose, the primal seed of mind,
(The sages have seen all this in their hearts
Sifting existence from non-existence.)
Its rays above, below and sideways spread.

Creative then became the glory,
With self-sustaining principle below,
And Creative Energy above.

Who knew the way? Who there declared
Whence this arose? Projection whence?
For after this projection came the gods.
Who therefore knew indeed, came out this whence?

This projection whence arose,
Whether held or whether not,
He the ruler in the supreme sky, of this
He, O Sharman! knows, or knows not.

•

One Mass, devoid of form, name, and colour,
Timeless, devoid of time past and future,
Spaceless, voiceless, boundless devoid of all—
Where rests hushed even speech of negation.

From thence, down floweth the river causal,
Wearing the form of desire radiant,
Its heaving waters angrily roaring
The constant roar, "I am", "I am".

In that ocean of desire limitless,
Appear shining waves, countless, infinite,
Oh, of what power manifold they are,
Of what forms myriad, of what repose,
Of what movements varied, who can reckon?

Millions of moons, millions of suns,
Taking their birth in that very ocean,
Rushing headlong with din tumultuous,
Overspread the whole firmament, drowning
The points of heaven in light effulgent.

In it arise and reside what beings,
Quick with life, dull, and lifeless—unnumbered,
And pleasure and pain, disease, birth, and death!
Verily, the Sun is He, His the ray,
Nay, the Sun is He, and He is the ray.

(Rigveda, X. 129)

India Awake

Once more awake!
For sleep it was, not death, to bring thee life
Anew, and rest to lotus-eyes for visions
Daring yet. The world in need awaits, O Truth!
No death for thee!

Resume thy march,
With gentle feet that would not break the
Peaceful rest even of the roadside dust
That lies so low. Yet strong and steady,
Blissful, bold, and free. Awakener, ever
Forward! Speak thy stirring words.

Thy home is gone,
Where loving hearts had brought thee up and
Watched with joy thy growth. But Fate is strong—
This is the law—all things come back to the source
They sprung, their strength to renew.

Then start afresh
From the land of thy birth, where vast cloud-belted
Snows do bless and put their strength in thee,
For working wonders new. The heavenly
River tune thy voice to her own immortal song;
Deodar shades give thee eternal peace.

And all above,
Himala's daughter Uma, gentle, pure,
The Mother that resides in all as Power
And Life, who works all works and

Makes of One the world, whose mercy
Opens the gate to Truth and shows
The One in All, give thee untiring
Strength, which is Infinite Love.

They bless thee all,
The seers great, whom age nor clime
Can claim their own, the fathers of the
Race, who felt the heart of Truth the same,
And bravely taught to man ill-voiced or
Well. Their servant, thou hast got
The secret—'tis but One.

Then speak, O Love!
Before thy gentle voice serene, behold how
Visions melt and fold on fold of dreams
Departs to void, till Truth and Truth alone
In all its glory shines.

And tell the world—
Awake, arise, and dream no more!
This is the land of dreams, where Karma
Weaves unthreaded garlands with our thoughts
Of flowers sweet or noxious, and none
Has root or stem, being born in naught, which
The softest breath, of Truth drives back to
Primal nothingness. Be bold, and face
The Truth! Be one with it! Let visions cease,
Or, if you cannot, dream but truer dreams,
Which are Eternal Love and Service Free.

Nirvana

-.-

Translation of a poem by Shankaracharya

I am neither the mind, nor the intellect, nor the ego, nor
the mind-stuff;
I am neither the body, nor the changes of the body;
I am neither the senses of hearing, taste, smell, or sight,
Nor am I the ether, the earth, the fire, the air;
I am Existence Absolute, Knowledge Absolute,
Bliss Absolute—
I am He, I am He. (Shivoham, Shivoham).

I am neither the Prana, nor the five vital airs;
I am neither the materials of the body, nor the five sheaths;
Neither am I the organs of action, nor object of the senses;
I am Existence Absolute, Knowledge Absolute,
Bliss Absolute—
I am He, I am He. (Shivoham, Shivoham).

I have neither aversion nor attachment, neither greed nor
delusion;
Neither egotism nor envy, neither Dharma nor Moksha;
I am neither desire nor object of desire;
I am Existence Absolute, Knowledge Absolute,
Bliss Absolute—
I am He, I am He. (Shivoham, Shivoham).

I am neither sin nor virtue, neither pleasure nor pain;
Nor temple nor worship, nor pilgrimage nor scriptures,
Neither the act of enjoying the enjoyable nor the enjoyer;
I am Existence Absolute, Knowledge Absolute,
Bliss Absolute—

I am He, I am He. (Shivoham, Shivoham).

I have neither death nor fear of death, nor caste;
Nor was I ever born, nor had I parents, friends, and relations;
I have neither Guru, nor disciple;
I am Existence Absolute, Knowledge Absolute, Bliss Absolute—
I am He, I am He. (Shivoham, Shivoham).

I am untouched by the senses, I am neither Mukti nor knowable;
I am without form, without limit, beyond space, beyond time;
I am in everything; I am the basis of the universe; everywhere am I.
I am Existence Absolute, Knowledge Absolute, Bliss Absolute—
I am He, I am He. (Shivoham, Shivoham).

Kali the Mother

The stars are blotted out,
    The clouds are covering clouds,
It is darkness vibrant, sonant.
    In the roaring, whirling wind
Are the souls of a million lunatics
    Just loose from the prison-house,
Wrenching trees by the roots,
    Sweeping all from the path.

The sea has joined the fray,
    And swirls up mountain-waves,
To reach the pitchy sky.
    The flash of lurid light
Reveals on every side
    A thousand, thousand shades
Of Death begrimed and black—
    Scattering plagues and sorrows,

Dancing mad with joy,
    Come, Mother, come!
For Terror is Thy name,
    Death is in Thy breath,

And every shaking step
    Destroys a world for e'er.
Thou "Time", the All-Destroyer!
    Come, O Mother, come!
Who dares misery love,
    And hug the form of Death,
Dance in Destruction's dance,
    To him the Mother comes.

Hold on Yet a While, Brave Heart

-.-

If the sun by the cloud is hidden a bit,
If the welkin shows but gloom,
Still hold on yet a while, brave heart,
The victory is sure to come.

No winter was but summer came behind,
Each hollow crests the wave,
They push each other in light and shade;
Be steady then and brave.

The duties of life are sore indeed,
And its pleasures fleeting, vain,
The goal so shadowy seems and dim,
Yet plod on through the dark, brave heart,
With all thy might and main.

Not a work will be lost, no struggle vain,
Though hopes be blighted, powers gone;
Of thy loins shall come the heirs to all,
Then hold on yet a while, brave soul,
No good is e'er undone.

Though the good and the wise in life are few,
Yet theirs are the reins to lead,
The masses know but late the worth;
    Heed none and gently guide.

With thee are those who see afar,
With thee is the Lord of might,
All blessings pour on thee, great soul,
    To thee may all come right!

Angels Unawares

One bending low with load of life—
That meant no joy, but suffering harsh and hard—
And wending on his way through dark and dismal paths
Without a flash of light from brain or heart
To give a moment's cheer, till the line
That marks out pain from pleasure, death from life,
And good from what is evil was well-nigh wiped from sight,
Saw, one blessed night, a faint but beautiful ray of light
Descend to him. He knew not what or wherefrom,
But called it God and worshipped.
Hope, an utter stranger, came to him and spread
Through all his parts, and life to him meant more
Than he could ever dream and covered all he knew,
Nay, peeped beyond his world. The Sages
Winked, and smiled, and called it "superstition".
But he did feel its power and peace
And gently answered back—
—"O Blessed Superstition!"

One drunk with wine of wealth and power
And health to enjoy them both, whirled on
His maddening course, till the earth, he thought,
Was made for him, his pleasure-garden, and man,
The crawling worm, was made to find him sport,
Till the thousand lights of joy, with pleasure fed,
That flickered day and night before his eyes,
With constant change of colours, began to blur
His sight, and cloy his senses; till selfishness,
Like a horny growth, had spread all o'er his heart;
And pleasure meant to him no more than pain,
Bereft of feeling; and life in the sense,
So joyful, precious once, a rotting corpse between his arms,
Which he forsooth would shun, but more he tried, the more
It clung to him; and wished, with frenzied brain,
A thousand forms of death, but quailed before the charm,
Then sorrow came—and Wealth and Power went—
And made him kinship find with all the human race
In groans and tears, and though his friends would laugh,
His lips would speak in grateful accents—
—"O Blessed Misery!"

One born with healthy frame—but not of will
That can resist emotions deep and strong,
Nor impulse throw, surcharged with potent strength—

And just the sort that pass as good and kind,
Beheld that he was safe, whilst others long
And vain did struggle gainst the surging waves.
Till, morbid grown, his mind could see, like flies
That seek the putrid part, but what was bad.

Then Fortune smiled on him, and his foot slipped.
That ope'd his eyes for e'er, and made him find
That stones and trees ne'er break the law,
But stones and trees remain; that man alone
Is blest with power to fight and conquer Fate,
Transcending bounds and laws.

From him his passive nature fell, and life appeared
As broad and new, and broader, newer grew,
Till light ahead began to break, and glimpse of That
Where Peace Eternal dwells—yet one can only reach
By wading through the sea of struggles—courage giving, came.
Then looking back on all that made him kin
To stocks and stones, and on to what the world
Had shunned him for, his fall, he blessed the fall,
And with a joyful heart, declared it—

—"Blessed Sin!"

O, Sannyasin

Wake up the note! the song that had its birth
Far off, where worldly taint could never reach,
In mountain caves and glades of forest deep,
Whose calm no sigh for lust or wealth or fame
Could ever dare to break; where rolled the stream
Of knowledge, truth, and bliss that follows both.
Sing high that note, Sannyasin bold! Say—
"Om Tat Sat, Om!"

Strike off thy fetters! Bonds that bind thee down,
Of shining gold, or darker, baser ore;
Love, hate—good, bad—and all the dual throng,
Know, slave is slave, caressed or whipped, not free;
For fetters, though of gold, are not less strong to bind;
Then off with them, Sannyasin bold! Say—
"Om Tat Sat, Om!"

Let darkness go; the will-o'-the-wisp that leads
With blinking light to pile more gloom on gloom.
This thirst for life, for ever quench; it drags
From birth to death, and death to birth, the soul.
He conquers all who conquers self. Know this
And never yield, Sannyasin bold! Say—
"Om Tat Sat, Om!"

"Who sows must reap," they say, "and cause must bring
The sure effect; good, good; bad, bad; and none
Escape the law. But whoso wears a form

Must wear the chain." Too true; but far beyond
Both name and form is Atman, ever free.
Know thou art That, Sannyasin bold! Say—
"Om Tat Sat, Om!"

They know not truth who dream such vacant dreams
As father, mother, children, wife, and friend.
The sexless Self! whose father He? whose child?
Whose friend, whose foe is He who is but One?
The Self is all in all, none else exists;
And thou art That, Sannyasin bold! Say—
"Om Tat Sat, Om!"

There is but One—The Free—The Knower—Self!
Without a name, without a form or stain.
In Him is Maya dreaming all this dream.
The witness, He appears as nature, soul.
Know thou art That, Sannyasin bold! Say—
"Om Tat Sat, Om!"

Where seekest thou? That freedom, friend, this world
Nor that can give. In books and temples vain
Thy search. Thine only is the hand that holds
The rope that drags thee on. Then cease lament,
Let go thy hold, Sannyasin bold! Say—
"Om Tat Sat, Om!"

Say, "Peace to all: From me no danger be
To aught that lives. In those that dwell on high.
In those that lowly creep, I am the Self in all!
All life both here and there, do I renounce,
All heavens and earths and hells, all hopes and fears."
Thus cut thy bonds, Sannyasin bold! Say—
"Om Tat Sat, Om!"

Heed then no more how body lives or goes,
Its task is done Let, Karma float it down;
Let one put garlands on, another kick

This frame; say naught. No praise or blame can be
Where praiser praised, and blamer blamed are one.
Thus be thou calm, Sannyasin bold! Say—
"Om Tat Sat, Om!"

Truth never comes where lust and fame and greed
Of gain reside. No man who thinks of woman
As his wife can ever perfect be;
Nor he who owns the least of things, nor he
Whom anger chains, can ever pass thro' Maya's gates.
So, give these up, Sannyasbin bold! Say—
"Om Tat Sat, Om!"

Have thou no home. What home can hold thee, friend?
The sky thy roof, the grass thy bed; and food
What chance may bring, well cooked or ill, judge not.
No food or drink can taint that noble Self
Which knows Itself. Like rolling river free
Thou ever be, Sannyasin bold! Say—
"Om Tat Sat, Om!"

Few only know the truth. The rest will hate
And laugh at thee, great one; but pay no heed.
Go thou, the free, from place to place, and help
Them out of darkness, Maya's veil. Without
The fear of pain or search for pleasure, go
Beyond them both, Sannyasin bold! Say—
"Om Tat Sat, Om!"

Thus, day by day, till Karma's powers spent
Release the soul for ever. No more is birth,
Nor I, nor thou, nor God, nor man. The "I"
Has All become, the All is "I" and Bliss.
Know thou art That, Sannyasin bold! Say—
"Om Tat Sat, Om!"

The Hymn of Samadhi

Lo! The sun is not, nor the comely moon,
All light extinct; in the great void of space
Floats shadow-like the image-universe.

In the void of mind involute, there floats
The fleeting universe, rises and floats,
Sinks again, ceaseless, in the current "I".

Slowly, slowly, the shadow-multitude
Entered the primal womb, and flowed ceaseless,
The only current, the "I am", "I am".

Lo! 'Tis stopped, ev'n that current flows no more,
Void merged into void—beyond speech and mind!
Whose heart understands, he verily does,

The Cup

This is your cup—the cup assigned
        to you from the beginning.
Nay, My child, I know how much
        of that dark drink is your own brew
Of fault and passion, ages long ago,
In the deep years of yesterday, I know.

This is your road—a painful road and drear.
I made the stones that never give you rest.
I set your friend in pleasant ways and clear,
And he shall come like you, unto My breast.
But you, My child, must travel here.

This is your task. It has no joy nor grace,
But it is not meant for any other hand,
And in My universe hath measured place,
Take it. I do not bid you understand.
I bid you close your eyes to see My face.

On the Seas

In blue sky floats a multitude of clouds—
White, black, of many shades and thicknesses;

An orange sun, about to say farewell,
Touches the massed cloud-shapes with streaks of red.

The wind blows as it lists, a hurricane
Now carving shapes, now breaking them apart:

Fancies, colours, forms, inert creations—
A myriad scenes, though real, yet fantastic.

There light clouds spread, heaping up spun cotton;
See next a huge snake, then a strong lion;
Again, behold a couple locked in love.
All vanish, at last, in the vapoury sky.

Below, the sea sings a varied music,
But not grand, O India, nor ennobling:
Thy waters, widely praised, murmur serene
In soothing cadence, without a harsh roar.

The Living God

He who is in you and outside you,
Who works through all hands,
Who walks on all feet,
Whose body are all ye,
Him worship, and break all other idols!

He who is at once the high and low,
The sinner and the saint,
Both God and worm,
Him worship—visible, knowable, real, omnipresent,
Break all other idols!

In whom is neither past life
Nor future birth nor death,
In whom we always have been
And always shall be one,
Him worship. Break all other idols!

Ye fools! who neglect the living God,
And His infinite reflections with which the world is full.

While ye run after imaginary shadows,
That lead alone to fights and quarrels,
Him worship, the only visible!
Break all other idols!

To an Early Violet

What though thy bed be frozen earth,
    Thy cloak the chilling blast;
What though no mate to cheer thy path,
    Thy sky with gloom o'ercast;

What though if love itself doth fail,
    Thy fragrance strewed in vain;
What though if bad o'er good prevail,
    And vice o'er virtue reign:

Change not thy nature, gentle bloom,
    Thou violet, sweet and pure,
But ever pour thy sweet perfume
    Unasked, unstinted, sure!

To My Own Soul

Hold yet a while, Strong Heart,
Not part a lifelong yoke
Though blighted looks the present, future gloom.

And age it seems since you and I began our
March up hill or down. Sailing smooth o'er
Seas that are so rare—
Thou nearer unto me, than oft-times I myself—
Proclaiming mental moves before they were!

Reflector true—Thy pulse so timed to mine,
Thou perfect note of thoughts, however fine—
Shall we now part, Recorder, say?

In thee is friendship, faith,
For thou didst warn when evil thoughts were brewing—
And though, alas, thy warning thrown away,
Went on the same as ever—good and true.

In Memorium

-.-

Written in memoriam to J.J. Goodwin,

Speed forth, a Soul! upon thy star-strewn path;
Speed, blissful one! where thought is ever free,
Where time and space no longer mist the view,
Eternal peace and blessings be with thee!

Thy service true, complete thy sacrifice,
Thy home the heart of love transcendent find;
Remembrance sweet, that kills all space and time,
Like altar roses fill thy place behind!

Thy bonds are broke, thy quest in bliss is found,
And one with That which comes as Death and Life;
Thou helpful one! unselfish e'er on earth.
Ahead! still help with love this world of strife!

Now Sister Mary

-.-

(This interesting correspondence in poetry was carried between the Swami and Mary Hale, one of the two daugthers of Mr. and Mrs. Hale whom he addressed as Father Pope and Mother Church. The 'hard raps' he mentions is a strong letter he wrote to her in vindication of his position. He was very close to both the sisters as well as their cousins. In it the Swami is seen in a new light, playful yet keen on the central theme of his life.)

Now Sister Mary,
You need not be sorry
For the hard raps I gave you,
You know full well,
Though you like me tell,
With my whole heart I love you.

The babies I bet,
The best friends I met,
Will stand by me in weal and woe.
And so will I do,
You know it too.

Life, name, or fame, even heaven forgo
For the sweet sisters four
Sans reproche et sans peur,
The truest, noblest, steadfast, best.

The wounded snake its hood unfurls,
The flame stirred up both blaze,

The desert air resounds the calls
Of heart-struck lion's rage.

The cloud puts forth its deluge strength
When lightning cleaves its breast,
When the soul is stirred to its inmost depth
Great ones unfold their best.

Let eyes grow dim and heart grow faint,
And friendship fail and love betray,
Let Fate its hundred horrors send,
And clotted darkness block the way.

All nature wear one angry frown,
To crush you out—still know, my soul,
You are Divine. March on and on,
Nor right nor left but to the goal.

Nor angel I, nor man, nor brute,
Nor body, mind, nor he or she,
The books do stop in wonder mute
To tell my nature; I am He.

Before the sun, the moon, the earth,
Before the stars or comets free,
Before e'en time has had its birth,
I was, I am, and I will be.

The beauteous earth, the glorious sun,
The calm sweet moon, the spangled sky,
Causation's laws do make them run;
They live in bonds, in bonds they die.

When from the crowd
A voice aloud
This question asked beseeching, seeking—
"Sir, tell me, pray,
Who were but they
These Sita Ram you were teaching, speaking!"

So Mary Hale,
Allow me tell,
You mar my doctrines wronging, baulking.
I never taught
Such queer thought
That all was God—unmeaning talking!

But this I say,
Remember pray,
The God is *true*, all else is *nothing*,
This world's a dream
Though true it seem,
And only truth is *He* the living!
The real *me* is none but *He*,
And never, never *matter* changing!
With undying love and gratitude to you all...

•

And then wrote Mary Hale:

The difference I clearly see
Twixt tweedledum and tweedledee—
That is a proposition sane,
But truly 'tis beyong my vein
To make your Eastern logic plain.

If "God is truth, all else is naught,"
This "world a dream", delusion up wrought,
What can exist which God is not?
All those who "many" see have much to fear,
He only lives to whom the "One" is clear.
So again I say
In my poor way,
I cannot see but that all's He,
If I'm in Him and He in me.

•

The Swami replies:

Of temper quick, a girl unique,
    A freak of nature she,
A lady fair, no question there,
    Rare soul is Miss Mary.
Her feelings deep she cannot keep,
    But creep they out at last,
A spirit free, I can foresee,
    Must be of fiery cast.

Tho' many a lay her muse can bray,
    And play piano too,
Her heart so cool, chills as a rule
    The fool who comes to woo.
Though, Sister Mary, I hear they say
    The sway your beauty gains,
Be cautious now and do not bow,
    However sweet, to chains.

For 'twill be soon, another tune
    The moon-struck mate will hear
If his will but clash, your words will hash
    And smash his life I fear.
These lines to thee, Sister Mary,
    Free will I offer, take
"Tit for tat"—a monkey chat,
    For monk alone can make.

Peace

Behold, it comes in might,
The power that is not power,
The light that is in darkness,
The shade in dazzling light.

It is joy that never spoke,
And grief unfelt, profound,
Immortal life unlived,
Eternal death unmourned.

It is not joy nor sorrow,
But that which is between,
It is not night nor morrow,
But that which joins them in.

It is sweet rest in music;
And pause in sacred art;
The silence between speaking;
Between two fits of passion—
It is the calm of heart.

It is beauty never seen,
And love that stands alone,
It is song that lives unsung,
And knowledge never known.

It is death between two lives,
And lull between two storms,
The void whence rose creation,
And that where it returns.

To it the tear-drop goes,
To spread the smiling form
It is the Goal of Life,
And Peace—its only home!

My Play Is Done

-.-

Ever rising, ever falling with the waves of time,
still rolling on I go
From fleeting scene to scene ephemeral,
with life's currents' ebb and flow.

Oh! I am sick of this unending force;
these shows they please no more.
This ever running, never reaching,
nor e'en a distant glimpse of shore!

From life to life I'm waiting at the gates,
alas, they open not.
Dim are my eyes with vain attempt
to catch one ray long sought.

On little life's high, narrow bridge
I stand and see below
The struggling, crying, laughing throng.
For what? No one can know.

In front yon gates stand frowning dark,
and say: "No farther way,
This is the limit; tempt not Fate,
bear it as best you may;

Go, mix with them and drink this cup
and be as mad as they.
Who dares to know but comes to grief;
stop then, and with them stay."

Alas for me, I cannot rest.
This floating bubble, earth—
Its hollow form, its hollow name,
its hollow death and birth—

For me is nothing. How I long
to get beyond the crust
Of name and form! Ah! open the gates;
to me they open must.
Open the gates of light, O Mother,
To me Thy tired son.

I long, oh, long to return home!
Mother, my play is done.
You sent me out in the dark to play,
and wore a frightful mask;

Then hope departed, terror came,
and play became a task.
Tossed to and fro, from wave to wave
in this seething, surging sea

Of passions strong and sorrows deep,
grief *is,* and joy *to be,*
Where life is living death, alas! and death—
who knows but 'tis

Another start, another round of this old wheel
of grief and bliss?
Where children dream bright, golden dreams,
too soon to find them dust,

And aye look back to hope long lost
and life a mass of rust!
Too late, the knowledge age doth gain;
scarce from the wheel we're gone

When fresh, young lives put their strength
to the wheel, which thus goes on
From day to day and year to year.
'Tis but delusion's toy,

False hope its motor; desire, nave;
its spokes are grief and joy.
I go adrift and know not whither.
Save me from this fire!

Rescue me, merciful Mother,
from floating with desire!
Turn not to me Thy awful face,
'tis more than I can bear.
Be merciful and kind to me,
to chide my faults forbear.

Take me, O Mother, to those shores
where strifes for ever cease;
Beyond all sorrows, beyond tears,
beyond e'en earthly bliss;

Whose glory neither sun, nor moon,
nor stars that twinkle bright,
Nor flash of lightning can express.
They but reflect its light.

Let never more delusive dreams
veil off Thy face from me.
My play is done, O Mother,
break my chains and make me free!

A Hymn to Shri Ramakrishna

आचण्डालाप्रतिहतरयो यस्य प्रेमप्रवाहः
लोकातीतोऽप्यहह न जहौ लोककल्याणमार्गम्।
त्रैलोक्येऽप्यप्रतिममहिमा जानकीप्राणबन्धो
भक्त्या ज्ञानं वृतबरवपुः सीतया यो हि रामः!! 1!!

He who was Shri Rama, whose stream of love flowed with resistless might even to the Chandala (the outcaste); Oh, who ever was engaged in doing good to the world though superhuman by nature, whose renown there is none to equal in the three worlds, Sita's beloved, whose body of Knowledge Supreme was covered by devotion sweet in the form of Sita.

स्तब्धीकृत्य प्रलयकलितं वाहवोत्थं महान्तं
हित्वा रात्रिं प्रकृतिसहजामन्धतामिस्रमिश्राम्।
गीतं शान्तं मधुरमपि यः सिंहनादं जगर्ज
सोऽयं जातः प्रथितपुरुषो रामकृष्णस्त्विदानीम्।। 2 !!

He who quelled the noise, terrible like that at the time of destruction, arising from the battle (of Kurukshetra), who destroyed the terrible yet natural night of ignorance (of Arjuna) and who roared out the Gita sweet and appeasing; That renowned soul is born now as Shri Ramakrishna.

नरदेव देव जय जय नरदेव।
शक्तिसमुद्रसमुत्थतरङ्गं
दर्शितप्रेमविजृम्भितरङ्गम्।।
संशयराक्षसनाशमहास्त्रं
यामि गुरुं शरणं भववैद्यम्।
नरदेव देव जय जय नरदेव।

Hail, O Lord of Men! Victory unto You! I surrender myself to my Guru, the physician for the malady of Samsâra (relative existence) who is, as it were, a wave rising in the ocean of Shakti (Power), who has shown various sports of Love Divine, and who is the weapon to destroy the demon of doubt. Hail, O Lord of Men! Victory unto You!

नरदेव देव जय जय नरदेव।
अद्वयतत्त्वसमाहितचित्तं
प्रोज्ज्वलभक्तिपटावृतवृत्तम्।।
कर्मकलेवरमद्भुतचेष्टं
यामि गुरुं शरणं भववैद्यम्।
नरदेव देव जय जय नरदेव।

Hail, O Lord of Men! Victory unto you! I surrender myself to my Guru the Man-God, the physician for the malady of this Samsara (relative existence), whose mind ever dwelt on the non-dualistic Truth, whose personality was covered by the cloth of Supreme Devotion, who was ever active (for the good of humanity) and whose actions were all superhuman. Hail, O Lord of Men! Victory unto You!

Light

I look behind and after
And find that all is right,
In my deepest sorrows
There is a soul of light.

❑❑❑

SELECT LECTURES AND WRITINGS

My Life and Mission

Ladies and gentlemen, I have been asked by your president and some of the ladies and gentlemen here to tell them something about my work and what I have been doing. It may be interesting to some here, but not so much so to me. In fact, I do not quite know how to tell it to you, for this will have been the first time in my life that I have spoken on that subject.

Now, to understand what I have been trying to do in my small way, I will take you, in imagination, to India. We have not time to go into all the details and all the ramifications of the subject; nor is it possible for you to understand all the complexities in a foreign race in this short time. Suffice it to say, I will at least try to give you a little picture of what India is like.

India is like a gigantic building all tumbled down in ruins. At first sight, then, there is little hope. It is a nation gone and ruined. But you wait and study, then you see something beyond that. The truth is that so long as the principle, the ideal, of which the outer man is the expression, is not hurt or destroyed, the man lives, and there is hope for that man. If your coat is stolen twenty times, that is no reason why you should be destroyed. You can get a new coat. The coat is unessential. The fact that a rich man is robbed does not hurt the vitality of the man, does not mean death. The man will survive.

Standing on this principle, we look in and we see—what? India is no longer a political power; it is an enslaved race. Indians have no say, no voice in their own government; they are three hundred millions of slaves—nothing more! The average income of a man in India is two shillings a month. The common state of the vast mass of the people is starvation, so that, with the least decrease in income, millions die. A little famine means death. So there, too, when I look on that side of India, I see ruin—hopeless ruin.

But we find that **the Indian race never stood for wealth.** Although they acquired immense wealth, perhaps more than any other nation ever acquired, yet the nation did not stand for wealth. It was a powerful race for ages, yet we find that nation never stood for power, **never went out of the country to conquer.** Quite content within their own boundaries, they never fought anybody. The Indian nation never stood for imperial glory. **Wealth and power, then, were not the ideals of the race.**

What then? Whether they were wrong or right—that is not the question we discuss—**that nation, among all the children of men, has believed, and believed intensely, that this life is not real. The real is God;** and they must cling unto that God through thick and thin. In the midst of their degradation, religion came first. The Hindu man drinks religiously, sleeps religiously, walks religiously, marries religiously, robs religiously.

Did you ever see such a country? If you want to set up a gang of robbers, the leader will have to preach some sort of religion, then formulate some bogus metaphysics, and say that this method is the clearest and quickest way to get God. Then he finds a following, otherwise not. That shows that **the vitality of the race, the mission of the race is religion; and because that has not been touched, therefore that race lives.**

See Rome. **Rome's mission was imperial power,** expansion. And so soon as that was touched, Rome fell to pieces, passed out. **The mission of Greece was intellect,** as soon as that was touched, why, Greece passed out. So in modern times, Spain and all these modern countries. **Each nation has a mission for the world. So long as that mission is not hurt, that nation lives,** despite every difficulty. But as soon as its mission is destroyed, the nation collapses.

Now, **that vitality of India has not been touched yet.** They have not given up that, and it is still strong—in spite of all their superstitions. Hideous superstitions are there, most revolting some of them. Never mind. **The national life-current is still there**—the mission of the race.

The Indian nation never will be a powerful conquering people—never. They will never be a great political power; that is not their business, that is not the note India has the play in the great harmony of nations. But what has she to play? God, and God alone. She clings unto that like grim death. Still there is hope there.

So then, after your analysis, you come to the conclusion that all these things, all this poverty and misery, are of no consequence—the man is living still, and therefore there is hope.

Well! You see religious activities going on all through the country. I do not recall a year that has not given birth to several new sects in India. The stronger the current, the more the whirlpools and eddies. Sects are not signs of decay, they are a sign of life. Let sects multiply, till the time comes when every one of us is a sect, each individual. We need not quarrel about that.

Now, take your country (I do not mean any criticism). Here the social laws, the political formation—everything is made to facilitate man's journey in this life. He may live very happily so long as he is on this earth. Look at your streets—how clean! Your beautiful cities! And in how many ways a man can make money! How many channels to get enjoyment in this life! But, if a man here should say, "Now look here, I shall sit down under this tree and meditate; I do not want to work," why, he would have to go to jail. See! There would be no chance for him at all. None. A man can live in this society only if he falls in line. He has to join in this rush for the enjoyment of good in this life, or he dies.

Now let us go back to India. There, if a man says, "I shall go and sit on the top of that mountain and look at the tip of my nose all the rest of my days," everybody says, "Go, and Godspeed to you!" He need not speak a word. Somebody brings him a little cloth, and he is all right. But if a man says, "Behold, I am going to enjoy a little of this life," every door is closed to him.

I say that the ideas of both countries are unjust. I see no reason why a man here should not sit down and look at the tip of his nose if he likes. Why should everybody here do just what the majority does? I see no reason.

Nor why, in India, a man should not have the goods of this life and make money. But you see how those vast millions are forced to accept the opposite point of view by tyranny. This is the tyranny of the sages. This is the tyranny of the great, tyranny of the spiritual, tyranny of the intellectual, tyranny of the wise. And the tyranny of the wise, mind you, is much more powerful than the tyranny of the ignorant. The wise, the intellectual, when they take to forcing their opinions upon others, know a hundred thousand ways to make bonds and barriers which it is not in the power of the ignorant to break.

Now, I say that this thing has got to stop. There is no use in sacrificing millions and millions of people to produce one spiritual giant. **If it is possible to make a society where the spiritual giant will be produced and all the rest of the people will be happy as well, that is good; but if the millions have to be ground down, that is unjust. Better that the one great man should suffer for the salvation of the world.**

In every nation you will have to work through their methods. To every man you will have to speak in his own language. Now, in England or in America, if you want to preach religion to them, you will have to work through political methods—make organisations, societies, with voting, balloting, a president, and so on, because that is the language, the method of the Western race. On the other hand, if you want to speak of politics in India, you must speak through the language of religion. You will have to tell them something like this: "The man who cleans his house every morning will acquire such and such an amount of merit, he will go to heaven, or he comes to God." Unless you put it that way, they will not listen to you. It is a question of language. The thing done is the same. But with every race, you will have to speak their language in order to reach their hearts. And that is quite just. We need not fret about that.

In the Order to which I belong we are called Sannyasins. The word means "a man who has renounced". This is a very, very, very ancient Order. Even Buddha, who was 560 years before Christ, belonged to that Order. He was one of the reformers of his Order. That was all. So ancient! You find it mentioned way back in the Vedas, the oldest book in the world. In old India there was the regulation that every man and woman, towards the end of their lives, must get out of social life altogether and think of nothing except God and their own salvation. This was to get ready for the great event—death. So old people used to become Sannyasins in those early days. Later on, young people began to give up the world. And young people are active. They could not sit down under a tree and think all the time of their own death, so they went about preaching and starting sects, and so on. Thus, Buddha, being young, started that great reform. Had he been an old man, he would have looked at the tip of his nose and died quietly.

The Order is not a church, and the people who join the Order are not priests. There is an absolute difference between the priests and the Sannyasins. In India, priesthood, like every other business in a social life, is a hereditary profession. A priest's son will become a priest, just as a carpenter's son will be a carpenter, or a blacksmith's son a blacksmith. The priest must always be married. The Hindu does not think a man is complete unless he has a wife. An unmarried man has no right to perform religious ceremonies.

The Sannyasins do not possess property, and they do not marry. Beyond that there is no organisation. The only bond that is there is the bond between the teacher and the taught—and that is peculiar to India. The teacher is not a man who comes just to teach me, and I pay him so much, and there it ends. In India it is really like an adoption. The teacher is more than my own father, and I am truly his child, his son in every respect. I owe him obedience and reverence first, before my own father even; because, they say, the father gave me this body, but *he* showed me the way to salvation, so he is greater than father. And we carry this love, this respect for our teacher all our lives. And that is the only organisation that exists. I adopt my disciples. Sometimes the teacher will be a young man and the disciple a very old man. But never mind, he is the son, and he calls me "Father," and I have to address him as my son, my daughter, and so on.

Now, **I happened to get an old man to teach me, and he was very peculiar.** He did not go much for intellectual scholarship, scarcely studied books; but when he was a boy he was seized with the tremendous idea of getting truth direct. First he tried by studying his own religion. **Then he got the idea that he must get the truth of**

other religions; and with that idea he joined all the sects, one after another. For the time being he did exactly what they told him to do—lived with the devotees of these different sects in turn, until he interpenetrated with the particular ideal of that sect. After a few years he would go to another sect. When he had gone through with all that, **he came to the conclusion that they were all good** He had no criticism to offer to anyone; **they are all so many paths leading to the same goal.** And then he said, "That is a glorious thing, that there should be so many paths, because if there were only one path, perhaps it would suit only an individual man. The more the number of paths, the more the chance for every one of us to know the truth. If I cannot be taught in one language, I will try another, and so on." Thus his benediction was for every religion.

Now, all the ideas that I preach are only an attempt to echo his ideas. Nothing is mine originally except the wicked ones, everything I say which is false and wicked. But every word that I have ever uttered which is true and good is simply an attempt to echo his voice.

Well, there at his feet I conceived these ideas—there with some other young men. I was just a boy. I went there when I was about sixteen. Some of the other boys were still younger, some a little older—about a dozen or more. And together we conceived that this ideal had to be spread. And not only spread, but made practical. That is to say, we must show the spirituality of the Hindus, the mercifulness of the Buddhists, the activity of the Christians, the brotherhood of the Mohammedans, by our practical lives. **"We shall start a universal religion now and here," we said, "we will not wait".**

Our teacher was an old man who would never touch a coin with his hands. He took just the little food offered, just so many yards of cotton cloth, no more. He could never be induced to take any other gift. With all these marvellous ideas, he was strict, because that made him free. The monk in India is the friend of the prince today, dines with him; and tomorrow he is with the beggar, sleeps under a tree. He must come into contact with everyone, must always move about. As the saying is, "The rolling stone gathers no moss." **The last fourteen years of my life, I have never been for three**

months at a time in anyone place—continually rolling. So do we all.

Now, this handful of boys got hold of these ideas, and all the practical results that sprang out of these ideas. Universal religion, great sympathy for the poor, and all that are very good in theory, but one must practise.

Then came the sad day when our old teacher died. We nursed him the best we could. We had no friends. Who would listen to a few boys, with their crank notions? Nobody. At least, in India, boys are nobodies. Just think of it—dozen boys, telling people vast, big ideas, saying they are determined to work these ideas out in life. Why, everybody laughed. From laughter it became serious; it became persecution. Why, the parents of the boys came to feel like spanking everyone of us. And the more we were derided, the more determined we became.

Then came a terrible time—for me personally and for all the other boys as well. But to me came such misfortune! On the one side was my mother, my brothers. My father died at that time, and we were left poor. Oh, very poor, almost starving all the time! I was the only hope of the family, the only one who could do anything to help them. I had to stand between my two worlds. On the one hand, I would have to see my mother and brothers starve unto death; on the other, I had believed that this man's ideas were for the good of India and the world, and had to be preached and worked out. And so the fight went on in my mind for days and months. Sometimes I would pray for five or six days and nights together without stopping. Oh, the agony of those days! I was living in hell! The natural affections of my boy's heart drawing me to my family—I could not bear to see those who were the nearest and dearest to me suffering. On the other hand, nobody to sympathies with me. Who would sympathies with the imaginations of a boy—imaginations that caused so much suffering to others? Who would sympathise with me? None—except one.

That one's sympathy brought blessing and hope. She was a woman. Our teacher, this great monk, was married when he was a boy and she a mere child. When he became a young man, and all this religious zeal was upon him, she came to see him. Although they had been married for long, they had not seen very much of each other until they were grown up. Then he said to his wife, "Behold, I am your husband; you have a right to this body. But I cannot live the sex life, although I have married you. I leave it to your judgment." And she wept and said, "God speed you! The Lord bless you! Am I the woman to degrade you? If I can, I will help you. Go on in your work."

That was the woman. The husband went on and became a monk in his own way; and from a distance the wife went on helping as much as she could. And later when the man had become a great spiritual giant, she came—really, she was the first disciple—and she spent the rest of her life taking care of the body of this man. He never knew whether he was living or dying or anything. Sometimes, when talking, he would get so excited that if he sat on live charcoals, he did not know it. Live charcoals! Forgetting all about his body, all the time.

Well, that lady, his wife, was the only one who sympathised with the idea of those boys. But she was powerless. She was poorer than we were. Never mind! We plunged into the breach. I believed, that these ideas were going to rationalise India and bring better days to many lands and foreign races. With that belief, came the realisation that it is better that a few persons suffer than that such ideas should die out of the world. What if a mother or two brothers die? It is a sacrifice. Let it be done. No great thing can be done without sacrifice. The heart must be plucked out and the bleeding heart placed upon the altar. Then great things are done. Is there any other way? None have found it. I appeal to each one of you, to those who have accomplished any great thing. Oh, how much it has cost! What agony! What torture! What terrible suffering is behind every deed of success in every life! You know that, all of you.

And thus we went on, that band of boys. The only thing we got from those around us was a kick and a curse—that was all. Of course, we had to beg from door to door for our food: got hips and haws—the refuse of everything—a piece of bread here and there. **We got hold of a broken-down old house, with hissing cobras living underneath; and because that was the cheapest, we went into that house and lived there.**

Thus we went on for some years, in the meanwhile making excursions all over India, trying to bring about the idea gradually. **Ten years were spent without a ray of light! Ten more years!** A thousand times despondency came; but there was one thing always to keep us hopeful—the tremendous faithfulness to each other, the tremendous love between us. I have got a hundred men and women around me; if I become the devil himself tomorrow, they will say, "Here we are still! We will never give you up!" That is a great blessing. In happiness, in misery, in famine, in pain, in the grave, in heaven, or in hell who never gives me up is my friend. Is such friendship a joke? A man may have salvation through such friendship. That brings salvation if we can love like that. If we have that faithfulness, why, there is the essence of all concentration. You need not worship any gods in the world if you have that faith, that strength, that love. And that was there with us all throughout that hard time. That was there. That made us go from the Himalayas to Cape Comorin, from the Indus to the Brahmaputra.

This band of boys began to travel about. Gradually we began to draw attention: ninety per cent was antagonism, very little of it was helpful. For we had one fault: we were boys—in poverty and with all the roughness of boys. He who has to make his own way in life is a bit rough, he has not much time to be smooth and suave and polite—"my lady and my gentleman," and all that. You have seen that in life, always. He is a rough diamond, he has not much polish, he is a jewel in an indifferent casket.

And there we were. "No compromise" was the watchword. "This is the ideal, and this has got to be carried out. If we meet the king, though we die, we must give him a bit of our minds; if the peasant, the same." Naturally, we met with antagonism.

But, mind you, this is life's experience; if you really want the good of others, the whole universe may stand against you and cannot hurt you. It must crumble before your power of the Lord Himself in you if you are sincere and really unselfish. And those boys were that. They came as children, pure and fresh from the hands of nature. Said our Master: 'I want to offer at the altar of the Lord only those flowers that have not even been smelled, fruits that have not been touched with the fingers.' The words of the great man sustained us all. For he saw through the future life of those boys that he collected from the streets of Calcutta, so to say. People used to laugh at him when he said, "You will see—this boy, that boy, what he becomes." His faith was unalterable: "Mother showed it to me. I may be weak but when she says this is so—She can never make mistakes—it must be so."

So things went on and on for ten years without any light, but with my health breaking all the time. It tells on the body in the long run: sometimes one meal at nine in the evening, another time a meal at eight in the morning, another after two days, another after three days—and always the poorest and roughest thing. Who is going to give to the beggar the good things he has? And then, they have not much in India. And most of the time walking, climbing snow peaks, sometimes ten miles of hard mountain climbing, just to get a meal. They eat unleavened bread in India, and sometimes they have it stored away for twenty or thirty days, until it is harder than bricks; and then they will give a square of that. I would have to go from house to house to collect sufficient for one meal. And then the bread was so hard, it made my mouth bleed to eat it. Literally, you can break your teeth on that bread. Then I would put it in a pot and pour over it water from the river. For months and months I existed that way—of course it was telling on the health.

Then I thought, I have tried India: it is time for me to try another country. At that time your Parliament of Religions was to be held, and someone was to be sent from India, I was just a vagabond, but I said, "If you send me, I am going. I have not much to lose, and I do not care if I lose that." It was very difficult to find the money, but after a long struggle they got together just enough to pay for my passage—and I came. Came one or two months earlier, so that I found myself drifting about in the streets here, without knowing anybody.

But finally the Parliament of Religions opened, and I met kind friends, who helped me right along. I worked a little, collected funds, started two papers, and so on. After that I went over to England and worked there. At the same time I carried on the work for India in America too.

My plan for India, as it has been developed and centralised, is this: I have told you of our lives as monks there, how we go from door to door, so that religion is brought to everybody without charge, except, perhaps, a broken piece of bread. That is why you see the lowest of the low in India holding the most exalted religious ideas. It is all through the work of these monks. But ask a man, "Who are the English?"—he does not know. He says perhaps, "They are the children of those giants they speak of in those books, are they not?" "Who governs you?" "We do not know." "What is the government?" They do not know. But they know philosophy. It is a practical want of intellectual education about life on this earth they suffer from. These millions and millions of people are ready for life beyond this world—is not that enough for them? Certainly not. They must have a better piece of bread and a better piece of rag on their bodies. **The great question is: How to get that better bread and better rag for these sunken millions.**

First, I must tell you, there is great hope for them, because, you see, they are the gentlest people on earth. Not that they are timid. When they want to fight, they fight like demons. The best soldiers the English have are recruited from the peasantry of India. Death is a thing of no importance to them. Their attitude is "Twenty times I have died before, and I shall die many times after this. What of that?" They never turn back. They are not given to much emotion, but they make very good fighters.

Their instinct, however, is to plough. If you rob them, murder them, tax them, do anything to them, they will be quiet and gentle, so long as you leave them free to practise their religion. They never interfere with the religion of others. "Leave us liberty to worship our gods, and take everything else!" That is their attitude. When the English touch them there, trouble starts. That was the real cause of the 1857 Mutiny—they would not bear religious repression. The great Mohammedan governments were simply blown up because they touched the Indians' religion.

But aside from that, they are very peaceful, very quiet, very gentle, and above all, not given to vice. **The absence of any strong drink, oh, it makes them infinitely superior to the mobs of any other country.** You cannot compare the decency of life among the poor in India with life in the slums here. A slum means poverty, but poverty does not mean sin, indecency, and vice in India. In other countries, the opportunities are such that only the indecent and the lazy need be poor. There is no reason for poverty unless one is a fool or a blackguard—the sort who want city life and all its luxuries. They will not go into the country. They say, "We are here with all the fun, and you must give us bread." But that is not the case in India, where the poor fellows work hard from morning to sunset, and somebody else takes the bread out of their hands, and their children go hungry. Notwithstanding the millions of tons of wheat raised in India, scarcely a grain passes the mouth of a peasant. He lives upon the poorest corn, which you would not feed to your canary-birds.

Now there is no reason why they should suffer such distress—these people; oh, so pure and good! We hear so much talk about the sunken millions and the degraded women of India—but none come to our help. What do they say? They say, "You can only be helped, you can only be good by ceasing to be what you are. It is useless to help Hindus." These people do not know the history of races. There will be no more India if they change their religion and their institutions, because that is the vitality of that race. It will disappear; so, really you will have nobody to help.

Then there is the other great point to learn: that you can never help really. What can we do for each other? You are growing in your own life, I am growing in my own. It is possible that I can give you a push in your life, knowing that, in the long run, all roads lead to Rome. It is a steady growth. No national civilisation is perfect yet. Give that civilisation a push, and it will arrive at its own goal; do not strive to change it. Take away a nation's institutions, customs, and manners, and what will be left? They hold the nation together.

But here comes the very learned foreign man, and he says, "Look here, you give up all those institutions and customs of thousands of years, and take my tomfool tin-pot and be happy." This is all nonsense.

We will have to help each other, but we have to go one step further: the first thing is to become unselfish in help. "If you do just what I tell you to do, I will help you; otherwise not." Is that help?

And so, if the Hindus want to help you spiritually there will be no question of limitations: perfect unselfishness. I give, and there it ends. It is gone from me. My mind, my powers, my everything that I have to give is given: given with the idea to give, and no more. I have seen many times people who have robbed half the world, and they gave $20,000 "to convert the heathen." What for? For the benefit of the heathen, or for their own souls? Just think of that.

And the Nemesis of crime is working. We men try to hoodwink our own eyes. But inside the heart, He has remained, the real Self. He never forgets. We can never delude Him. His eyes will never be hoodwinked. Whenever there is any impulse of real charity, it tells, though it be at the end of a thousand years. Obstructed, it yet wakens once more to burst like a thunderbolt. And every impulse where the motive is selfish, self-seeking—though it may be launched forth with all the newspapers blazoning, all the mobs standing and cheering—it fails to reach the mark.

I am not taking pride in this. But, mark you, I have told the story of that group of boys. Today there is not a village, not a man, not a woman in India that does not know their work and bless them. There is not a famine in the land where these boys do not plunge in and try to work and rescue as many as they can. And that strikes to the heart. The people come to know it. So help whenever you can, but mind what your motive is. If it is selfish, it will neither benefit those you help, nor yourself. If it is unselfish, it will bring blessings upon them to whom it is given, and infinite blessings upon you, sure as you are living. The Lord can never be hood-winked. The law of Karma can never be hoodwinked.

Well then, **my plans are, therefore, to reach these masses of India.** Suppose you start schools all over India for the poor, still you cannot educate them. How can you? The boy of four years would better go to the plough or to work, than to your school. He cannot go to your school. It is impossible. Self-preservation is the first instinct. But if the mountain does not go to Mohammed, then Mohammed can come to the mountain. Why should not education go from door to door, say I. If a ploughman's boy cannot come to education, why not meet him at the plough, at the factory, just wherever he is? Go along with him, like his shadow. But there are these hundreds and thousands of monks, educating the people on the spiritual plane; why not let these men do the same work on the intellectual plane? Why should they not talk to the masses a little about history—about many things? The ears are the best educators. The best principles in our lives were those which we heard from our mothers through our ears. Books came much later. Book-learning is nothing. Through the ears we get the best formative principles. Then, as they get more and more interested, they may come to your books too. First, let it roll on and on—that is my idea.

Well, I must tell you that **I am not a very great believer in monastic systems. They have great merits, and also great defects. There should be a perfect balance between the monastics and the householders.** But monasticism has absorbed all the power in India. We represent the greatest power. The monk is greater than the prince. There is no reigning sovereign in India who dares to sit down when the "yellow cloth" is there. He gives up his seat and stands. Now, that is bad, so much power, even in the hands of good men—although these monastics have been the bulwark of the people. They stand between the priestcraft and knowledge. They are the centres of knowledge and reform. They are just what the prophets were among the Jews. The prophets were always preaching against the priests, trying to throw out superstitions. So are they in India. But all the same, so much power is not good there; better methods should be worked out. But you can only work in the line of least resistance. The whole national soul there is upon monasticism. You go to India and preach any religion as a householder: the Hindu people will turn back and go out. If you have given up the world, however, they say, "He is good, he has given up the world. He is sincere man, he wants to do what he preaches." What I mean to say is this that it represents a tremendous power. What we can do is just to transform it, give it another form. This tremendous power in the hands of the roving Sannyasins of India has got to be transformed, and it will raise the masses up.

Now, you see, **we have brought the plan down nicely on paper;** but I have taken it, at the same time, from the regions of idealism.

So far the plan was loose and idealistic. As years went on, it became more and more condensed and accurate; I began to see by actual working its defects, and all that.

What did I discover in its working on the material plane? First, **there must be centres to educate these monks in the method of education.** For instance, I send one of my men, and he goes about with a camera: he has to be taught in those things himself. In India, you will find every man is quite illiterate, and that teaching requires tremendous centres. And what does all that mean? Money. From the idealistic plane you come to everyday work. Well, I have worked hard, four years in your country, and two in England. And I am very thankful that some friends came to the rescue. One who is here today with you is amongst them. **There are American friends and English friends who went over with me to India,** and there has been a very rude beginning. Some English people came and joined the orders. One poor man worked hard and died in India. There are an Englishman and an Englishwoman who have retired; they have some means of their own, and they have started a centre in the Himalayas, educating the children. I have given them one of the papers I have started—a copy you will find there on the table—*The Awakened India.* And there they are instructing and working among the people. I have another centre in Calcutta. Of course, all great movements must proceed from the capital. For what is a capital? It is the heart of a nation. All the blood comes into the heart and thence it is distributed; so all the wealth, all the ideas, all the education, all spirituality will converge towards the capital and spread from it.

I am glad to tell you **I have made a rude beginning. But the same work I want to do, on parallel lines, for women.** And my principle is: each one helps himself. My help is from a distance. There are Indian women, English women, and I hope American women will come to take up the task. As soon as they have begun, I wash my hands off it. No man shall dictate to a woman nor a woman to a man. Each one is independent. What bondage there may be is only that of love. Women will work out their own destinies—much better, too, than men can ever do for them. All the mischief to women has come because men undertook to shape the destiny of women. And I do not want to start with any initial mistake. One little mistake made then will go on multiplying; and if you succeed, in the long run that mistake will have assumed gigantic proportions and become hard to correct. So, if I made this mistake of employing men to work out this women's part of the work, why, women will never get rid of that—it will have become a custom. But I have got an opportunity. I told you of the lady who was my Master's wife. We have all great respect for her. She never dictates to us. So it is quite safe.

That part has to be accomplished.

(*Lecture delivered at the Shakespeare Club, Pasadena, California, on 27 Jan. 1900*)

What is Religion?

A huge locomotive has rushed on over the line and, a small worm that was creeping upon one of the rails saved its life by crawling out of the path of the locomotive. Yet this little worm, so insignificant that it can be crushed in a moment, is a living something, while this locomotive, so huge, so immense, is only an engine, a machine. You say the one has life and the other is only dead matter and all its powers and strength and speed are only those of a dead machine, a mechanical contrivance. Yet the poor little worm which moved upon the rail and which the least touch of the engine would have deprived of its life is a majestic being compared to that huge locomotive. It is a small part of the Infinite and, therefore, it is greater than this powerful engine.

Why should that be so? How do we know the living from the dead? The machine mechanically performs all the movements its maker made it to perform, its movements are not those of life. How can we make the distinction between the living and the dead, then? In the living there is freedom, there is intelligence; in the dead all is bound and no freedom is possible, because there is no intelligence. This freedom that distinguishes us from mere machines is what we are all striving for. To be more free is the goal of all our efforts, for only in perfect freedom can there be perfection. This effort to attain freedom underlies all forms of worship, whether we know it or not.

If we were to examine the various sorts of worship all over the world, we would see that **the rudest of mankind are worshipping ghosts, demons, and the spirits of their forefathers**—serpent worship, worship of tribal gods, and worship of the departed ones. **Why do they do this? Because they feel that in some unknown**

way these beings are greater, more powerful than themselves, and limit their freedom. They, therefore, seek to propitiate these beings in order to prevent them from molesting them, in other words, to get more freedom. They also seek to win favour from these superior beings, to get by gift of the gods what ought to be earned by personal effort.

On the whole, this shows that the world is expecting a miracle. This expectation never leaves us, and however we may try, we are all running after the miraculous and extraordinary. **What is mind but that ceaseless inquiry into the meaning and mystery of life?** We may say that only uncultivated people are going after all these things, but the question still is there: Why should it be so? The Jews were asking for a miracle. The whole world has been asking for the same these thousands of years. There is, again, the universal dissatisfaction. We make an ideal but we have rushed only half the way after it when we make a newer one. We struggle hard to attain to some goal and then discover we do not want it. This dissatisfaction we are having time after time, and what is there in the mind if there is to be only dissatisfaction? What is the meaning of this universal dissatisfaction? It is because **freedom is every man's goal. He seeks it ever, his whole life is a struggle after it.** The child rebels against law as soon as it is born. Its first utterance is a cry, a protest against the bondage in which it finds itself. **This longing for freedom produces the idea of a being who is absolutely free. The concept of God is a fundamental element in the human constitution.** In the Vedanta, Sat-chit-ananda (Existence-Knowledge-Bliss) is the highest concept of God possible to the mind. It is the essence of knowledge and is by its nature the essence of bliss. We have been stifling that inner voice long enough, seeking to follow law and quieten the human nature, but there is that human instinct to rebel against nature's laws. We may not understand what the meaning is, but there is that unconscious struggle of the human with the spiritual, of the lower with the higher mind, and the struggle attempts to preserve one's separate life, what we call our "individuality".

Even hells stand out with this miraculous fact that we are born rebels; and the first fact of life—the inrushing of life itself—against this we rebel and cry out: "No law for us." As long as we obey the laws we are like machines, and on goes the universe, and we cannot break it. Laws as laws become man's nature. The first inkling of life on its higher level is in seeing this struggle within us to break the bond of nature and to be free. **"Freedom, O Freedom! Freedom, O Freedom!" is the song of the soul.** Bondage, alas, to be bound in nature, seems its fate.

Why should there be serpent, or ghost, or demon worship and all these various creeds and forms for having miracles? Why do we say that there is life, there is being in anything? There must be a meaning in all this search, this endeavour to understand life, to explain being. It is not meaningless and vain. It is man's ceaseless endeavour to become free. The knowledge which we now call science has been struggling for thousands of years in its attempt to gain freedom, and people ask for freedom. Yet there is no freedom in nature. It is all law. Still the struggle goes on. Nay, the whole of nature from the very sun to the atoms is under law, and even for man there is no freedom. But we cannot believe it. We have been studying laws from the beginning and yet cannot—nay, will not—believe that man is under law. The soul cries ever, "Freedom, O Freedom!" With the conception of God as a perfectly free Being, man cannot rest eternally in this bondage. Higher he must go, and unless the struggle were for himself, he would think it too severe. Man says to himself, "I am a born slave, I am bound; nevertheless, there is a Being who is not bound by nature. He is free and Master of nature."

The conception of God, therefore, is as essential and as fundamental a part of mind as is the idea of bondage. Both are the outcome of the idea of freedom. There cannot be life, even in the plant, without the idea of freedom. In the plant or in the worm, life has to rise to the individual concept. It is there, unconsciously working, the plant living its life to preserve the variety, principle, or form, not nature. The idea of nature controlling every step onward overrules the idea of freedom. Onward goes the idea of the material world, onward moves the idea of freedom. Still the fight goes on. We are hearing about all the quarrels of creeds and sects, yet creeds and sects are just and proper, they must be there. The chain is lengthening and naturally the struggle increases, but there need be no quarrels if we only knew that we are all striving to reach the same goal.

The embodiment of freedom, the Master of nature, is what we call God. You cannot deny Him. No, because you cannot move or live without the idea of freedom. Would you come here if you did not believe you were free? It is quite possible that the biologist can and will give some explanation of this perpetual effort to be free. Take all that for granted, still the idea of freedom is there. It is a fact, as much so as the other fact that you cannot apparently get over, the fact of being under nature.

Bondage and liberty, light and shadow, good and evil must be there, but the very fact of the bondage shows also this freedom hidden there. If one is a fact, the other is equally a fact. There must be this idea of freedom. While now we cannot see that this idea of bondage, in uncultivated man, is his struggle for freedom, yet the idea of freedom is there. The bondage of sin and impurity in the uncultivated savage is to his consciousness very small, for his nature is only a little higher than the animal's. What he struggles against is the bondage of physical nature, the lack of physical gratification, but out of this lower consciousness grows and broadens the higher conception of a mental or moral bondage and a longing for spiritual freedom. Here we see the divine dimly shining through the veil of ignorance. The veil is very dense at first and the light may be almost obscured, but it is there, ever pure and undimmed—the radiant fire of freedom and perfection. Man personifies this as the Ruler of the Universe, the One Free Being. He does not yet know that the universe is all one, that the difference is only in degree, in the concept.

The whole of nature is worship of God. Wherever there is life, there is this search for freedom and that **freedom is the same as God. Necessarily this freedom gives us mastery over all nature and is impossible without knowledge. The more we are knowing, the more we are becoming masters of nature.** Mastery alone is making us strong and if there be some being entirely free and master of nature, that being must have a perfect knowledge of nature, must be omnipresent and omniscient. Freedom must go hand in hand with these, and that being alone who has acquired these will be beyond nature.

Blessedness, eternal peace, arising from perfect freedom, is the highest concept of religion underlying all the ideas of God in Vedanta—absolutely free Existence, not bound by anything, no change, no nature, nothing that can produce a change in Him. This same freedom is in you and in me and is the only real freedom.

God is still, established upon His own majestic changeless Self. You and I try to be one with Him, but plant ourselves upon nature, upon the trifles of daily life, on money, on fame, on human love, and all these changing forms in nature which make for bondage. When nature shines, upon what depends the shining? Upon God and not upon the sun, nor the moon, nor the stars. Wherever anything shines, whether it is the light in the sun or in our own consciousness, it is He. He shining, all shines after Him.

Now we have seen that **this God is self-evident, impersonal, omniscient, the Knower and Master of nature, the Lord of all.** He is behind all worship and it is being done according to Him, whether we know it or not. I go one step further. That at which all marvel, that which we call evil, is His worship too. This too is a part of freedom. Nay, I will be terrible even and tell you that, when you are doing evil, the impulse behind is also that freedom. It may have been misguided and misled, but it was there;. and there cannot be any life or any impulse unless that freedom be behind it. Freedom breathes in the throb of the universe. Unless there is unity at the universal heart, we cannot understand variety. Such is the conception of the Lord in the Upanishads. Sometimes it rises even higher, presenting to us an ideal before which at first we stand aghast—that we are in essence one with God. He who is the colouring in the wings of the butterfly, and the blossoming of the rose-bud, is the power that is in the plant and in the butterfly. **He who gives us life is the power within us. Out of His fire comes life, and the direst death is also His power.** He whose shadow is death, His shadow is immortality also. Take a still higher conception. See how we are flying like hunted hares from all that is terrible, and like them, hiding our heads and thinking we are safe. See how the whole world is flying from everything terrible.

Once when I was in Varanasi, I was passing through a place where there was a large tank of water on one side and a high wall on the other. It was in the grounds where there were many monkeys. The monkeys of Varanasi are huge brutes and are sometimes surly. They now took it into their heads not to allow me to pass through their street, so they howled and shrieked and clutched at my feet as I passed. As they pressed closer, I began to run, but the faster I ran, the faster came the monkeys and they began to bite at me. It seemed impossible to escape, but just then I met a stranger who called out to me, "Face the brutes." I turned and faced the monkeys, and they fell back and finally fled. That is a lesson for all life—face the terrible, face it boldly. Like the monkeys, the hardships of life fall back when we cease to flee before them. **If we are ever to gain freedom, it must be by conquering nature, never by running away.** Cowards never win victories. We have to fight fear and troubles and ignorance if we expect them to flee before us.

What is death? What are terrors? Do you not see the Lord's face in them? Fly from evil and terror and misery, and they will follow you. Face them, and they will flee. The whole world worships ease and pleasure, and very few dare to worship that which is painful. To rise above both is the idea of freedom. Unless man passes through this gate he cannot be free. We all have to face these. We strive to worship the Lord, but the body rises between, nature rises between Him and us and blinds our vision. We must learn how to worship and love Him in the thunderbolt, in shame, in sorrow, in sin. All the world has ever been preaching the God of virtue. I preach a God of virtue and a God of sin in one. Take Him if you dare—that is the one way to salvation; then alone will come to us the Truth Ultimate which comes from the idea of oneness. Then will be lost the idea that one is greater than another. The nearer we approach the law of freedom, the more we shall come under the Lord, and troubles will vanish. Then we shall not differentiate the door of hell from the gate of heaven, nor differentiate between men and say, "I am greater than any being in the universe." Until we see nothing in the world but the Lord Himself, all these evils will beset us and we shall make all these distinctions; because **it is only in the Lord, in the Spirit, that we are all one; and until we see God everywhere, this unity will not exist for us.**

Two birds of beautiful plumage, inseparable companions, sat upon the same tree, one on the top and one below. The beautiful bird below was eating the fruits of the tree, sweet and bitter, one moment a sweet one and another a bitter. The moment he ate a bitter fruit, he was sorry, but after a while he ate another and when it too was bitter, he looked up and saw the other bird who ate neither the sweet nor the bitter, but was calm and majestic, immersed in his own glory. And then the poor lower bird forgot and went on eating the sweet and bitter fruits again, until at last he ate one that was extremely bitter; and then he stopped again and once more looked up at the glorious bird above. Then he came nearer and nearer to the other bird; and when he had come near enough, rays of light shone upon him and enveloped him, and he saw he was transformed into the higher bird. He became calm, majestic, free, and found that there had been but one bird all the time on the tree. The lower bird was but the reflection of the one above. **So we are in reality one with the Lord, but the reflection makes us seem many, as when the one sun reflects in a million dew-drops and seems a million tiny suns.** The reflection must vanish if we are to identify ourselves with our real nature which is divine. The universe itself can never be the limit of our satisfaction. That is why the miser gathers more and more money, that is why the robber robs, the sinner sins, that is why you are learning philosophy. All have one purpose. There is no other purpose in life, save to reach this freedom. Consciously or unconsciously, we are all striving for perfection. Every being must attain to it.

The man who is groping through sin, through misery, the man who is choosing the path through hells, will reach it, but it will take time. We cannot save him. Some hard knocks on his head will help him to turn to the Lord. The path of virtue, purity, unselfishness, spirituality, becomes known at last and what all are doing unconsciously, we are trying to do consciously. The idea is expressed by St. Paul, "The God that ye ignorantly worship, Him declare I unto you." This is the lesson for the whole world to learn. What have these philosophies and theories of nature to do, if not to help us to attain to this one goal in life? **Let us come to that consciousness of the identity of everything and let man see himself in everything.**

Let us be no more the worshippers of creeds or sects with small limited notions of God, but see Him in everything in the universe. If you are knowers of God, you will everywhere find the same worship as in your own heart.

Get rid, in the first place, of all these limited ideas and see God in every person—working through all hands, walking through all feet, and eating through every mouth. **In every being He lives, through all minds He thinks. He is self-evident, nearer unto us than ourselves. To know this is religion, is faith,** and may it please the Lord to give us this faith! **When we shall feel that oneness, we shall be immortal.** We are physically immortal even, one with the universe. So long as there is one that breathes throughout the universe, I live in that one. I am not this limited little being, I am the universal. I am the life of all the sons of the past. I am the soul of Buddha, of Jesus, of Mohammed. I am the soul of the teachers, and I am all the robbers that robbed, and all the murderers that were hanged, I am the universal. Stand up then; this is the highest worship. You are one with the universe. That only is humility—not crawling upon all fours and calling yourself a sinner. That is the highest evolution when this veil of differentiation is torn off. The highest creed is Oneness. I am so-and-so is a limited idea, not true of the real "I". I am the universal; stand upon that and **ever worship the Highest through the highest form, for God is Spirit and should be worshipped in spirit and in truth.** Through lower forms of worship, man's material thoughts rise to spiritual worship and the Universal Infinite One is at last worshipped in and through the spirit. That which is limited is material. The Spirit alone is infinite. God is Spirit, is infinite; man is Spirit and, therefore, infinite, and the Infinite alone can worship the Infinite. We will worship the Infinite; that is the highest spiritual worship.

The grandeur of realising these ideas, how difficult it is! I theorise, talk, philosophise; and the next moment something comes against me, and I unconsciously become angry, I forget there is anything in the universe but this little limited self, I forget to say, "I am the Spirit, what is this trifle to me? I am the Spirit." I forget it is all myself playing, I forget God, I forget freedom.

Sharp as the blade of a razor, long and difficult and hard to cross, is the way to freedom. The sages have declared this again and again. Yet do not let these weaknesses and failures bind you. **The Upanishads have declared, "Arise! Awake! and stop not until the goal is reached."** We will then certainly cross the path, sharp as it is like the razor, and long and distant and difficult though it be. Man becomes the master of gods and demons. No one is to blame for our miseries but ourselves. Do you think there is only a dark cup of poison if man goes to look for nectar? The nectar is there and is for every man who strives to reach it. The Lord Himself tells us, "Give up all these paths and struggles. Do thou take refuge in Me. I will take thee to the other shore, be not afraid.'"

We hear that from all the scriptures of the world that come to us. The same voice teaches us to say, "Thy will be done upon earth, as it is in heaven," for "Thine is the kingdom and the power and the glory." It is difficult, all very difficult. I say to myself, "This moment I will take refuge in Thee, O Lord. Unto Thy love I will sacrifice all, and on Thine altar I will place all that is good and virtuous. My sins, my sorrows, my actions, good and evil, I will offer unto Thee; do Thou take them and I will never forget." One moment I say, "Thy will be done," and the next moment something comes to try me and I spring up in a rage. **The goal of all religions is the same, but the language of the teachers differs.** The attempt is to kill the false "I", so that the real "I", the Lord, will reign.

"I the Lord thy God am a jealous God. Thou shalt have no other gods before me," say the Hebrew scriptures. God must be there all alone. We must say, "Not I, but Thou," and then we should give up everything but the Lord. He, and He alone, should reign. Perhaps we struggle hard, and yet the next moment our feet slip, and then we try to stretch out our hands to Mother. We find we cannot stand alone. Life is infinite, one chapter of which is, "Thy will be done," and unless we realise all the chapters we cannot realise the whole.

"Thy will be done"—every moment the traitor mind rebels against it, yet it must be said, again and again, if we are to conquer the lower self. We cannot serve a traitor and yet be saved. There is salvation for all except the traitor and we stand condemned as traitors, traitors against our own selves, against the majesty of Mother, when we refuse to obey the voice of our higher Self. Come what will, we must give our bodies and minds up to the Supreme Will. Well has it been said by the Hindu philosopher, "If man says twice, 'Thy will be done,' he commits sin." "Thy will be done," what more is needed, why say it twice? What is good is good. No more shall we take it back. "Thy will be done on earth as it is in heaven, for Thine is the kingdom and the power and the glory for evermore."

The Hindu Theories of God, Life and Karma

The first group of religious ideas that we see coming up—I mean recognised religious ideas, and not the very low ideas, which do not deserve the name of religion—all include the idea of inspiratian and revealed books and so forth. **The first group of religious ideas starts with the idea af God.** Here is the universe, and this universe is created by a certain Being. Everything that is in this universe has been created by Him. Along with that, **at a later stage comes the idea of Soul**—that there is this body, and something inside this body which is not the body. This is the most primitive idea of religion that we know. We can find a few followers of that in India, but it was given up very early.

The Indian religions take a peculiar start. It is only by strict analysis, and much calculation and conjecture, that we can ever think that that stage existed in Indian religions. **The tangible state in which we find them is the next step, not the first one.** At the earliest step the idea of creation is very peculiar, and it is that the whole universe is created out of zero, at the will of God; **that all this universe did not exist, and out of this nothingness all this has come. In the next stage we find this conclusion is questioned.** How can existence be produced out of non-existence? At the first step in the Vedanta this question is asked. If this universe is existent it must have came out of something, because it was very easy to see that nothing comes out of nothing, anywhere. All work that is done by human hands requires materials. If a house is built, the material was existing before; if a boat is made the material existed before; if any implements are made, the materials were existing before. So the effect is produced. Naturally, therefore, **the first idea that this world was created out of nothing was rejected, and some material out of which this world was created was wanted. The whole history of religion, in fact, is this search after that material.**

Out of what has all this been produced? Apart from the question of the efficient cause, or God, apart from the question that God created the universe, the great question of all questions is: Out of what did He create it? All the philosophies are turning, as it were, on this question. **One solution is that nature, God, and soul are eternal existences,** as if three lines are running parallel eternally, of which nature and soul comprise what they call the dependent, and God the independent Reality. Every soul, like every particle of matter, is perfectly dependent on the will of God. **Before going to the other steps we will take up the idea of soul, and then find that with all the Vedantic philosophers, there is one tremendous departure from all Western philosophy.** All of them have a common psychology. Whatever their philosophy may have been, their psychology is the same in India, the old Sankhya psychology.

Sankhya: The Dualistic Theory

According to this, perception occurs by the transmission of the vibrations which first come to the external sense-organs, from the external to the internal organs, from the internal organs to the mind, from the mind to the Buddhi, from the Buddhi or intellect, to something which is a unit, which they call the Atman. Coming to modern physiology, we know that it has found centres for all the different sensations. First it finds the lower centres, and then a higher grade of centres, and these two centres exactly correspond with the internal organs and the mind, but not one centre has been found which controls all the other centres. So physiology cannot tell what unifies all these centres. Where do the centres get united? **The centres in the brain are all different, and there is not one centre which controls all the other centres; therefore, so far as it goes, the Indian psychology stands unchallenged upon this point.** We must have this unification, something upon which the sensations will be reflected, to form a complete whole. Until there is that something, I cannot have any idea af you, ar a picture, or anything else. If we had not that unifying something, we would only see, then after a while breathe, then hear, and so on, and while I heard a man talking I would not see him at all, because all the centres are different.

This body is made of particles which we call matter, and it is dull and insentient. So is what the Vedantists call the fine body. The fine body, according to them, is a material but transparent body, made of very fine particles, so fine that no microscope can see them. What is the use of that? It is the receptacle of the fine forces. Just as this gross body is the receptacle af the gross forces, so that fine body is the receptacle af the fine forces, which we call thought, in its various modifications. First is the body, which is gross matter, with gross force. Force cannot exist without matter. It must require some matter to exist, so the grosser forces work in the body; and those very forces become finer; the very force which is working in a gross form, works in a fine form, and becomes thought. There is no distinction between them, simply one is the gross and the other the fine manifestation af the same thing. Neither is there any distinction between this fine body and the gross body. The fine body is also material, only very fine matter; and just as this gross body is the instrument that works the gross forces, so the fine body is the instrument that works the fine forces.

From where do all these forces come? **According to Vedanta philosophy, there are two things in nature, one of which they call Akasha, which is the substance, infinitely fine, and the other they call Prana, which is the force.** Whatever you see, or feel, or hear, as air, earth, or anything, is material—the product of Akasha. It goes on and becomes finer and finer, or grosser and grosser, changing under the action of Prana. **Like Akasha, Prana is omnipresent, and interpenetrating everything.** Akasha is like the water, and everything else in the universe is like blocks of ice, made out of that water, and floating in the water, and **Prana is the power that changes**

this Akasha into all these various forms. The gross body is the instrument made out of Akasha, for the manifestatian af Prana in gross forms, as muscular motion, or walking, sitting, talking, and so forth. That fine body is also made of Akasha, a very fine form of Akasha, for the manifestation of the same Prana in the finer form of thought. So, **first there is this gross body. Beyond that is this fine body, and beyond that is the Jiva, the real man.** Just as the nails can be pared off many times and yet are still part of our bodies, not different, so is our gross body related to the fine. It is not that a man has a fine and also a gross body; it is the one body only, the part which endures longer is the fine body, and that which dissolves sooner is the gross. Just as I can cut this nail any number af times, so, millions of times I can shed this gross body, but the fine body will remain. According to the dualists, this Jiva or the real man is very fine, minute.

So far we see that man is a being, who has first a gross body which dissolves very quickly, then a fine body which remains through aeons, and then a Jiva. **This Jiva, according ta the Vedanta philosophy, is eternal, just as God is eternal.** Nature is also eternal, but changefully eternal. The material of nature—Prana and Akasha—is eternal, but it is changing into different forms eternally. But the Jiva is not manufactured either af Akasha ar Prana; it is immaterial and, therefore, will remain for ever. It is not the result of any combination of Prana and Akasha, and **whatever is not the result of combination, will never be destroyed,** because destructian is going back to causes. The gross body is a compound of Akasha and Prana and, therefore, will be decomposed. The fine body will also be decomposed, after a long time, but the Jiva is simple, and will never be destroyed. **It was never born for the same reason. Nothing simple can be born.** The same argument applies. That which is a compound only can be born.

The whole of nature comprising millions and millions of souls is under the will of God. God is all-pervading, omniscient, formless, and He is working through nature day and night. The whole of it is under His control. He is the eternal Ruler. So say the dualists. Then the question comes: If God is the ruler of this universe, why did He create such a wicked universe, why must we suffer so much? They say, it is not God's fault. It is our fault that we suffer. Whatever we sow we reap. He did not do anything to punish us. Man is born poor, or blind, or some other way. What is the reason? He had done something before, he was born that way. **The Jiva has been existing for all time, was never created. It has been doing all sorts of things all the time. Whatever we do reacts upon us. If we do good, we shall have happiness, and if evil, unhappiness.** So the Jiva goes on enjoying and suffering, and doing all sorts of things.

What comes after death? All these Vedanta philosophers admit that this Jiva is by its own nature pure. But ignorance covers its real nature, they say. As by evil deeds it has covered itself with ignorance, so by good deeds it becomes conscious of its own nature again. Just as it is eternal, so its nature is pure. The nature of every being is pure.

When through good deeds all its sins and misdeeds have been washed away, then the Jiva becomes pure again, and when it becomes pure, it goes to what is called Devayana. Its organ of speech enters the mind. You cannot think without words. Wherever there is thought, there must be words. **As words enter the mind, so the mind is resolved into the Prana, and the Prana into the Jiva. Then the Jiva gets quickly out of the body, and goes to the solar regions.** This universe has sphere after sphere. This earth is the world sphere, in which are moons, suns, and stars. Beyond that there is the solar sphere, and beyond that another which they call the lunar sphere. Beyond that there is the sphere which they call the sphere of lightning, the electric sphere, and when the Jiva goes there, **there comes another Jiva, already perfect, to receive it, and takes it to another world, the highest heaven, called the Brahmaloka, where the Jiva lives eternally,** no more to be born or to die. It enjoys through eternity, and gets all sorts of powers, except the power of creation.

There is only one ruler of the universe, and that is God. No one can become God; the dualists maintain that if you say you are God, it is a blasphemy. **All powers except the creative come to the Jiva, and if it likes to have bodies, and work in different parts of the world, it can do so.** If it orders all the gods to come before it, if it wants its forefathers to come, they all appear at its command. Such are its powers that it never feels any more pain, and if it wants, it can live in the Brahmaloka through all eternity. This is the highest man, who has attained the love of God, who has become perfectly unselfish, perfectly purified, who has given up all desires, and who does not want to do anything except worship and love God.

There are others that are not so high, who do good works, but want some reward. They say they will give so much to the poor, but want to go to heaven in return. When they die, what becomes of them? The speech enters the mind, the mind enters the Prana, the Prana enters the Jiva, and the Jiva gets out, and goes to the lunar sphere, where it has a very good time for a long period. There it enjoys happiness, so long as the effect of its good deeds endures. When the same is exhausted, it descends, and once again enters life on earth according to its desires. **In the lunar sphere the Jiva becomes what we call a god, or what the Christians or Mohammedans call an angel.** These gods are the names of certain positions; for instance, Indra, the king of the gods, is the name of a position; thousands of men get to that position. When a virtuous man who has performed the highest of Vedic rites dies, he becomes a king of the gods; by that time the old king has gone down again, and become man. Just as kings change here, so the gods, the Devas, also have to die. In heaven they will all die. The only deathless place is Brahmaloka, where alone there is no birth and death.

So the Jivas go to heaven, and have a very good time, except now and then when the demons give them chase. In our mythology it is said there are demons, who sometimes trouble the gods. In all mythologies, you read how these demons and the gods fought, and the demons sometimes conquered the gods, although many times, it seems, the demons did not do so many wicked things as the gods. **In all mythologies, for instance, you find the Devas fond of**

women. So after their reward is finished, they fall down again, come through the clouds, through the rains, and thus get into some grain or plant and find their way into the human body, when the grain or plant is eaten by men. The father gives them the material out of which to get a fitting body. When the material suits them no longer, they have to manufacture other bodies. Now there are the very wicked fellows, who do all sorts of diabolical things; they are born again as animals, and if they are very bad, they are born as very low animals, or become plants, or stones.

In the Deva form they make no Karma at all; only man makes Karma. Karma means work which will produce effect When a man dies and becomes a Deva, he has only a period of pleasure, and during that time, makes no fresh Karma; it is simply a reward for his past good Karma. When the good Karma is worked out, then the remaining Karma begins to take effect, and he comes down to earth. He becomes man again, and if he does very good works, and purifies himself, he goes ta Brahmaloka and comes back no more.

The animal is a state af sojourn for the Jiva evolving from lower forms. In course of time the animal becomes man. It is a significant fact that as the human population is increasing, the animal population is decreasing. The animal souls are all becoming men. So many species of animals have become men already. Where else have they gone?

In the Vedas, there is no mention af hell. But our Puranas, the later books of our scriptures, thought that no religion could be complete, unless hells were attached to it, and so they invented all sorts of hells. In some af these, men are sawed in half, and continually tortured, but do not die. They are continually feeling intense pain, but the books are merciful enough to say it is only for a period. Bad Karma is worked out in that state and then they come back on earth, and get another chance. So this human form is the great chance. It is called the Karma-body, in which we decide our fate. We are running in a huge circle, and this is the point in the circle which determines the future. So this is considered the most important form that there is. Man is greater than the gods.

So far with dualism, pure and simple. Next comes the higher Vedantic philosophy which says, that this cannot be. God is both the material and the efficient cause of this universe. If you say there is a God who is an infinite Being, and a soul which is also infinite, and a nature which is also infinite, you can go on multiplying infinites without limit which is simply absurd; you smash all logic. So God is both the material and the efficient cause of the universe; He projects this universe out of Himself. Then how is it that God has become these walls and this table, that God has become the pig, and the murderer, and all the evil things in the world? We say that God is pure. How can He become all these degenerate things? Our answer is: just as I am a soul and have a body, and in a sense, this body is not different from me, yet I, the real I, in fact, am not the body. For instance, I say, I am a child, a young man, or an old man, but my soul has not changed. It remains the same soul. Similarly, the whole universe, comprising all nature and an infinite number of souls, is, as it were, the infinite body of God. He is interpenetrating the whole of it. He alone is unchangeable, but nature changes, and soul changes. He is unaffected by changes in nature and soul.

Two Other Theories

In whot way does nature change? In its fresh forms; it takes fresh forms. But the soul cannot change that way. The soul contracts and expands in knowledge. It contracts by evil deeds. Those deeds which contract the real natural knowledge and purity of the soul are called evil deeds. Those deeds, again, which bring out the natural glory of the soul, are called good deeds. All these souls were pure, but they have become contracted, through the mercy of God, and by doing good deeds, they will expand and recover their natural purity. Everyone has the same chance, and in the long run, must get out. But this universe will not cease, because it is eternal. This is the second theory. The first is called dualism. **The second theory holds that there are God, soul, and nature, and soul and nature form the body of God, and, therefore, these three form one unit. It represents a higher stage of religious development and goes by**

the name of Qualified Monism. In dualism, the universe is conceived as a large machine set going by God while in qualified monism, it is conceived as an organism, inter-penetrated by the Divine Self.

The last are the Non-Dualists. They raise the question also, that God must be both the material and the efficient cause of this universe. As such, God has become the whole of this universe and there is no going against it. And when these other people say that God is the soul, and the universe is the body, and the body is changing, but God is changeless, the non-dualists say, all this is nonsense. In that case what is the use of calling God the material cause of this universe? The material cause is the cause become effect; the effect is nothing but the cause in another form. Wherever you see an effect, it is the cause reproduced. If the universe is the effect, and God the cause, it must be the reproduction of God. If you say that the universe is the body of God, and that the body becomes contracted and fine, and becomes the cause, and out of that the universe is evolved, the non-dualists say that it is God Himself who has become this universe.

Now comes a very fine question. If this God has become this universe, you and all these things are God. Certainly. This book is God, everything is God. My body is God, and my mind is God, and my soul is God. Then why are there so many Jivas? Has God become divided into millions of Jivas? Does that one God turn into millions of Jivas? Then how did it become so? How can that infinite power and substance, the one Being of the universe, become divided? It is impossible to divide infinity. How can that pure Being become this universe? If He has become the universe, He is changeful, and if He is changeful, He is part of nature, and whatever is nature and changeful is born and dies. If our God is changeful, He must die some day. Take note of that. Again, how much of God has become this universe? If you say X, the unknown algebraical quantity, then God is God minus X now, and, therefore, not the same God as before this creation, because so much has become this universe.

So the non-dualists say: "This universe does not exist at all; it is all illusion. The whole of this universe, these Devas, gods, angels, and all the other beings born and dying, all this infinite number of souls coming up and going down, are all dreams." There is no Jiva at all. How can there be many? It is the one Infinity. As the one sun, reflected on various pieces of water, appears to be many, and millions of globules of water reflect so many millions of suns, and in each globule will be a perfect image of the sun, yet there is only one sun, so are all these Jivas but reflections in different minds. These different minds are like so many different globules, reflecting this one Being. God is being reflected in all these different Jivas. But a dream cannot be without a reality, and that reality is that one Infinite Existence. **You, as body, mind, or soul, are a dream, but what you really are, is Existence, Knowledge, Bliss. You are the God of this universe. You are creating the whole universe and drawing it in. Thus says the Advaitist. So all these births and rebirths, coming and going are the figments of Maya.** You are infinite. Where can you go? The sun, the moon, and the whole universe are but drops in your transcendent nature.

How can you be born or die? I never was born, never will be born. I never had father or mother, friends or foes, for I am Existence, Knowledge, Bliss Absolute. I am He, I am He. So, what is the goal, according to this philosophy? That those who receive this knowledge are one with the universe. For them, all heavens and even Brahmaloka are destroyed, the whole dream vanishes, and they find themselves the eternal God of the universe. They attain their real individuality, with its infinite knowledge and bliss, and become free. Pleasures in little things cease. We are finding pleasure in this little body, in this little individuality. How much greater the pleasure when this whole universe is my body! If there is pleasure in one body, how much more when all bodies are mine! Then is freedom attained. And this is called Advaita, the non-dualistic Vedanta philosophy.

These are the three steps which Vedanta philosophy has taken, and we cannot go any further, because we cannot go beyond unity. When a science reaches a unity, it cannot by any manner of means go any further. You cannot go beyond this idea of the Absolute.

All people cannot take up this Advaita philosophy; it is hard. First of all, it is very hard to understand it intellectually. It requires the sharpest of intellects, a bold understanding. **Secondly, it does not suit the vast majority of people.** So there are these three steps. Begin with the first one. Then by thinking of that and understanding it, the second will open itself. Just as a race advances, so individuals have to advance. The steps which the human race has taken to reach to the highest pinnacles of religious thought, every individual will have to take. Only, while the human race took millions of years to reach from one step to another, individuals may live the whole life of the human race in a much shorter duration. But each one of us will have to go through these steps. Those of you who are non-dualists look back to the period of your lives when you were strong dualists. As soon as you think you are a body and a mind, you will have to take the whole of this dream. If you take one portion; you must take the whole.

The man who says, here is this world, and there is no Personal God, is a fool; because if there is a world, there will have to be a cause, and that is what is called God. You cannot have an effect without knowing that there is a cause. God will only vanish when this world vanishes; then you will become God Absolute, and this world will be no longer for you. So long as the dream that you are a body exists, you are bound to see yourself as being born and dying; but as soon as that dream vanishes, so will the dream vanish that you are being born and dying, and so will the other dream that there is a universe vanish. That very thing which we now see as the universe will appear to us as God Absolute, and that very God who has so long been external will appear to be internal, as our own Self.

The Vedanta Philosophy

The Vedanta philosophy, as it is generally called at the present day, **really comprises all the various sects that now exist In India.** Thus there have been various inter-pretations, and to my mind they have been progressive, beginning with the dualistic or Dvaita and ending with the non-dualistIc or Advaita. The word Vedanta literally means the end of the Vedas—the Vedas being the scriptures of the Hindus. Sometimes in the West by **the Vedas are meant only the hymns and rituals of the Vedas. But at the present time these parts have almost gone out of use, and usually by the word Vedas in India, the Vedanta is meant.** All our commentators, when they want to quote a passage from the scriptures, as a rule, quote from the Vedanta, which has another technical name with the commentators —the Shrutis.

Now, all the books known by the name of the Vedanta were not entirely written after the ritualistic portions of the Vedas. For instance, one of them—the Isha Upanishad—forms the fortieth chapter of the Yajurveda, that being one of the oldest parts of the Vedas. There are other Upanishads which form portions of the Brahmanas or ritualistic writings; and the rest of the Upanishads are independent, not comprised in any of the Brahmanas or other parts of the Vedas; but there is no reason to suppose that they were entirely independent of other parts, for, as we well know, many of these have been lost entirely and many of the Brahmanas have become extinct. So it is quite possible that the independent Upanishads belonged to some Brahmanas, which in course of time fell into disuse, while the Upanishads remained. These Upanishads are also called Forest Books or Aranyakas.

The Vedanta, then, practically forms the scriptures of the Hindus, and all systems of philosophy that are orthodox have to take it as their foundation. Even the Buddhists and Jains, when it suits their purpose, will quote a passage from the Vedanta as authority. **All schools of philosophy in India, although they claim to have been based upon the Vedas, took different names for their systems. The last one, the system of Vyasa, took its stand upon the doctrines of the Vedas more than the previous systems did, and made an attempt to harmonise the preceding philosophies, such as the Sankhya and the Nyaya, with the doctrines of the Vedanta.** So it is especially called the Vedanta philosophy; and the Sutras or aphorisms of Vyasa are, in modern India, the basis of the Vedanta philosophy. Again, these Sutras of Vyasa have been variously explained by different commentators. **In general there are three sorts of commentators in India now; interpretations have arisen three systems of philosophy and sects.** One is the dualistic, or Dvaita; a second is the qualified non-dualistic, or **Vishishtadvaita**; and a third is the non-dualistic, or **Advaita**. Of these the dualistic and the qualified non-dualistic include the largest number of the Indian people. The non-dualists are comparatively few in number.

Now I will try to lay before you the ideas that are contained in all these three sects; but before going on, I will make one remark—that these different Vedanta systems have one common psychology, and that is, the psychology of the Sankhya system. The Sankhya psychology is very much like the psychologies of the Nyaya and Vaisheshika systems, differing only in minor particulars.

All the Vedantists agree on three points. They believe in God, in the Vedas as revealed, and in cycles. We have already considered the Vedas. The belief about cycles is as follows: All matters throughout the universe is the outcome of one primal matter called Akasha; and all force, whether gravitation, attraction or repulsion, or life, is the outcome of one primal force called Prana. **Prana acting on Akasha is creating or projecting the universe.** At the beginning of a cycle, Akasha is motionless, un-manifested. Then Prana begins to act, more and more, creating grosser and grosser forms out of Akasha—plants, animals, men, stars, and so on. After an incalculable time this evolution ceases and involution begins, everything being resolved back through finer and finer forms into the original Akasha and Prana, when a new cycle follows. Now there is something beyond Akasha and Prana. Both can be resolved into a third thing called **Mahat—the Cosmic Mind.** This Cosmic Mind does not create Akasha and Prana, but changes itself into them.

We will now take up the beliefs about mind, soul, and God. According to the universally accepted Sankhya psychology, in perception—in the case of vision, for instance—there are, first of all, the instruments of vision, the eyes. Behind the instruments—the eyes—is the organ of vision or Indriya—the optic nerve and its centres—which is not the external instrument, but without which the eyes will not see. More still is needed for perception. The mind or Manas must come and attach itself to the organ. And besides this, the sensation must be carried to the intellect or Buddhi—the determinative, reactive state of the mind. When the reaction comes from Buddhi, along with it flashes the external world and egoism. Here then is the will; but everything is not complete. Just as every picture, being composed of successive impulses of light, must be united on something stationary to form a whole, **so all the ideas in the mind must be gathered and projected on something that is stationary—relatively to the body and mind—that is, on what is called the Soul or Purusha or Atman.**

According to the Sankhya philosophy, the reactive state of the mind called Buddhi or intellect is the outcome, the change, or a certain manifestation of the Mahat or Cosmic Mind. The Mahat becomes changed into vibrating thought; and that becomes in one part changed into the organs, and in the other part into the fine particles of matter. Out of the combination of all these, the whole of this universe is produced. **Behind even Mahat, the Sankhya conceives of a certain state which is called Avyakta or unmanifested, where even the manifestation of mind is not present, but only the causes exist. It is also called Prakriti. Beyond this Prakriti, and eternally separate from it, is the Purusha, the soul of the Sankhya which is without attributes and omnipresent.** The Purusha is not the doer but the witness. The illustration of the crystal is used to explain the Purusha. The latter is said to be like a crystal without any colour, before which different, colours are placed, and then it seems to be coloured by the colours before it, but in reality it is not.

The Vedantists reject the Sankhya ideas of the soul and nature. They claim that between them there is a huge gulf to be bridged over. On the one hand the Sankhya system comes to nature, and then at once it has to jump over to the other side and come to the soul, which is entirely separate from nature. How can these different colours, as the Sankhya calls them, be able to act on that soul which by its nature is colourless? **So the Vedantists, from the very first affirm that this soul and this nature are one.** Even the dualistic Vedantists admit that the Atman or God is not only the efficient cause of this universe, but also the material cause. But they only say so in so many words. They do not really mean it, for they try to escape from their conclusions, in this way: They say there are three existences in this universe—God, soul, and nature. Nature and soul are, as it were, the body of God, and in this sense it may be said that God and the whole universe are one. But this nature and all these various souls remain different from each other through all eternity. Only at the beginning of a cycle do they become manifest; and when the cycle ends, they become fine, and remain in a fine state.

The Advaita Vedantists—the non-dualists—reject this theory of the soul, and, having nearly the whole range of the Upanishads in their favour, build their philosophy entirely upon them. All the books contained in the Upanishads have one subject, one task before them—to prove the following theme: "Just as by the knowledge of one lump of clay we have the knowledge of all the clay in the universe, so what is that, knowing which we know everything in the universe?" **The idea of the Advaitists is to generalise the whole universe into one**—that something which is really the whole of this universe. And **they claim that this whole universe is one, that it is one Being manifesting itself in all these various forms.** They admit that what the Sankhya calls nature exists, but say that nature is God. It is this Being, the Sat, which has become converted into all this—the universe, man, soul, and everything that exists. Mind and Mahat are but the manifestations of that one Sat.

But the the difficulty arises that this would be pantheism. How come that Sat which is unchangeable, as they admit (for that which is absolute is unchangeable), to be changed into that which is changeable, and perishable? The Advaitists here have a theory which they call Vivarta Vada or apparent manifestation. According to the dualists and the Sankhyas, the whole of this universe is the evolution of primal nature. According to some of the Advaitists and some of the dualists, the whole of this universe is evolved from God. And according to the Advaitists proper, the followers of Shankaracharya, the whole universe is the *apparent* evolution of God. God is the material cause of this universe, but not really, only apparently.

The celebrated illustration used is that of the rope and the snake, where the rope appeared to be the snake, but was not really so. The rope did not really change into the snake. Even so this whole universe as it exists is that Being. It is unchanged, and all the changes we see in it are only apparent. These changes are caused by Desha, Kala and Nimitta, space, time, and causation, or, according to a higher psychological generalisation, by Nama and Rupa, name and form. It is by name and form that one thing is differentiated from another. The name and form alone cause the difference. In reality they are one and the same. Again, it is not, the Vedantists say, that there is something as phenomenon and something as noumenon. The rope is changed into the snake apparently only; and when the delusion ceases, the snake vanishes.

When one is in ignorance, he sees the pnenomenon and does not see God. When he sees God, this universe vanishes entirely for him. Ignorance or Maya, as it is called, is the cause of all this phenomenon—the Absolute, the Unchangeable, being taken as this manifested universe. This Maya is not absolute zero, nor non-existence. It is defined as neither existence nor non-existence. It is not existence, because that can be said only of the Absolute, the Unchangeable, and in this sense, Maya is non-existence. Again, it cannot be said it is non-existence; for if it were, it could never produce the phenomenon. So it is something which is neither; and in the Vedanta philosophy it is called Anirvachaniya or inexpressible. Maya, then, is the real cause of this universe. Maya gives the name and form to what Brahman or God gives the material; and the latter seems to have been transformed into all this. **The Advaitists, then, have no place for the individual soul. They say individual souls are created by Maya. In reality they cannot exist.**

If there were only one existence throughout, how could it be that I am one, and you are one, and so forth? We are all one, and the cause of evil is the perception of duality. As soon as I begin to feel that I am separate from thus universe, then first comes fear, and then comes misery. "Where one hears another, one sees another, that is small. Where one does not see another, where one does not hear another, that is the greatest, that is God. In that greatest is perfect happiness. In small things there is no happiness."

According to the Advaita philosophy, then, this differentiation of matter, these phenomena, are, as it were, for a time, hiding the real nature of man; but the latter really has not been changed at all. In the lowest worm, as well as in the highest human being, the same divine nature is present. The worm form is the lower form in which the divinity has been more overshadowed by Maya; that is the highest form in which it has been least overshadowed. Behind everything the same divinity is existing, and out of this comes the basis of morality. Do not injure another. Love everyone as your own self, because the whole universe is one. In injuring another, I am injuring myself; in loving another, I am loving myself. From this also springs that principle of Advaita morality which has been summed up in one word—self-abnegation. The Advaitist says, this little personalised self is the cause of all my misery. This individualised self, which makes me different from all other beings, brings hatred and jealousy and misery, struggle and all other evils. And when this idea has been got rid of, all struggle will cease, all misery vanish. So this is to be given up. We must always hold ourselves ready, even to give up our lives for the lowest beings.

When a man has become ready even to give up his life for a little insect, he has reached the perfection which the Advaitist wants to attain; and at that moment when he has become thus ready, the veil of ignorance falls away from him, and he will feel his own nature. Even in this life, he will feel that he is one with the universe. For a time, as it were, the whole of this phenomenal world will disappear for him, and he will realise what he is. But so long as the Karma of this body remains, he will have to live. This state, when the veil has vanished and yet the body remains for some time, is what the Vedantists call the Jivanmukti, the living freedom. If a man is deluded by a mirage for some time, and one day the mirage disappears—if it comes back again the next day, or at some future time, he will not be deluded. Before the mirage first broke, the man could not distinguish between the reality and the deception. But when it has once broken, as long as he has organs and eyes to work with, he will see the image, but will no more be deluded. That fine distinction between the actual world and the mirage he has caught, and the latter cannot delude him any more. So when the Vedantist has realised his own nature, the whole world has vanished for him. It will come back again, but no more the same world of misery. The prison of misery has become changed into Sat, Chit, Ananda—Existence Absolute, Knowledge Absolute, Bliss Absolute—and the attainment of this is the goal of the Advaita Philosophy.

Reason-Checking of Religion

A sage called Narada went to another sage named Sanatkumara to learn about truth, and Sanatkumara inquired what he had studied already. Narada answered that he had studied the Vedas, Astronomy, and various other things, yet he had got no satisfaction. Then there was a conversation between the two, in the course of which Sanatkumara remarked that all this knowledge of the Vedas, of Astronomy, and of Philosophy, was but secondary; sciences were but secondary. That which made us realise the Brahman was the supreme, the highest knowledge. This idea we find in every religion, and that is why religion always claimed to be supreme knowledge. Knowledge of the sciences covers, as it were, only part of our lives, but the knowledge which religion brings to us is eternal, as infinite as the truth it preaches. **Claiming this superiority, religions have many times looked down, unfortunately, on all secular knowledge, and not only so, but many times have refused to be justified by the aid of secular knowledge.**

In conseqence, all the world over there have been fights between secular knowledge and religious knowledge, the one claiming infallible authority as its guide, refusing to listen to anything that secular knowledge has to say on the point, the other, with its shining instrument of reason, wanting to cut to pieces everything religion could bring forward. This fight has been and is still waged in every country. Religions have been again and again defeated, and almost exterminated. The worship of the goddess of Reason during the French Revolution was not the first manifestation of that phenomenon in the history of humanity, it was a reenactment of what had happened in ancient times, but in modern times it has assumed greater proportions. The physical sciences are better equipped now than formerly, and religions have become less and less equipped. The foundations have been all undermined, and **the modern man, whatever he may say in public, knows in the privacy of his heart that he can no more "believe".** Believing certain things because an organised body of priests tells him to believe, believing because it is written in certain books, believing because his people like him to believe, the modern man knows to be impossible for him. **There are, of course, a number of people who seem to acquiesce in the so-called popular faith, but we also know for certain that they do not think. Their idea of belief may be better translated as "not-thinking-carelessness".** This fight cannot last much longer without breaking to pieces all the buildings of religion.

The question is: Is there a way out? To put it in a more concrete form: Is religion to justify itself by the discoveries of reason, through which every other science justifies itself? **Are the same methods of investigation, which we apply to sciences and knowledge outside, to be applied to the science of Religion? In my opinion this must be so, and I am also of opinion that the sooner it is done the better. If a religion is destroyed by such investigations, it was then all the time useless, unworthy superstition; and the sooner it goes the better.** I am thoroughly convinced that its destruction would be the best thing that could happen. All that is dross will be taken off, no doubt, but the essential parts of religion will emerge triumphant out of this investigation. Not only will it be made scientific—as scientific, at least, as any of the conclusions of physics or chemistry—but will have greater strength, because physics or chemistry has no internal mandate to vouch for its truth, which religion has.

People who deny the efficacy of any rationalistic investigation into religion seem to me somewhat to be contradicting themselves. For instance, the Christian claims that his religion is the only true one, because it was revealed to so-and-so. The Mohammedan makes the same claim for his religion; his is the only true one, because it was revealed to so-and-so. But the Christian says to the Mohammedan, "Certain parts of your ethics do not seem to be right. For instance, your books say, my Mohammendan friend, that an infidel may be converted to the religion of Mohammedan by force, and if he will not accept the Mohammedan religion he may be killed; and the Mohammedan who kills such an infidel will get a sure entry into heaven, whatever may have been his sins or misdeeds." The Mohammedan will retort by saying, "It is right for me to do so, because my book enjoins it. It will be wrong on my part not to do so." The Mohammedan replies, "I do not know; I am not bound by the authority of your book; my book says, 'Kill all the infields."

How do you know which is right and which is wrong? Surely what is written in my book is right and what your book says, 'Do not kill,' is wrong. You also say the same thing, my Christian friend; you say that what Jehovah declared to the Jews is right to do, and what he forbade them to do is wrong. So say I, Allah declared in my book that certain things should not be done, and that is all the test of right and wrong." In spite of that the Chirstian is not satisfied; he insists on a comparison of the morality of the Sermon on the Mount with the morality of the Koran. How is this to be decided? Certainly not by the books, because the books, fighting between themselves, cannot be the judges. Decidedly then we have to admit that there is something more universal than these books, something higher than all the ethical codes that are in the world, something which can judge between the strength of inspirations of different nations. Whether we declare it boldly, clearly, or not—it is evident that here we appeal to reason.

Now, the question arises if this light of reason is able to judge between inspiration and inspiration, and if this light can uphold its standard when the quarrel is between prophet and prophet, if it has the power of understanding anything whatsoever of religion. If it has not, **nothing can determine the hopeless fight of books and prophets which has been going on through ages;** for it means that all religions are mere lies, hopelessly contradictory, without any constant idea of ethics. **The proof of religion depends on the truth of the constitution of man, and not on any books.** These books are the outgoings, the effects of man's constitution; man made these books. We are yet to see the books that made man. Reason is equally an effect of that common cause, the constitution of man, where our appeal must be. And yet, as reason alone is directly connected with this constitution, it should be resorted to, as long as it follows faithfully the same. What do I mean by reason? I mean what every educated man or woman is wanting to do at the present time, to apply the discoveries of secular knowledge to religion.

The first principle of reasoning is that the particular is explained by the general, the general by the more general, until we come to the universal. For instance, we have the idea of law. If something happens and we believe that it is the effect of such and such a law, we are satisfied; that is an explanation for us. What we mean by that explanation is that it is proved that this one effect, which had dissatisfied us, is only one particular of a general mass of occurrences which we designate by the word "law". When one apple fall, Newton was disturbed; but when he found that all apples fell, it was gravitation, and he was satisfied. This is one principle of human knowledge. I see a particular being, a human being, in the street. I refer him to the bigger conception of man, and I am satisfied; I know he is a man by referring him to the more general. So the particulars are to be referred to the general, the general to the more general, and everything at last to the universal, the last concept that we have, the most universal—that of existence. **Existence is the most universal concept.**

We are all human beings; that is to say, each one of us, as it were, a particular part of the general concept, humanity. A man, and a cat, and a dog, are all animals. These particular examples, as man, or dog, or cat, are parts of a bigger and more general concept, animal. The man, and the cat, and the dog, and the plant, and the tree, all come under the still more general concept, life. Again, all these, all beings and all materials, come under the one concept of existence, for we all are in it. This explanation merely means referring the particular to a higher concept, finding more of its kind. The mind, as it were, has stored up numerous classes of such generalisations. It is, as it were, full of pigeon-holes where all these ideas are grouped together, and whenever we find a new thing the mind immediately tries to find out its type in one of these pigeon-holes. If we find it, we put the new thing in there and are satisfied, and we are said to have known the thing. This is what is meant by knowledge, and no more. And if we do not find that there is something like it, we are dissatisfied, and have to wait until we find a further classification for it, already existing in the mind. Therefore, as I have already pointed out, knowledge is more or less classification.

There is something more. A second explanation of knowledge is that the explanation of a thing must come from inside and not from outside. There had been the belief that, when a man threw up a stone and it fell, some demon dragged it down. Many occurrences which are really natural phenomena are attributed by people to unnatural beings. That a ghost dragged down the stone was an explanation that was not in the thing itself, it was an explanation from outside; but the second explanation of gravitation is something in the nature of the stone; the explanation is coming from inside. This tendency you will find throughout modern thought; in one word, **what is meant by science is that the explanations of things are in their own nature, and that no external beings or existences are required to explain what is going on in the universe.** The chemist never requires demons, or ghosts, or anything of that sort, to explain his phenomena. The physicist never requires anyone of these to explain the things he knows, nor does any other scientist.

And this is one of the features of science which I mean to apply to religion. In this religions are found wanting and that is why they are crumbling into pieces. Every science wants its explanations from inside, from the very nature of things; and the religions are not able to supply this. There is an ancient theory of a personal deity entirely separate from the universe, which has been held from the very earliest time. The arguments in favour of this have been repeated again and again, how it is necessary to have a God entirely separate from the universe, an extra-cosmic deity, who has created the universe out of his will, and is conceived by religion to be its ruler. We find, apart from all these arguments, **the Almighty God painted as the All-merciful, and at the same time, inequalities remain in the world.** These things do not concern the philosopher at all, but he says the heart of the thing was wrong; it was an explanation from outside, and not inside. What is the cause of the universe? Something outside of it, some being who is moving this universe! And just as it was found insufficient to explain the phenomenon of the falling stone, so this was found insufficient to explain religion. And religions are falling to pieces, because they cannot give a better explanation than that.

Another idea connected with this, the manifestation of the same principle, that the explanation of everything comes from inside it, is **the modern law of evolution**. The whole meaning of evolution is simply that the nature of a thing is reproduced, that the effect is nothing but the cause in another form, that all the potentialities of the effect were present in the cause, **that the whole of creation is but an evolution and not a creation.** That is to say, every effect is a reproduction of a preceding cause, changed only by the circumstances, and thus it is going on throughout the universe, and we need not go outside the universe to seek the causes of these changes; they are within. It is unnecessary to seek for any cause outside. This also is breaking down religion. **What I mean by breaking down religion is that religions that have held on to the idea of an extra-cosmic deity, that he is a very big man and nothing else, can no more stand on their feet;** they have been pulled down, as it were.

Can there be a religion "satisfying these two principles? I think there can be. In the first place we have seen that we have to satisfy the principle of generalisation. The generalisation principle ought to be satisfied along with the principle of evolution. We have to come to an ultimate generalisation, which not only will be the most universal of all generalisations, but out of which everything else must come. It will be of the same nature as the lowest effect; the cause, the highest, the ultimate, the primal cause, must be the same as the lowest and most distant of its effects, a series of evolutions. **The Brahman of the Vedanta fulfils that condition**, because Brahman is the last generalisation to which we can come. It has no attributes but is Existence, Knowledge, and Bliss-Absolute. Existence, we have seen, is the very ultimate generalisation which the human mind can come to. Knowledge does not mean the knowledge we have, but the essence of that, that which is expressing itself in the course of evolution in human beings or in other animals as knowledge. The essence of that knowledge is meant, the ultimate fact beyond, if I may be allowed to say so, even consciousness. That is what is meant by knowledge and what we see in the universe as the essential things.

To my mind, if modem science is proving anything again and again, it is this, that we are one—mentally, spiritually, and physically. It is wrong to say we are even physically different. Supposing we are materialists, for argument's sake, we shall have to come to this, that the whole universe is simply an ocean of matter, of which you and I are like little whirlpools. Masses of matter are coming into each whirlpool, taking the whirlpool form, and coming out as matter again. **The matter that is in my body may have been in yours a few years ago, or in the sun, or may have been the matter in a plant, and so on, in a continuous state of flux.** What is meant by your body and my body? It is the oneness of the body. **So with thought. It is an ocean of thought, one infinite mass, in which your mind and my mind are like whirlpools.** Are you not seeing the effect now, how my thoughts are entering into yours, and yours into mine? The whole of our lives *is* one; we are one, even in thought. Coming to a still further generalisation, the essence of matter and thought is their potentiality of spirit; this is the unity from which all have come, and that must essentially be one.

We are absolutely one, we are physically one, we are mentally one, and as spirit, it goes without saying, that we are one, if we believe in spirit at all. This oneness is the one fact that is being proved every day by modern science. To proud man it is told: You are the same as that little worm there; think not that you are something enormously different from it; you are the same. You have been that in a previous incarnation, and **the worm has crawled up to this man state, of which you are so proud.** This grand preaching, the oneness of things, making us one with everything that exists, is the great lesson to learn, for **most of us are very glad to be made one with higher beings, but nobody wants to be made one with lower beings.** Such is human ignorance, that if anyone's ancestors were men whom society honoured, even if they were brutish, if they were robbers, even robber barons, everyone of us would try to trace our ancestry to them; but if among our ancestors we had poor, honest gentlemen, none of us wants *to* trace our ancestry to them. But the scales are falling from our eyes, truth is beginning to manifest itself more and more, and that is a great gain to religion. That is exactly the teaching of the Advaita, about which I am lecturing to you. The Self is the essence of this universe, the essence of all souls; He is the essence of your own life, nay, "Thou art That."' You are one with this universe. He who says he is different from others, even by a hair's breadth, immediately becomes miserable. Happiness belongs to him who knows this oneness, who knows he is one with this universe.

Thus we see that the religion of the Vedanta can satisfy the demands of the scientific world by referring it to the higest generalisation and to the law of evolution. That the explanation of a thing comes from within itself is still more completely satisfied by Vedanta. The Brahman, the God of the Vedanta, has nothing outside of Himself; nothing at all. All this indeed is He: He is in the universe: He is the universe Himself. "Thou art the man, Thou art the woman, Thou art the young man walking in the pride of youth, Thou art the old man tottering in his step." He is here. Him we see and feel: in

Him we live, and move, and have our being. You have that conception in the New Testament. It is that idea, God immanent in the universe, the very essence, the heart, the soul of things. He manifests Himself, as it were, in this universe. You and I are little bits, little points, little channels, little expressions, all living inside of that infinite ocean of Existence, Knowlege, and Bliss.

The diffrence between man and man, between angels and man, between man and animals, between animals and plants, between plants and stones is not in kind, because everyone from the highest angel to the lowest particle of matter is but an expression of that one infinite ocean, and the difference is only in degree. I am a low manifestation, you may be a higher, but in both the materials are the same. You and I are both outlets of the same channel, and that is God; as such, your nature is God, and so is mine. You are of the nature of God by your birthright; so am I. You may be an angel of purity, and I may be the blackest of demons. Nevertheless, my birth-right is that infinite ocean of Existence, Knowledge, and Bliss. So is You have manifested yourself more today.

Wait; I will manifest myself more yet, for I have it all within me. No extraneous explanation is sought; none is asked for. The sum total of this whole universe is God Himself. Is God then matter? No, certainly not, for matter is that God perceived by the five senses; that God as perceived through the intellect is mind; and when the spirit sees, He is seen as spirit. He is not matter, but whatever is real in matter is He. Whatever is real in this chair is He, for the chair requires two things to make it. Something was outside which my senses brought to me, and to which my mind contributed something else, and the combination of these two is the chair. That which existed eternally, independent of the senses and of the intellect, was the Lord Himself. Upon Him the senses are painting chairs, and tables, and rooms, houses, and worlds, and moons, and suns, and stars, and everything else.

How is it, then, that we all see this same chair, that we are all alike painting these various things on the Lord, on this Existence,

Knowledge, and Bliss? It need not be that all paint the same way, but those who paint the same way are on the same plane of existence and therefore they see one another's paintings as well as one another. There may be millions of beings between you and me who do not paint the Lord in the same way, and them and their paintings we do not see.

On the other hand, as you all know, the modern physical researches are tending more and more to demonstrate that what is real is but the finer; the grass is simply appearance. However that may be, we have seen that if any theory of religion can stand the test of modern reasoning, it is the Advaita, because it fulfils its two requirements. It is the highest generalisation, beyond even personality, generalisation which is common to every being. **A generalisation ending in the Personal God can never be universal, for, first of all, to conceive of a Personal God we must say, He is all-merciful, all-good. But this world is a mixed thing, same good and same bad.** We cut off what we like, and generalise that into a Personal God! Just as you say a Personal God is this and that, so you have also to say that He is not this and not that. And you will always find that the idea of a Personal God has to carry with it a personal devil. That is how we clearly see that the idea of a Personal God is not a true generalisation, we have to go beyond, to the Impersonal. In that the universe exists, with all its joys and miseries, for whatever exists in it has all come from the Impersonal.

What sort of a God can He be to whom we attribute evil and other things? The idea is that both good and evil are different aspects, or manifestations of the same thing. The idea that they were two was a very wrong idea from the first, and it has been the cause of a good deal of the misery in this world of ours—the idea that right and wrong are two separate things, cut and dried, independent of each other, that good and evil are two eternally separable and separate things. I should be very glad to see a man who could show me something which is good all the time, and something which is bad all the time. As if one could stand and gravely define some occurrences in this life of ours as good and good alone, and some which are bad and bad alone. That which is good today may be evil tomorrow. That which is bad today may be good tomorrow. What is good for me may be bad for you. The conclusion is, that like every other thing, there is an evolution in good and evil too. There is something which in its evolution, we call, in one degree, good, and in another, evil. The storm that kills my friend I call evil, but that may have saved the lives of hundreds of thousands of people by killing the bacilli in the air. They call it good, but I call it evil. So both good and evil belong to the relative world, to phenomena. The Impersonal God we propose is not a relative God; therefore it cannot be said that it is either good or bad, but that it is something beyond, because it is neither good nor evil. Good, however, is a nearer manifestation of it than evil.

What is the effect of accepting such an Impersonal Being, an Impersonal Deity? What shall we gain? Will religion stand as a factor in human life, our consoler, our helper? What becomes of the desire of the human heart to pray for help to some being? That will all remain. The Personal God will remain, but on a better basis. He has been strengthened by the Impersonal. We have seen that without the Impersonal, the Personal cannot remain. **If you mean to say there is a Being entirely separate from this universe, who has created this universe just by His will, out of nothing, that cannot be proved.** Such a state of things cannot be. But if we understand the idea of the Impersonal, then the idea of the Personal can remain there also. This universe, in its various forms, is but the various readings of the same Impersonal. When we read it with the five senses, we call it the material world. If there be a being with more senses than five, he will read it as something else. If one of us gets the electrical sense, he will see the universe as something else again. There are various forms of that same Oneness, of which all these various ideas of worlds are but various readings, and the Personal God is the highest reading that can be attained, of that Impersonal, by the human intellect. So that the Personal God is true as much as this chair is true, as much as this world is true, but no more. It is not absolute truth. That is to say, the Personal God is that very Impersonal God and, therefore, it is true, just as I, as a human being, am true and not true at the same time.

It is not true that I am what you see I am; you can satisfy yourself on that point. I am not the being that you take me to be. You can satisfy your reason as to that, because light, and various vibrations, or conditions of the atmosphere, and all sorts of motions inside me have contributed to my being looked upon as what I am, by you. If anyone of these conditions change, I am different again. You may satisfy yourself by taking a photograph of the same man under different conditions of light. So I am what I appear in relation to your senses, and yet, in spite of all these facts, there is an unchangeable something of which all these are different states of existence, the impersonal me, of which thousands of me's are different persons. I was a child, I was young, I am getting older. Every day of my life, my body and thoughts are changing, but in spite of all these changes, the sum-total of them constitutes a mass which is a constant quantity. That is the impersonal me, of which all these manifestations form, as it were, parts.

Similarly, the sum-total of this universe is immovable, we know, but everything pertaining to this universe consists of motion, everything is in a constant state of flux, everything changing and moving. At the same time, we see that the universe as a whole is immovable, because motion is a relative term. I move with regard to the chair, which does not move. There must be at least two to make motion. If this whole universe is taken as a unit there is no motion; with regard to what should it move? Thus the Absolute is unchangeable and immovable, and all the movements and changes are only in the phenomenal world, the limited. That whole is Impersonal, and within this Impersonal are all these various persons beginning with the lowest atom, up to God, the Personal God, the Creator, the Ruler of the Universe, to whom we pray, before whom we kneel, and so on. Such a Personal God can be established with a great deal of reason. **Such a Personal God is explicable as the highest manifestation of the Impersonal.** You and I are very low manifestations, and the Personal God is the highest of which we can conceive. Nor can you or I become that Personal God.

When the Vedanta says you and I are God, it does not mean the Personal God. To take an example. Out of a mass of clay a huge elephant of clay is manufactured, and out of the same clay, a little clay mouse is made. Would the clay mouse ever be able to become the clay elephant? But put them both in water and they are both clay; as clay they are both one, but as mouse and elephant there will be an eternal difference between them. The Infinite, the Impersonal, is like the clay in the example. We and the Ruler of the Universe are one, but as manifested beings, men, we are His eternal slaves, His worshippers. Thus we see that the Personal God remains. Everything else in this relative world remains, and religion is made to stand on a better foundation. Therefore it is necessary that we first know the Impersonal in order to know the Personal.

As we have seen, the law of reason says, the particular is only known through the general. So all these particulars, from man to God, are only known through the Impersonal, the highest generalisation. Prayers will remain, only they will get a better meaning. All those senseless ideas of prayer, the low stages of prayer, which are simply giving words to all sorts of silly desires in our minds, perhaps, will have to go. **In all sensible religions, they never allow prayers to God; they allow prayers to gods. That is quite natural. The Roman Catholics pray to the saints;** that is quite good. But to pray to God is senseless. To ask God to give you a breath of air, to send down a shower of rain, to make fruits grow in your garden, and so on, is quite unnatural. **The saints, however, who were little beings like ourselves, may help us.** But to pray to the Ruler of the Universe, praying every little need of ours, and from our childhood saying, "O Lord, I have a headache; let it go," is ridiculous. There have been millions of souls that have died in this world, and they are all here; they have become gods and angels; let them come to your help. But God! It cannot be. Unto Him we must go for higher things. A fool indeed is he who, resting on the banks of the Ganga, digs a little well for water; a fool indeed is he who, living near a mine of diamonds, digs for bits of crystal.

And indeed we shall be fools if we go to the Father of all mercy, Father of all love, for trivial earthly things. Unto Him, therefore, we shall go for light, for strength, for love. But so long as there is weakness and a craving for servile dependence in us, there will be these little prayers and ideas of the worship of the Personal God. But those who are highly advanced do not care for such little helps, they have well nigh forgotten all about this seeking things for themselves, wanting things for themselves. The predominant idea in them is—not I, but thou, my brother. Those are the fit persons to worship the Impersonal God. **And what is the worship of the Impersonal God? No slavery there—"O Lord, I am nothing, have mercy on me."** You know the old Persian poem, translated into English: "I came to see my beloved. The doors were closed. I knocked and a voice came from inside. 'Who art thou?' 'I am so-and-so.' The door was not opened. A second time I came and knocked; I was asked the same question, and gave the same answer. The door opened not. I came a third time, and the same question came. I answered, 'I am thee, my love,' and the door opened." Worship of the Impersonal God is through truth.

And what is truth? That I am He. When I say that I am not Thou, it is untrue. When I say I am separate from you it is a lie, a terrible lie. I am one with this universe, born one. It is self-evident to my senses that I am one with the universe. I am one with the air that surrounds me, one with heat, one with light, eternally one with the whole Universal Being, who is called this universe, who is mistaken for the universe, for it is He and nothing else, the eternal subject in the heart who says, "I am," in every heart—the deathless one, the sleepless one, ever awake, the immortal, whose glory never dies, whose powers never fail. I am one with That.

This is all the worship of the Impersonal, and what is the result? The whole life of man will be changed. Strength, strength it is that we want so much in this life, for what we call sin and sorrow have all one cause, and that is our weakness. With weakness comes ignorance, and with ignorance comes misery. It will make us strong. Then miseries will be laughed at, then the violence of the vile will be smiled at, and the ferocious tiger will reveal, behind its tiger's nature, my own Self. That will be the result. That soul is strong that has become one with the Lord; none else is strong.

In your own Bible, what do you think was the cause of that strength of Jesus of Nazareth, that immense, infinite strength which laughed at traitors, and blessed those that were willing to murder him? It was that, "I and my Father are one"; it was that prayer, "Father, just as I am one with you, so make them all one with me." That is the worship of the Impersonal God. Be one with the universe, be one with Him. And this Impersonal God requires no demonstrations, no proofs. He is nearer to us than even our senses, nearer to us than our own thoughts; it is in and through Him that we see and think. To see anything, I must first see Him. To see this wall I first see Him, and then the wall, for He is the eternal subject.

Who is seeing whom? He is here in the heart of our hearts. Bodies and minds change; misery, happiness, good and evil come and go; days and years roll on; life comes and goes; but He dies not. The same voice, "I am, I am," is eternal, unchangeable. In Him and through Him we know everything. In Him and through Him we see everything. In Him and through Him we sense, we think, we live, and we are. And that "I," which we mistake to be a little "I" limited, is not only my "I," but yours, the "I" of everyone, of the animals, of the angels, of the lowest of the low. That "I am" is the same in the murderer as in the saint, the same in the rich as in the poor, the same in man as in woman, the same in man as in animals.

From the lowest amoeba to the highest angel, He resides in every soul, and eternally declares, "I am He, I am He." When we have understood that voice eternally present there, when we have learnt this lesson, the whole universe will have expressed its secret. Nature will have given up her secret to us. Nothing more remains to be Known. Thus we find the truth for which all religions search, that all this knowledge of material sciences is but secondary. That is the only true knowledge which makes us one with this Universal God of the Universe.

(*A talk delivered in England*)

Practical Vedanta

I have been asked to say something about the practical position of the Vedanta philosophy. As I have told you, theory is very good indeed, but how are we to carry it into practice? If it be absolutely impracticable, no theory is of any value whatever, except as intellectual gymnastics. The Vedanta, therefore, as a religion must be intensely practical. We must be able to carry it out in every part of our lives. And not only this, the fictitious differentiation between religion and the life of the world must vanish, for the Vedanta teaches oneness—one life throughout. The ideals of religion must cover the whole field of life, they must enter into all our thoughts, and more and more into practice. I will enter gradually on the practical side as we proceed. But this series of lectures is intended to be a basis, and so we must first apply ourselves to theories and understand how they are worked out, proceeding from forest caves to busy streets and cities; and one peculiar feature we find is that many of these thoughts have been the outcome, not of retirement into forests, but have emanated from persons whom we expect to lead the busiest lives—from ruling monarchs.

Shvetaketu was the son of Aruni, a sage, most probably a recluse. He was brought up in the forest, but he went to the city of the Panchalas and appeared at the court of the king, Pravahana Jaivali. The king asked him, "Do you know how beings depart hence at death?" "No, sir." "Do you know how they return hither?" "No, sir."

"Do you know the way of the fathers and the way of the gods?" "No, sir." Then the king asked other questions. Shvetaketu could not answer them. So the king told him that he knew nothing. The boy went back to his father, and the father admitted that he himself could not answer these questions. It was not that he was unwilling to answer these questions. It was not that he was unwilling to teach the boy, but he did not know these things. So he went to the king and asked to be taught these secrets. **The king said that these things had been hitherto known only among kings; the priests never knew them.** He, however, proceeded to teach him what he desired to know. **In various Upanishads we find that this Vedanta philosophy is not the outcome of meditation in the forests only, but that the very best parts of it were thought out and expressed by brains which were busiest in the everyday affairs of life.** We cannot conceive any man busier than an absolute monarch, a man who is ruling over millions of people, and yet, some of these rulers were deep thinkers.

Everything goes to show that this philosophy must be very practical; and later on, when we come to the Bhagavad-gita—most of you, perhaps, have read it, it is the best commentary we have on the Vedanta philosophy —curiously enough the scene is laid on the battlefield, where Krishna teaches this philosophy to Arjuna; and the doctrine which stands out luminously in every page of the Gita is intense activity, but in the midst of it, eternal calmness. This is the secret of work, to attain which is the goal of the Vedanta. Inactivity, as we understand it in the sense of passivity, certainly cannot be the goal. Were it so, then the walls around us would be the most intelligent; they are inactive. Clods of earth, stumps of trees, would be the greatest sages in the world; they are inactive. Nor does inactivity become activity when it is combined with passion. Real activity, which is the goal of Vedanta, is combined with eternal calmness, the calmness which cannot he ruffled, the balance of mind which is never disturbed, whatever happens. And we all know from our experience in life that is the best attitude for work.

I have been asked many times how we can work if we do not have the passion which we generally feel for work. I also thought in that way years ago, but as I am growing older, getting more experience, I find it is not true. The less passion there is, the better we work. The calmer we are, the better for us, and the more the amount of work we can do. When we let loose our feelings, we waste so much energy, shatter our nerves, disturb our minds, and accomplish very little work. The energy which ought to have gone out as work is spent as mere feeling which counts for nothing. It is only when the mind is very calm and collected that the whole of its energy is spent in doing good work. And if you read the lives of the great workers which the world has produced, you will find that they were wonderfully calm men. Nothing, as it were, could throw them off their balance. That is why the man who becomes angry never does a great amount of work, and the man whom nothing can make angry accomplishes so much. The man who gives way to anger, or hatred, or any other passion, cannot work; he only breaks himself to pieces, and does nothing practical. It is the calm, forgiving, equable, well-balanced mind that does the greatest amount of work.

The Vedanta preaches the ideal; and the ideal, as we know, is always far ahead of the real, of the practical, as we may call it. There are two tendencies in human nature: one to harmonise the ideal with the life, and the other to elevate the life to the ideal. It is a great thing to understand this, for the former tendency is the temptation of our lives. I think that I can only do a certain class of work. Most of it, perhaps, is bad; most of it, perhaps, has a motive power of passion behind it, anger, or greed, or selfishness. Now if any man comes to preach to me a certain ideal, the first step towards which is to give up selfishness, to give up self-enjoyment, I think that is impractical. But when a man brings an ideal which can be reconciled with my selfishness, I am glad at once and jump at it. That is the ideal for me. As the word "orthodox" has been manipulated into various forms, so has been the word "practical". "My doxy is orthodoxy; your doxy is heterodoxy." So with practicality. What I think is practical, is to me the only practicality in the world. If I am a shopkeeper, I think shopkeeping the only practical pursuit in the world. If I am a thief, I think stealing is the best means of being practical; others are not practical.

You see how we all use this word practical for things we like and can do. Therefore I will ask you to understand that Vedanta, though it is intensely practical, is always so in the sense of the ideal. It does not preach an impossible ideal, however high it be, and it is high enough for an ideal. In one word, this ideal is that you are divine, "Thou art That". This is the essence of Vedanta; after all its ramifications and intellectual gymnastics, you know the human soul to be pure and omniscient, you see that such superstitions as birth and death would be entire nonsense when spoken of in connection with the soul. The soul was never born and will never die, and all these ideas that we are going to die and are afraid to die are mere superstitions. And all such ideas as that we can do this or cannot do that are superstitions.

We can do everything. **The Vedanta teaches men to have faith in themselves first.** As certain religions of the world say that a man who does not believe in a Personal God outside of himself is an atheist, so **the Vedanta says, a man who does not believe in himself is an atheist.** Not believing in the glory of our own soul is what the Vedanta calls atheism. To many this is, no doubt, a terrible idea; and most of us think that this ideal can never be reached; but the Vedanta insists that it can be realised by everyone. There is neither man nor woman or child, nor difference of race or sex, nor anything that stands as a bar to the realisation of the ideal, because Vedanta shows that it is realised already, it is already there.

All the powers in the universe are already ours. It is we who have put our hands before our eyes and cry that it is dark. **Know that there is no darkness around us.** Take the hands away and there is the light which was from the beginning. **Darkness never existed, weakness never existed. We who are fools cry that we are weak; we who are fools cry that we are impure.** Thus Vedanta not only insists that the ideal is practical, but that it has been so all the time; and this ideal, this reality, is our own nature. Everything else that you see is false, untrue. As soon as you say, "I am a little mortal being," you are saying something which is not true, you are giving the lie to yourselves, you are hypnotising yourselves into something vile and weak and wretched.

The Vedanta recognises no sin, it only recognises error. And the greatest error, says the Vedanta, is to say that you are weak, that you are a sinner, a miserable creature, and that you have no power and you cannot do this and that. Every time you think in that way, you, as it were, rivet one more link in the chain that binds you down, you add one more layer of hypnotism on to your own soul. Therefore, whosoever thinks he is weak is wrong, whosoever thinks he is impure is wrong, and is throwing a bad thought into the world.

This we must always bear in mind that in the Vedanta there is no attempt at reconciling the present life—the hypnotised life, this false life which we have assumed—with the ideal; but this false life must go, and the real life which is always existing must manifest itself, must shine out. No man becomes purer and purer, it is a matter of greater manifestation. The veil drops away, and the native purity of the soul begins to manifest itself. Everything is ours already—infinite purity, freedom, love, and power.

The Vedanta also says that not only can this be realised in the depths of forests or caves, but by men in all possible conditions of life. We have seen that the people who discovered these truths were neither living in caves nor forests, nor following the ordinary vocations of life, but men who, we have every reason to believe, led the busiest of lives, men who had to command armies, to sit on thrones, and look to the welfare of millions—and all these, in the days of absolute monarchy, and not as in these days when a king is to a great extent a mere figurehead. Yet they could find time to think out all these thoughts, to realise them, and to teach them to humanity. How much more then should it be practical for us whose lives, compared with theirs, are lives of leisure? That we cannot realise them is a shame to us, seeing that we are comparatively free all the time, having very little to do my requirements are as nothing compared with those of an ancient absolute monarch. My wants are as nothing compared with the demands of Arjuna on the battlefield of Kurukshetra, commanding a huge army; and yet he could find time in the midst of the din and turmoil of battle to talk the highest philosophy and to carry it into his life also. Surely we ought to be able to do as much in this life as ours—comparatively free, easy, and comfortable.

Most of us here have more time than we think we have, if we really want to use it for good. With the amount of freedom we have we can attain to two hundred ideals in this life, if we will, but we must not degrade the ideal to the actual. One of the most insinuating things comes to us in the shape of persons who apologise for our mistakes and teach us how to make special excuses for all our foolish wants and foolish desires; and we think that their ideal is the only ideal we need to have. But it is not so. The Vedanta teaches no such thing. The actual should be reconciled to the ideal, the present life should be made to coincide with life eternal.

For you must always remember that the one central ideal of Vedanta is this oneness. There are no two in anything, no two lives, nor even two different kinds of life for the two worlds. You will find the Vedas speaking of heavens and things like that at first, but later on, when they come to the highest ideals of their philosophy, they brush away all these things. There is but one life, one world, one existence. Everything is that One, the difference is in degree and not in kind. The difference between our lives is not in kind. **The Vedanta entirely denies such ideas as that animals are separate from men, and that they were made and created by God to be used for our food.**

Some people have been kind enough to start an anti-vivisection society. I asked a member, "Why do you think, my friend, that it is quite lawful to kill animals for food, and not to kill one or two for scientific experiments?" He replied, "Vivisection is most horrible, but animals have been given to us for food." Oneness includes all animals. If man's life is immortal, so also is the animal's. The difference is only in degree and not in kind. The amoeba and I are the same, the difference is only in degree; and from the standpoint of the highest life, all these differences vanish. A man may see a great deal of difference between grass and a little tree but if you mount very high, the grass and the biggest tree will appear much the same. So, from the standpoint of the highest ideal, the lowest animal and the highest man are the same. If you believe there is a God, the animal and the highest creatures must be the same.

A God who is partial to his children called men, and cruel to his children called beasts, is worse than a demon. I would rather die a hundred times than worship such a God. My whole life would be a fight with such a God. But there is no difference, and those who say there is, are irresponsible, heartless people who do not know. Here is a case of the word 'practical' used in a wrong sense. I myself may not be a very strict vegetarian, but I understand the ideal. When I eat meat I know it is wrong. Even if I am bound to eat it under certain circumstances, I know it is cruel. I must not drag my ideal down to the actual and apologise for my weak conduct in this way.

The ideal is not to eat flesh, not to injure any being, for all animals are my brothers. If you can think of them as your brothers you have made a little headway towards the brotherhood of all souls, not to speak of the brotherhood of man! That is child's play. You generally find that this is not very acceptable to many, because it teaches them to give up the actual, and go higher up to the ideal. But if you bring out a theory which is reconciled with their present conduct, they regard it as entirely practical.

There is this strongly conservative tendency in human nature: we do not like to move one step forward. I think of mankind just as I read of persons who become frozen in snow; all such, they say, want to go to sleep, and if you try to drag them up, they say, "Let me sleep; it is so beautiful to sleep in the snow," and they die there in that sleep. So is our nature. That is what we are doing all our life, getting frozen from the feet upwards, and yet wanting to sleep. Therefore you must struggle towards the ideal, and if a man comes who wants to bring that ideal down to your level, and teach a religion that does not carry that highest ideal, do not listen to him. To me that is an impracticable religion. But if a man teaches a religion which presents the highest ideal, I am ready for him. Beware when anyone is trying to apologise for sense vanities and sense weaknesses. If anyone wants to preach that way to us, poor, sense-bound clods of earth as we have made ourselves by following that teaching, we shall never progress. I have seen many of these things, I have had some experience of the world, and **my country is the land where religious sects grow like mushrooms. Every year new sects arise. But one thing I have marked, that it is only those that never want to reconcile the man of flesh with the man of truth that make progress.** Wherever there is this false idea of reconciling fleshly vanities with the highest ideals, of dragging down God to the level of man, there comes decay. Man should not be degraded to worldly slavery, but should be raised up to God.

At the same time, there is another side to the question. We must not look down with contempt on others. All of them are going towards the same goal. The difference between weakness and strength is one of degree; the difference between virtue and vice is one of degree; the difference between heaven and hell is one of degree; the difference between life and death is one of degree; **all differences in this world are of degree, and not of kind,** because oneness is the secret of everything. All is One, which manifests Itself, either as thought, or life, or soul, or body, and the difference is only in degree. As such, **we have no right to look down with contempt upon those who are not developed exactly in the same degree as we are.** Condemn none; if you can stretch out a helping hand, do so. If you cannot, fold your hands, bless your brothers, and let them go their own way. Dragging down and condemning is not the way to work. Never is work accomplished in that way. We spend our energies in condemning others. Criticism and condemnation is a vain way of spending our energies, for in the long run we come to learn that all are seeing the same thing, are more or less approaching the same ideal, and that most of our differences are merely differences of expression.

Take the idea of sin. I was telling you just now the Vedantic idea of it, and the other idea is that man is a sinner. They are practically the same, only the one takes the positive and the other the negative side. One shows to man his strength and the other his weakness. There may be weakness, says the Vedanta, but never mind, we want to grow. Disease was found out as soon as man was born. Everyone knows his disease; it requires no one to tell us what our diseases are. But thinking all the time that we are diseased will not cure us— medicine is necessary. We may forget anything outside, we may try to become hypocrites to the external world, but in our heart of hearts we all know our weakness.

But, says the Vedanta, being reminded of weakness does not help much; give strength, and strength does not come by thinking of weakness all the time. The remedy for weakness is not brooding over weakness, but thinking of strength. Teach men of the strength that is already within them. **Instead of telling them they are sinners, the Vedanta takes the opposite position, and says, "You are pure and perfect, and what you call sin does not belong to you."** Sins are very low degrees of Self-manifestation; manifest your Self in a high degree. That is the one thing to remember; all of us can do that. Never say, "No," never say, "I cannot," for you are infinite. Even time and space are as nothing compared with your nature. **You can do anything and everything, you are almighty.**

These are the principles of ethics, but we shall now come down lower and work out the details. We shall see how this Vedanta can be carried into our everyday life, the city life. the country life, the national life, and the home life of every nation. For, if a religion cannot help man wherever he may be, wherever he stands, it is not of much use; it will remain only a theory for the chosen few. Religion, to help mankind, must be ready and able to help him in whatever condition he is, in servitude or in freedom, in the depths of degradation or on the heights of purity; everywhere, equally, it should be able to come to his aid. The principles of Vedanta, or the ideal of religion or whatever you may call it, will be fulfilled by its capacity for performing this great function.

The ideal of faith in ourselves is of the greatest help to us. If faith in ourselves had been more extensively taught and practised, I am sure a very large portion of the evils and miseries that we have would have vanished. Throughout the history of mankind, if any motive power has been more potent than another in the lives of all great men and women, it is that of faith in themselves. Born with the consciousness that they were to be great, they became great. Let a man go down as low as possible; there must come a time when out of sheer desperation he will take an upward curve and will learn to have faith in himself. But it is better for us that we should know it from the very first. Why should we have all these bitter experiences in order to gain faith in ourselves? We can see that all the difference between man and man is owing to the existence or non-existence of faith in himself. Faith in ourselves will do everything.

I have experienced it in my own life, and am still doing so; and as I grow older that faith is becoming stronger and stronger. He is an atheist who does not believe in himself. The old religions said that he was an atheist who did not believe in God. The new religion says that he is the atheist who does not believe in himself. But it is not selfish faith, because the Vedanta, again, is the doctrine of oneness. It means faith in all, because you are all. Love for yourselves means love for all, love for animals, love for everything, for you are all one. It is the great faith which will make the world better. I am sure of that. He is the highest man who can say with truth, "I know all about myself." Do you know how much energy, how many powers, how many forces are still lurking behind that frame of ours?

What scientist has known all that is in man? Millions of years have passed since man first came here, and yet but one infinitesimal part of his powers has been manifested. Therefore, you must not say that you are weak. How do you know what possibilities lie behind that degradation on the surface? You know but little of that which is within you. For behind you is the ocean of infinite power and blessedness.

"This Atman is first to be heard of." Hear day and night that you are that Soul. Repeat it to yourselves day and night till it enters into your very veins, till it tingles in every drop of blood, till it is in your flesh and bone. Let the whole body be full of that one ideal, "I am the birthless, the deathless, the blissful, the omniscient, the omnipotent, everglorious Soul." Think on it day and night; think on it till it becomes part and parcel of your life. Meditate upon it, and out of that will come work. "Out of the fullness of the heart the mouth speaketh," and out of the fullness of the heart the hand worketh also. Action will come. Fill yourselves with the ideal; whatever you do, think well on it. All your actions will be magnified, transformed, deified, by the very power of the thought. **If matter is powerful, thought is omnipotent.** Bring this thought to bear upon your life, fill yourselves with the thought of your almightiness, your majesty, and your glory. Would to God no superstitions had been put into your head! Would to God we had not been surrounded from our birth by all these superstitious influences and paralysing ideas of our weakness and vileness! Would to God that mankind had had an easier path through which to attain to the noblest and highest truths! But man had to pass through all this; do not make the path more difficult for those who are coming after you.

These are sometimes terrible doctrines to teach. I know people who get frightened at these ideas, but for those who want to be practical, this is the first thing to learn. Never tell yourselves or others that you are weak.

Do good if you can, but do not injure the world. You know in your inmost heart that many of your limited ideas, this humbling of yourself and **praying and weeping to imaginary beings are superstitions. Tell me one case where these prayers have been answered.** All the answers that came were from your own hearts.

You know there are no ghosts, but no sooner are you in the dark than you feel a little creepy sensation. That is so because in our childhood we have had all these fearful ideas put into our heads. But do not teach these things to others through fear of society and public opinion, through fear of incurring the hatred of friends, or for fear of losing cherished superstitions. Be masters of all these. What is there to be taught more in religion than the oneness of the universe and faith in one's self?

All the works of mankind for thousands of years past have been towards this one goal, and mankind is yet working it out. It is your turn now and you already know the truth. For it has been taught on all sides. Not only philosophy and psychology, but materialistic sciences have declared it. Where is the scientific man today who fears to acknowledge the truth of this oneness of the universe? Who is there who dares talk of many worlds? All these are superstition. There is only one life and one world, and this one life and one world is appearing to us as manifold. This manifoldness is like a dream. When you dream, one dream passes away and another comes. You do not live in your dreams. The dreams come one after another, scene after scene unfolds before you. So it is in this world of ninety per cent misery and ten per cent happiness. Perhaps after a while it will appear as ninety per cent happiness, and we shall call it heaven, but a time comes to the sage when the whole thing vanishes, and this world appears as God Himself, and his own soul as God. It is not therefore that there are many worlds, it is not that there are many lives. All this manifoldness is the manifestation of that One. That One is manifesting Himself as many, as matter, spirit, mind, thought, and everything else. It is that One, manifesting Himself as many. Therefore the first step for us to take is to teach the truth to ourselves and to others.

Let the world resound with this ideal, and let superstitions vanish. Tell it to men who are weak and persist in telling it. **You are the Pure One; awake and arise, O mighty one, this sleep does not become you. Awake and arise, it does not befit you.** Think not that you are weak and miserable. Almighty, arise and awake, and manifest your own nature. It is not fitting that you think yourself a sinner. It is not fitting that you think yourself weak. Say that to the world, say it to yourselves, and see what a practical result comes, see how with an electric flash everything is manifested, how everything is changed. Tell that to mankind, and show them their power. Then we shall learn how to apply it in our daily lives.

To be able to use what we call Viveka (discrimination), to learn how in every moment of our lives, in every one of our actions, to discriminate between what is right and wrong, true and false, we shall have to know the test of truth, which is purity, oneness. Everything that makes for oneness is truth, Love is truth, and hatred is false, because hatred makes for multiplicity. It is hatred that separates man from man; therefore, it is wrong and false. It is a disintegrating power; it separates and destroys.

Love binds, love makes for that oneness. You become one, the mother with the child, families with the city, the whole world becomes one with the animals. For love is Existence, God Himself; and all this is the manifestation of that One Love, more or less expressed. The difference is only in degree, but it is the manifestation of that One Love throughout. Therefore in all our actions we have to judge whether it is making for diversity or for oneness. If for diversity we have to give it up, but if it makes for oneness we are sure it is good. So with our thoughts; we have to decide whether they make for disintegration, multiplicity, or for oneness, binding soul to soul and bringing one influence to bear. If they do this, we will take them up, and if not, we will throw them off as criminal.

The whole idea of ethics is that it does not depend on anything unknowable, it does not teach anything unknown, but in the language of the Upanishad, "The God whom you worship as an unknown God, the same I preach unto thee." It is through the Self that you know anything. I see the chair; but to see the chair, I have first to perceive myself and then the chair. It is in and through the Self that the chair is perceived. It is in and through the Self that you are known to me, that the whole world is known to me; and therefore to say this Self is unknown is sheer nonsense. Take off the Self and the whole universe vanishes. In and through the Self all knowledge comes. Therefore it is the best known of all. It is yourself, that which you call I. You may wonder how this I of me can be the I of you. You may wonder how this limited I can be the unlimited Infinite, but it is so. The limited is a mere fiction. The Infinite has been covered up, as it were, and a little of It is manifesting as the I. Limitation can never come upon the unlimited; it is a fiction. The Self is known, therefore, to everyone of us—man, woman, or child—and even to animals. Without knowing Him we can neither live nor move, nor have our being; without knowing this Lord of all, we cannot breathe or live a second. The God of the Vedanta is the most known of all and is not the outcome of imagination.

If this is not preaching a practical God, how else could you teach a practical God? Where is there a more practical God than He whom I see before me—a God omnipresent, in every being, more real than Our senses? For you are He, the Omnipresent God Almighty, the Soul of your souls, and if I say you are not, I tell an untruth. I know it, whether at all times I realise it or not. He is the Oneness, the Unity of all, the Reality of all life and all existence.

These ideas of the ethics of Vedanta have to be worked out in detail, and, therefore, you must have patience. As I have told you, we want to take the subject in detail and work it up thoroughly, to see how the ideas grow from very low ideals, and how the one great ideal of oneness has developed and become shaped into the universal love; and we ought to study these in order to avoid dangers. The world cannot find time to work it up from the lowest steps. But what is the use of our standing on higher steps if we cannot give the truth to others coming afterwards? Therefore, it is better to study it in all its workings; and first, it is absolutely necessary to clear the intellectual portion, although we know that intellectuality is almost nothing; for it is the heart that is of most importance. It is through the heart that the Lord is seen, and not through the intellect.

The intellect is only the street-cleaner, cleansing the path for us, a secondary worker, the policeman; but the policeman is not a positive necessity for the workings of society. He is only to stop disturbances, to check wrong-doing, and that is all the work required of the intellect. When you read intellectual books, you think when you have mastered them, "Bless the Lord that I am out of them," because the intellect is blind and cannot move of itself, it has neither hands nor feet. It is feeling that works, that moves with speed infinitely superior to that of electricity or anything else. Do you feel?—that is the question. If you do, you will see the Lord: It is the feeling that you have today that will be intensified, deified, raised to the highest platform, until it feels everything, the oneness in everything, till it feels God in itself and in others. The intellect can never do that. "Different methods of speaking words, different methods of explaining the texts of books, these are for the enjoyment of the learned, not for the salvation of the soul." *(Vivekachudamani,* 58)

Those of you who have read Thomas a Kempis know how in every page he insists on this, and almost every holy man in the world has insisted on it. Intellect is necessary, for without it we fall into crude errors and make all sorts of mistakes. Intellect checks these; but beyond that, do not try to build anything upon it. It is an inactive, secondary help, the real help is feeling, love. Do you feel for others? If you do, you are growing in oneness. If you do not feel for others, you may be the most intellectual giant ever born, but you will be nothing; you are but dry intellect, and you will remain so. And if you feel, even if you cannot read any book and do not know any language, you are in the right way. The Lord is yours.

Do you not know from the history of the world where the power of the prophets lay? Where was it? In the intellect? Did any of them write a fine book on philosophy, on the most intricate ratiocinations of logic? Not one of them. They only spoke a few words. Feel like Christ and you will be a Christ; feel like Buddha and you will be a Buddha. **It is feeling that is the life, the strength, the vitality, without which no amount of intellectual activity can reach God. Intellect is like limbs without the power of locomotion. It is only when feeling enters and gives them motion that they move and work on others.** That is so all over the world, and it is a thing which you must always remember. It is one of the most practical things in Vedantic morality, for **it is the teaching of the Vedanta that you are all prophets, and all must be prophets.** The book is not the proof of your conduct, but you are the proof of the book. How do you know that a book teaches truth? Because you are truth and feel it. That is what the Vedanta says

What is the proof of the Christs and Buddhas of the world? That you and I feel like them. That is how you and I understand that they were true. Our prophet-soul is the proof of their prophet-soul. Your godhead is the proof of God Himself. If you are not a prophet, there never has been anything true of God. **If you are not God, there never was any God, and never will be. This, says the Vedanta, is the ideal to follow.** Every one of us will have to become a prophet, and you are that already. Only *know* it. Never think there is anything impossible for the soul. It is the greatest heresy to think so. **If there is sin, this is the only sin—to say that you are weak, or others are weak.**

The Social Ideal of Vedanta

As we have seen in the dualistic form of Vedic doctrines, in the earlier forms there was a dearly defined particular and limited soul for every being. There have been a great many theories about this particular soul in each individual, but the main discussion was between the ancient Vedantists and the ancient Buddhists, the former believing in the individual soul as complete in itself, the latter denying *in toto* the existence of such an individual soul.

As I have told you it is pretty much the same discussion you have in Europe as to substance and quality, one set holding that behind the qualities there is something as substance in which the qualities inhere; and the other denying the existence of such a substance as being unnecessary, for the qualities may live by themselves. The most ancient theory of the soul, of course, is based upon the argument of self-identity—"I am I'—that the I of yesterday is the I of today, and the I of today will be the I of tomorrow; that in spite of all the changes that are happening to the body, I yet believe that I am the same I. This seems to have been the central argument with those who believed in a limited, and yet perfectly complete, individual soul.

On the other hand, the ancient Buddhists denied the necessity of such an assumption. They brought forward the argument that all that we know, and all that we possibly can know, are simply these changes. The positing of an unchangeable and unchanging substance is simply superfluous, and even if there were any such unchangeable thing, we could never understand it, nor should we ever be able to cognise it in any sense of the word. The same discussion you will find at the present time going on in Europe between the religionists and the idealists on the one side, and the modem positivists and agnostics on the other; one set believing there is something which does not change, of whom the latest representative is your Herbert Spencer, that we catch a glimpse of something which is unchangeable. And the other is represented by the modern Comtists and modern Agnostics. Those of you who were interested a few years ago in the discussions between Herbert Spencer and Frederick Harrison might have noticed that it was the same old difficulty, the one party standing for a substance behind the changeful, and the other party denying the necessity for such an assumption. One party says we cannot conceive of changes without conceiving of something which does not change; the other party brings out the argument that this is superfluous; we can only conceive of something which is changing, and as to the unchanging, we can neither know, feel, nor sense it.

In India this great question did not find its solution in very ancient times, because we have seen that the assumption of a substance which is behind the qualities, and which is not the qualities, can never be substantiated; nay, even the argument from self-identity, from memory, —that I am the I of yesterday because I remember it, and therefore I have been a continuous something—cannot be substantiated. The other quibble that is generally put forward is a mere delusion of words. For instance, a man may take a long series of such sentences as "I do", "I go", "I dream", "I sleep", "I move", and here you will find it claimed that the doing, going, dreaming etc., have been changing, but what remained constant was that "I". As such they conclude that the "I" is something which is constant and an individual in itself, but all these changes belong to the body. This, though apparently very convincing and clear, is based upon the mere play on words. The "I" and the doing, going, and dreaming may be separate in black and white, but no one can separate them in his mind.

When I eat, I think of myself as eating—I am identified with eating. When I run, I and the running are not two separate things. Thus the argument from personal identity does not seem to be very strong. The other argument from memory is also weak. If the identity of my being is represented by my memory, many things which I have forgotten are lost from that identity. And we know that people under certain conditions forget their whole past. In many cases of lunacy a man will think of himself as made of glass, or as being an animal. If the existence of that man depends on memory, he has become glass, which not being the case we cannot make the identity of the Self depend on such a flimsy substance as memory. Thus we see that the soul as a limited yet complete and continuing identity cannot be established as separate from the qualities. We cannot establish a narrowed-down, limited existence to which is attached a bunch of qualities.

On the other hand, the argument of the ancient Buddhists seems to be stronger—that we do not know, and cannot know, anything that is beyond the bunch of qualities. According to them, the soul consists of a bundle of qualities called sensations and feelings. A mass of such is what is called the soul, and this mass is continually changing.

The Advaitist theory of the soul reconciles both these positions. The position of the Advaitist is that *it* is true that we cannot think of the substance as separate from the qualities, we cannot think of change and not-change at the same time; it would be impossible. But the very thing which is the substance is the quality; substance and quality are not two things. It is the unchangeable that is appearing as the changeable. The unchangeable substance of the universe is not something separate from it. The noumenon is not something different from the phenomena, but it is the very noumenon which has become the phenomena. There is a soul which is unchanging, and what we call feelings and perceptions, nay, even the body, are the very soul, seen from another point of view. We have got into the habit of thinking that we have bodies and souls and so forth, but really speaking, there is only one.

When I think of myself as the body, I am only a body; it is meaningless to say I am something else. And when I think of myself as the soul, the body vanishes, and the perception of the body does not remain. None can get the perception of the Self without his perception of the body having vanished, none can get perception of the substance without his perception of the qualities having vanished.

The ancient illustration of Advaita, of the rope being taken for a snake, may elucidate the point a little more. When a man mistakes the rope for a snake, the rope has vanished, and when he takes it for a rope, the snake has vanished, and the rope only remains. The ideas of dual or treble existence come from reasoning on insufficient data, and we read them in books or hear about them, until we come under the delusion that we really have a dual perception of the soul and the body; but such a perception never really exists. The perception is either of the body or of the soul. It requires no arguments to prove it, you can verify it in your own minds.

Try to think of yourself as a soul, as a disembodied something. You will find it to be almost impossible, and those few who are able to do so will find that at the time when they realise themselves as a soul they have no idea of the body. You have heard of, or perhaps have seen, persons who on particular occasions had been in peculiar states of mind, brought about by deep meditation, self-hypnotism, hysteria, or drugs. From their experience you may gather that when they were perceiving the internal something, the external had vanished for them. This shows that whatever exists is one. That one is appearing in these various forms, and all these various forms give rise to the relation of cause and effect. The relation of cause and effect is one of evolution—the one becomes the other, and so on. Sometimes the cause vanishes, as it were, and in its place leaves the effect. If the soul is the cause of the body, the soul, as it were, vanishes for the time being, and the body remains; and when the body vanishes, the soul remains. This theory fits the arguments of the Buddhists that were levelled against the assumption of the dualism of body and soul, by denying the duality, and showing that the substance and the qualities are one and the same thing appearing in various forms.

We have seen also that this idea of the unchangeable can be established only as regards the whole, but never as regards the part. The very idea of part comes from the idea of change or motion. Everything that is limited we can understand and know, because it is changeable; and the whole must be unchangeable, because there is no other thing besides it in relation to which change would be possible. Change is always in regard to something which does not change, or which changes relatively less.

According to Advaita, therefore, the idea of the soul as universal, unchangeable, and immortal can be demonstrated as far as possible. The difficulty would be as regards the particular. What shall we do with the old dualistic theories which have such a hold upon us, and which we have all to pass through—these beliefs in limited, little, individual souls?

We have seen that we are immortal with regard to the whole; but the difficulty is, we desire so much to be immortal as *parts* of the whole. We have seen that we are Infinite, and that that is our real individuality. But we want so much to make these little souls individual. What becomes of them when we find in our everyday experience that these little souls are individuals, with only this reservation that they are continuously growing individuals? They are the same, yet not the same. The I of yesterday is the I of today, and yet not so, it is changed somewhat. Now, by getting rid of the dualistic conception, that in the midst of all these changes there is something that does not change, and taking the most modern of conceptions, that of evolution, we find that the "I" is a continuously changing, expanding entity.

If it be true that man is the evolution of a mollusc, the mollusc individual is the same as the man, only it has to become expanded a great deal. From mollusc to man it has been a continuous expansion towards infinity. Therefore the limited soul can be styled an individual which is continuously expanding towards the Infinite Individual. Perfect individuality will only be reached when it has reached the Infinite, but on this side of the Infinite it is a continuously changing, growing personality. One of the remarkable features of the Advaitist system of Vedanta is to harmonise the preceding systems. In many cases it helped the philosophy very much; in some cases it hurt it. **Our ancient philosophers knew what you call the theory of evolution; that growth is gradual, step by step, and the recognition of this led**

them to harmonise all the preceding systems. Thus not one of these preceding ideas was rejected. The fault of the Buddhistic faith was that it had neither the faculty nor the perception of this continual, expansive growth, and for this reason it never even made an attempt to harmonise itself with the preexisting steps towards the ideal. They were rejected as useless and harmful.

This tendency in religion is most harmful. A man gets a new and better idea, and then he looks back on those he has given up, and forthwith decides that they were mischievous and unnecessary. He never thinks that, however crude they may appear from his present point of view, they were very useful to him, that they were necessary for him to reach his present state, and that everyone of us has to grow in a similar fashion, living first on crude ideas, taking benefit from them, and then arriving at a higher standard. **With the oldest theories, therefore, the Advaita is friendly. Dualism and all systems that had preceded it are accepted by the Advaita not in a patronising way, but with the conviction that they are true manifestations of the same truth, and that they all lead to the same conclusions as the Advaita has reached.**

With blessing, and not with cursing, should be pre-served all these various steps through which humanity has to pass. Therefore all these dualistic systems have never been rejected or thrown out, but have been kept intact in the Vedanta; and the dualistic conception of an individual soul, limited yet complete in itself, finds its place in the Vedanta.

According to dualism, man dies and goes to other worlds, and so forth; and these ideas are kept in the Vedanta in their entirety. For with the recognition of growth in the Advaitist system, these theories are given their proper place by admitting that they represent only a partial view of the Truth.

From the dualistic standpoint this universe can only be looked upon as a creation of matter or force, can only be looked upon as the play of a certain will, and that will again can only be looked upon as separate from the universe. Thus a man from such a standpoint has to see himself as composed of a dual nature, body and soul, and this soul, though limited, is individually complete in itself. Such a man's ideas of immortality and of the future life would necessarily accord with his idea of soul. These phases have been kept in the Vedanta, and it is, therefore, necessary for me to present to you a few of the popular ideas of dualism. According to this theory, we have a body, of course, and behind the body there is what they call a fine body. This fine body is also made of matter, only very fine. It is the receptacle of all our Karma, of all our actions and impressions, which are ready to spring up into visible forms.

Every thought that we think, every deed that we do, after a certain time becomes fine, goes into seed form, so to speak, and lives in the fine body in a potential form, and after a time it emerges again and bears its results. These results condition the life of man. Thus he moulds his own life. Man is not bound by any other laws excepting those which he makes for himself. Our thoughts, our words and deeds are the threads of the net which we throw round ourselves, for good or for evil. Once we set in motion a certain power, we have to take the full consequences of it. This is the law of Karma. Behind the subtle body, lives Jiva or the individual soul of man. There are various discussions about the form and the size of this individual soul. According to some, it is very small like an atom; according to others, it is not so small as that; according to others, it is very big, and so on. This Jiva is a part of that universal substance, and it is also eternal; without beginning it is existing, and without end it will exist. It is passing through all these forms in order to manifest its real nature which is purity. Every action that retards this manifestation is called an evil action; so with thoughts. And every action and every thought that helps the Jiva to expand, to manifest its real nature, is good.

One theory that is held in common in India by the crudest dualists as well as by the most advanced non-dualists is that all the possibilities and powers of the soul are within it, and do not come from any external source. They are in the soul in potential form, and the whole work of life is simply directed towards manifesting those potentialities.

They have also the theory of reincarnation which says that after the dissolution of this body, the Jiva will have another, and

after that has been dissolved, it will again have another, and so on, either here or in some other worlds; but this world is given the preference, as it is considered the best of all worlds for our purpose. Other worlds are conceived of as worlds where there is very little misery, but for that very reason, they argue, there is less chance of thinking of higher things there. As this world contains some happiness and a good deal of misery, the Jiva some time or other gets awakened, as it were, and thinks of freeing itself. But just as very rich persons in this world have the least chance of thinking of higher things, so the Jiva in heaven has little chance of progress, for its condition is the same as that of a rich man, only more intensified; it has a very fine body which knows no disease, and is under no necessity of eating or drinking, and all its desires are fulfilled.

The Jiva lives there, having enjoyment after enjoyment, and so forgets all about its real nature. Still there are some higher worlds, where in spite of all enjoyments, its further evolution is possible. Some dualists conceive of the goal as the highest heaven, where souls will live with God for ever. They will have beautiful bodies and will know neither disease nor death, nor any other evil, and all their desires will be fulfilled. From time to time some of them will come back to this earth and take another body to teach liuman beings the way to God; and the great teachers of the world have been such. They were already free, and were living with God in the highest sphere; but their love and sympathy for suffering humanity was so great that they came and incarnated again to teach mankind the way to heaven.

Of course we know that the Advaita holds that this cannot be the goal or the ideal; bodilessness must be the ideal. The ideal cannot be finite. Anything short of the Infinite cannot be the ideal, and there cannot be an infinite body. That would be impossible, as body comes from limitation. There cannot be infinite thought, because thought comes from limitation. We have to go beyond the body, and beyond thought too, says the Advaita. And we have also seen that, according to Advaita, this freedom is not to be attained, it is already ours. We only forget it and deny it. Perfection is not to be attained, it is already within us. Immortality and bliss are not to be acquired, we possess them already; they have been ours all the time.

If you dare declare that you are free, free you are this moment. If you say you are bound, bound you will remain. This is what Advaita boldly declares. I have told you the ideas of the dualists. You can take whichever you like.

The highest ideal of the Vedanta is very difficult to understand, and people are always quarrelling about it, and the greatest difficulty is that when they get hold of certain ideas, they deny and fight other ideas. Take up what suits you, and let others take up what they need. If you are desirous of clinging to this little individuality, to this limited manhood, remain in it, have all these desires, and be content and, pleased with them. If your experience of manhood has been very good and nice, retain it as long as you like; and you can do so, for you are the makers of your own fortunes; none can compel you to give up your manhood. You will be men as long as you like; none can prevent you. If you want to be angels, you will be angels, that is the law. But there may be others who do not want to be angels even. What right have you to think that theirs is a horrible notion? You may be frightened to lose a hundred pounds, but there may be others who would not even wink if they lost all the money they had in the world. There have been such men and still there are. Why do you dare to judge them according to your standard? You cling on to your limitations, and these little worldly ideas may be your highest ideal. You are welcome to them. It will be to you as you wish. But there are others who have seen the truth and cannot rest in these limitations, who have done with these things and want to get beyond. The world with all its enjoyments is a mere mud-puddle for them. Why do you want to bind them down to your ideas? You must get rid of this tendency once for all. **Accord a place to everyone.**

I once read a story about some ships that were caught in a cyclone in the South Sea Islands, and there was a picture of it in the *Illustrated London News.* All of them were wrecked except one English vessel, which weathered the storm. The picture showed the men who were going to be drowned, standing on the decks and cheering the people who were sailing through the storm. Be brave and generous like that. Do not drag others down to where you are. Another foolish notion is that if we lose our little individuality, there will be no morality, no hope for humanity. As if everybody had been dying for humanity all the time! God bless you! If in every country there were two hundred men and women really wanting to do good to humanity, the millennium would come in five days. We know how we are dying for humanity! These are all tall talks, and nothing else. **The history of the world shows that those who never thought of their little individuality were the greatest bendactors of the human race, and that the more men and women think of themselves, the less are they able to do for others.** One is unselfishness, and the other selfishness. Clinging on to little enjoyments, and to desire the continuation and repetition of this state of things is utter selfishness. It arises not from any desire for truth, its genesis is not in kindness for other beings, but in the utter selfishness of the human heart, in the idea, "I will have everything, and do not care for anyone else." This is as it appears to me. I would like to see more moral men in the world like some of those grand old prophets and sages of ancient times who would have given up a hundred lives if they could by so doing benefit one little animal! Talk of morality and doing good to others! Silly talk of the present time!

I would like to see moral men like Gautama Buddha, who did not believe in a Personal God or a personal soul, never asked about them, but was a perfect agnostic, and yet was ready to lay down his life for anyone, and worked all his life for the good of all, and thought only of the good of all. Well has it been said by his biographer, in describing his birth, that he was born for the good of the many, as a blessing to the many. He did not go to the forest to meditate for his own salvation; he felt that the world was burning, and that he must find a way out. "Why is there so much misery in the world?"—was the one question that dominated his whole life. Do you think we are so moral as the Buddha?

The more selfish a man, the more immoral he is. And so also with the race. That race which is bound down to itself has been the most cruel and the most wicked in the whole world. **There has not been a religion that has clung to this dualism more than that founded by the Prophet of Arabia, and there has not been a religion which has shed so much blood and been so cruel to other men.** In the Koran there is the doctrine that a man who does not believe these teachings should be killed; it is a mercy to kill him! And the surest way to get to heaven, where there are beautiful houris and all sorts of sense-enjoyments, is by killing these unbelievers. Think of the bloodshed there has been in consequence of such beliefs!

In the religion of Christ there was little of crudeness; there is very little difference between the pure religion of Christ and that of the Vedanta. You find there the idea of oneness; but Christ also preached dualistic ideas to the people in order to give them something tangible to take hold of, to lead them up to the highest ideal. The same Prophet who preached, "Our Father which art in heaven," also preached, "I and my Father are one," and the same Prophet knew that through the "Father in heaven" lies the way to the "I and my Father are one."

There was only blessing and love in the religion of Christ; but as soon as crudeness crept in, it was degraded into something not much better than the religion of the Prophet of Arabia. It was crudeness indeed—this fight for the little self, this clinging on to the "I", not only in this life, but also in the desire for its continuance even after death. This they declare to be unselfishness; this the foundation of morality! Lord help us, if this be the foundation of morality! And strangely enough, men and women who ought to know better think all morality will be destroyed if these little selves go and stand aghast at the idea that morality can only stand upon their destruction. **The watchword of all well-being, of all moral good is not "I" but "thou."** Who cares whether there is a heaven or a hell, who cares if there is a soul or not, who cares if there is an unchangeable or not? Here is the world, and it is full of misery. Go out into it as Buddha did, and struggle to lessen it or die in the attempt. Forget yourselves; this is the first lesson to be learnt, whether you are a theist or an atheist, whether you are an agnostic or a

Vedantist, a Christian or a Mohammedan. The one lesson obvious to all is the destruction of the little self and the building up of the Real Self.

Two forces have been working side by side in parallel lines. The one says "I", the other says "not I". Their manifestation is not only in man but in animals, not only in animals but in the smallest worms. The tigress that plunges her fangs into the warm blood of a human being would give up her own life to protect her young. The most depraved man who thinks nothing of taking the lives of his brother men will, perhaps, sacrifice himself without any hesitation to save his starving wife and children. Thus throughout creation these two forces are working side by side; where you find the one, you find the other too. The one is selfishness, the other is unselfishness. The one is acquisition, the other is renunciation. The one takes, the other gives. From the lowest to the highest, the whole universe is the playground of these two forces. It does not require any demonstration; it is obvious to all.

What right has any section of the community to base the whole work and evolution of the universe upon one of these two factors alone, upon competition and struggle? What right has it to base the whole working of the universe upon passion and fight? That these exist we do not deny; but what right has anyone to deny the working of the other force? Can any man deny that love, this "not I", this renunciation is the only positive power in the universe? That other is only the misguided employment of the power of love; the power of love brings competition, the real genesis of competition is in love. The real genesis of evil is in unselfishness. The creator of evil is good, and the end is also good. It is only misdirection of the power of good. A man who murders another is, perhaps, moved to do so by the love of his own child. His love has become limited to that one little baby, to the exclusion of the millions of other human beings in the universe. Yet, limited or unlimited, it is the same love.

Thus the motive power of the whole universe, in whatever way it manifests itself, is that one wonderful thing, unselfishness, renunciation, love, the real, the only living force in existence.

Therefore, the Vedantist insists upon that oneness. We insist upon this explanation because we cannot admit two causes of the universe. If we simply hold that by limitation the same beautiful, wonderful love appears to be evil or vile, we find the whole universe explained by the one force of love. If not, two causes of the universe have to be taken for granted, one good and the other evil, one love and the other hatred. Which is more logical? Certainly the one-force theory.

Let us now pass on to things which do not possibly belong to dualism. I cannot stay longer with the dualists, I am afraid. My idea is to show that the highest ideal of morality and unselfishness goes hand in hand with the highest metaphysical conception, and that you need not lower your conception to get ethics and morality, but, on the other hand, to reach a real basis of morality and ethics you must have the highest philosophical and scientific conceptions. Human knowledge is not antagonistic to human well-being. On the contrary, it is knowledge alone that will save us in every department of life in as knowledge is worship. The more we know the better for us. The Vedantist says, the cause of all that is apparently evil is the limitation of the unlimited. The love which gets limited into little channels and seems to be evil eventually comes out at the other end and manifests itself as God.

The Vedanta also says that the cause of all this apparent evil is in ourselves. Do not blame any supernatural being, neither be hopeless and despondent, nor think we are in a place from which we can never escape unless someone comes and lends us a helping hand. That cannot be, says the Vedanta. **We are like silkworms; we make the thread out of our own substance and spin the cocoon, and in course of time are imprisoned inside.** But this is not for ever. In that cocoon we shall develop spiritual realisation, and like the butterfly come out free. This network of Karma we have woven around ourselves; and in our ignorance we feel as if we are bound, and weep and wail for help. But help does not come from without; it comes from within ourselves. Cry to all the gods in the universe. I cried for years, and in the end I found that I was helped. But help came from within. And I had to undo what I had done by mistake. That is the only way.

I had to cut the net which I had thrown round myself, and the power to do this is within. Of this I am certain that not one aspiration, well-guided or ill-guided in my life, has been in vain, but that I am the resultant of all my past, both good and evil. I have committed many mistakes in my life; but mark you, I am sure of this that without every one of those mistakes I should not be what I am today, and so am quite satisfied to have made them. I do not mean that you are to go home and wilfully commit mistakes; do not misunderstand me in that way. But do not mope because of the mistakes you have committed, but know that in the end all will come out straight. It cannot be otherwise, because goodness is our nature, purity is our nature, and that nature can never be destroyed. Our essential nature always remains the same.

What we are to understand is this, that what we call mistakes or evil, we commit because we are weak, and we are weak because we are ignorant. I prefer to call them mistakes. The word sin, although originally a very good word, has got a certain flavour about it that frightens me. Who makes us ignorant? We ourselves. We put our hands over our eyes and weep that it is dark. Take the hands away and there is light; **the light exists always for us, the self-effulgent nature of the human soul.** Do you not hear what your modern scientific men say? What is the cause of evolution? Desire. The animal wants to do something, but does not find the environment favourable, and therefore develops a new body. Who develops it? The animal itself, its will. You have developed from the lowest amoeba. **Continue to exercise your will and it will take you higher still. The will is almighty.** If it is almighty, you may say, why cannot I do everything? But you are thinking only of your little self. Look back on yourselves from the state of the amoeba to the human being; who made all that? Your own will. Can you deny then that it is almighty? That which has made you come up so high can make you go higher still. What you want is character, strengthening of the will.

If I teach you, therefore, that your nature is evil, that you should go home and sit in sackcloth and ashes and weep your lives out because you took certain false steps, it will not help you, but will weaken you all the more, and I shall be showing you the road to more evil than good. If this room is full of darkness for thousands of years and you come in and begin to weep and wail, "Oh the darkness," will the darkness vanish? Strike a match and light comes in a moment. What good will it do you to think all your lives, "Oh, I have done evil, I have made many mistakes"! It requires no ghost to tell us that. Bring in the light and the evil goes in a moment. Build up your character, and manifest your real nature, the Effulgent, the Resplendent, the Ever-Pure, and call it up in everyone that you see. I wish that everyone of us had come to such a state that even in the vilest of human beings we could see the Real Self within, and instead of condemning them, say, "Rise thou effulgent one, rise thou who art always pure, rise thou birthless and deathless, rise almighty and manifest thy true nature. These little manifestations do not befit thee."

This is the highest prayer that the Advaita teaches. This is the one prayer, to remember our true nature, the God who is always within us, thinking of it always as infinite, almighty, ever-good, ever-beneficent, selfless, bereft of all limitations. And because that nature is selfless, it is strong and fearless; for only to selfishness comes fear. He who has nothing to desire for himself, whom does he fear, and what can frighten him? What fear has death for him? What fear has evil for him? So **if we are Advaitists, we must think from this moment that our old self is dead and gone. The old Mr., Mrs., and Miss so-and-so are gone, they were mere superstitions, and what remains is the ever-pure, the ever-strong, the almighty, the all-knowing**—that alone remains for us, and then all fear vanishes from us.

Who can injure us, the omnipresent? All weakness has vanished from us, and our only work is to arouse this knowledge in our fellow-beings. We see that they too are the same pure self, only they do not know it; we must teach them, we must help them to rouse up their infinite nature. This is what I feel to be absolutely necessary all over the world. These doctrines are old, older than many mountains possibly. All truth is eternal. Truth is nobody's property;

no race, no individual can lay any exclusive claim to it. Truth is the nature of all souls. Who can lay any special claim to it? But it has to be made practical, to be made simple—for the highest truths are always simple—so that it may penetrate every pore of human society, and become the property of the highest intellects and the commonest minds, of the man, woman, and child at the same time. All these ratiocinations of logic, all these bundles of metaphysics, all these theologies and ceremonies may have been good in their own time, but let us try to make things simpler and bring about the golden days when every man will be a worshipper, and the Reality in every man will be the object of worship.

(*Talk delivered in London, 10-18 Nov., 1896*)

Towards a Universal Religion

No search has been dearer to the human heart than that which brings to us light from God. No study has taken so much of human energy, whether in times past or present, as the study of the soul, of God, and of human destiny. However immersed we are in our daily occupations, in our ambitions, in our work, in the midst of the greatest of our struggles, sometimes there will come a pause; the mind stops and wants to know something beyond this world. Sometimes it catches glimpses of a realm beyond the senses, and a struggle to get at it is the result. Thus it has been throughout the ages, in all countries. Man has wanted to look beyond, wanted to expand himself; and all that we call progress, evolution, has been always measured by that one search, the search for human destiny, the search for God.

As our social struggles are represented amongst different nations by different social organisations, so is man's spiritual struggle represented by various religions; and as different social organisations are constantly quarrelling, are constantly at war with one another, so these spiritual organisations have been constantly at war with one another, constantly quarrelling. Men belonging to a particular social organisation claim that the right to live only belongs to them; and so long as they can, they want to exercise that right at the cost of the weak. We know that just now there is a fierce struggle of that sort going on in South Africa. Similarly, each religious sect has claimed the exclusive right to live. And thus **we find that though there is nothing that has brought to man more blessings than religion, yet at the same time, there is nothing that has brought more horror than religion.**

Nothing has made more for peace and love than religion; nothing has engendered fiercer hatred than religion. Nothing has made the brotherhood of man more tangible than religion; nothing has bred more bitter enmity between man and man than religion. Nothing has built more charitable institutions, more hospitals for men, and even for animals, than religion; nothing has deluged the world with more blood than religion. We know, at the same time, that there has always been an undercurrent of thought; there have been always parties of men, philosophers, students of comparative religion who have tried and are still trying to bring about harmony in the midst of all these jarring and discordant sects. As regards certain countries, these attempts have succeeded, but as regards the whole world, they have failed.

There are some religions which have come down to us from the remotest antiquity, which are imbued with the idea that all sects should be allowed to live, that every sect has a meaning, a great idea, embedded within itself, and, therefore it is necessary for the good of the world and ought to be helped. In modern times the same idea is prevailing and attempts are made from time to time to reduce it to practice. These attempts do not always come up to our expectations, up to the required efficiency. Nay, to our great disappointment, we sometimes find that we are quarrelling all the more.

Now, leaving aside dogmatic study, and taking a commonsense view of the thing, we find at the start that there is a tremendous life-power in all the great religions of the world. Some may say that they are ignorant of this, but ignorance is no excuse. If a man says, "I do not know what is going on in the external world, therefore, things that are going on in the external world do not exist,' that man is inexcusable. Now, those of you that watch the movement of religious thought all over the world are perfectly aware that not one of the great religions of the world has died; not only so, each one of them is progressive. Christians are multiplying, Mohammedans are multiplying, the Hindus are gaining ground, and the Jews also are increasing, and by their spreading all over the world and increasing rapidly, the fold of Judaism is constantly expanding.

Only one religion of the world—an ancient, great religion—has dwindled away, and that is the religion of Zoroastrianism, the religion of the ancient Persians. Under the Mohammedan conquest of Persia about a hundred thousand of these people came and took shelter in India and some remained in ancient Persia. Those that were in Persia, under the constant persecution of the Mohammedans, dwindled down till there are at most only ten thousand; in India there are about eighty thousand of them, but they do not increase. Of course, there is an initial difficulty; they do not convert others to their religion. And then, this handful of persons living in India, with the pernicious custom of cousin marriage, do not multiply. With this single exception, all the other religions are living, spreading, and increasing.

We must remember that **all the great religions of the world are very ancient, not one has been formed at the present time, and that every religion of the world owes its origin to the country between the Ganga and the Euphrates; not one great religion has arisen in Europe, not one in America,** not one; every religion is of Asiatic origin and belongs to that part of the world. If what the modern scientists say is true, that the survival of the fittest is the test, these religions prove by their still living that they are yet fit for some people. There is a reason why they should live, they bring good to many. Look at the Mohammedans, how they are spreading in some places in Southern Asia, and spreading like fire in Africa. The Buddhists are spreading all over Central Asia, all the time. The Hindus, like the Jews, do not convert others; still gradually, other races are coming within Hinduism and adopting the manners and customs of the Hindus and falling into line with them. Christianity, you all know, is spreading—though I am not sure that the results are equal to the energy put forth. The Christians' attempt at propaganda has one tremendous defect—and that is the defect of all Western institutions: the machine consumes ninety per cent of the energy, there is too much machinery. **Preaching has always been the business of the Asiatics. The Western people are grand in organisation, social institutions, armies, governments, etc.;** but when it comes to preaching religion, they cannot come near the Asiatic, whose business it has been all the time, and he knows it, and he does not use too much machinery.

This then is a fact in the present history of the human race, that all these great religions exist and are spreading and multiplying. Now, there is a meaning, certainly, to this; and had it been the will of an All-wise and All-merciful Creator that one of these religions should exist and the rest should die, it would have become. a fact long, long ago. If it were a fact that only one of these religions is true and all the rest are false, by this time it would have covered the whole ground. But this is not so; not one has gained all the ground. All religions sometimes advance—sometimes decline. Now, just think of this: in your own country there are more than sixty millions of people, and only twenty-one millions professing religions of all sorts. So it is not always progress. In every country, probably, if the statistics are taken, you would find that religions are sometimes progressing and sometimes going back. Sects are multiplying all the time. If the claims of a religion that it has all the truth and God has given it all this truth in a certain book were true, why are there so many sects? **Fifty years do not pass before there are twenty sects founded upon the same book.** If God has put all the truth in certain books, He does not give us those books in order that we may quarrel over texts.

That seems to be the fact. Why is its? Even if a book were given by God which contained all the truth about religion, it would not serve the purpose because nobody could understand the book. Take the Bible, for instance, and all the sects that exist amongst Christians; each one puts its own interpretation upon the same text, and each says that it alone understands that text and all the rest are wrong. So with every religion. There are many sects among the Mohammedans and among the Buddhists, and hundreds among the Hindus. Now, I bring these facts before you in order to show you that **any attempt to bring all humanity to one method of thinking in spiritual things has been a failure and always will be a failure.** Every man that starts a theory, even at the present day, finds that if he goes twenty miles away from his followers, they will make twenty sects. You see that happening all the time. You cannot make all conform to the same ideas: that is a fact, and I thank God that it is so.

I am not against any sect. I am glad that sects exist, and I only wish they may go on multiplying more and more. Why? Simply because of this: If you and I and all who are present here were to think exactly the same thoughts, there would be no thoughts for us to think. We know that two or more forces must come into collision in order to produce motion. **It is the clash of thought, the differentiation of thought, that awakes thought.** Now, if we all thought alike, we would be like Egyptian mummies in a museum looking vacantly at one another's faces—no more than that! Whirls and eddies occur only in a rushing, living stream. There are no whirlpools in stagnant, dead water. When religions are dead, there will be no more sects; it will be the perfect peace and harmony of the grave. **But so long as mankind thinks, there will be sects.** Variation is the sign of life, and it must be there. I pray that they may multiply so that at last there will be as many sects as human beings, and each one will have his own method, his individual method of thought in religion.

But this thing exists already. Each one of us is thinking in his own way, but his natural course has been obstructed all the time and is still being obstructed. If the sword is not used directly, other means will be used. **Just hear what one of the best preachers in New York says: he preaches that the Filipinos should be conquered because that is the only way to teach Christianity to them! They are already Catholics; but he wants to make them Presbyterians, and for this, he is ready to lay all this terrible sin of bloodshed upon his race.** How terrible! And this man is one of the greatest preachers of this country, one of the best informed men. Think of the state of the world when a man like that is not ashamed to stand up and utter such arrant nonsense; and think of the state of the world when an audience cheers him! Is this civilisation? It is the old blood-thirstiness of the tiger, the cannibal, the savage, coming out once more under new names, new circumstances. What else can it be? If the state of things is such now, think of the horrors through which the world passed in olden times, when every sect was trying by every means in its power to tear to pieces the other sects.

History shows that. The tiger in us is only asleep; it is not dead. When opportunities come, it jumps up and, as of old, uses its claws and fangs. Apart from the sword, apart from material weapons, there are weapons still more terrible—contempt, social hatred, and social ostracism. Now, these are the most terrible of all inflictions that are hurled against persons who do not think exactly in the same way as we do. And why should everybody think just as we do? I do not see any reason. If I am a rational man, I should be glad they do not think just as I do. I do not want to live in a gravelike land; I want to be a man in a world of men. Thinking beings must differ; difference is the first sign of thought. If I am a thoughtful man, certainly I ought to like to live amongst thoughtful persons where there are differences of opinion.

Then arises the question: How can all these varieties be true? If one thing is true, its negation is false. How can contradictory opinions be true at the same time? This is the question which I intend to answer. But I will first ask you: Are all the religions of the world really contradictory? I do not mean the external forms in which great thoughts are clad. I do not mean the different buildings, languages, rituals, books, etc., employed in various religions, but I mean the internal soul of every religion. Every religion has a soul behind it, and that soul may differ from the soul of another religion; but are they contradictory? Do they contradict or supplement each other?—that is the question.

I took up the question when I was quite a boy, and have been studying it all my life. Thinking that my conclusion may be of some help to you, I place it before you. **I believe that they are not contradictory; the are supplementary. Each religion, as it were, take up one part of the great universal truth and spends its whole force embodying and typifying that part of the great truth. It is, therefore, addition, not exclusion.** That is the idea. System after system arises, I each one embodying a great idea, and ideals must be added to ideals. **And this is the march of humanity. Man never progresses from error to truth, but from truth, but from truth to truth, from lesser truth to higher truth**—but it is never from error to truth. The child may develop more than the father, but was the father inane? The child is the father plus something else. If your present state of knowledge is much greater than it was when you were a child, would you look down upon that stage now? Will you look back and call it inanity? Why, your present stage is the knowledge of the child plus something more.

Then, again, we also know that there may be almost contradictory points of view of the same thing, but they will all indicate the same thing. Suppose a man is journeying towards the sun, and as he advances he takes a photograph of the sun at every stage. When he comes back, he has many photographs of the sun, which he places before us. We see that not two are alike, and yet, who will deny that all these are photographs of the same sun, from different standpoints? Take four photographs of this church from different corners: how different they would look, and yet they would all represent this church. In the same way, we are all looking at truth from different standpoints, which vary according to our birth, education, surroundings, and so on. We are viewing truth, getting as much of it as these circumstances will permit, colouring the truth with our own heart, understanding it with our own intellect, and grasping it with our own mind. We can only know as much of truth as is related to us, as much of it as we are able to receive. This makes the difference between man and man, and on occasions sometimes even contradictory ideas; yet we all belong to the same great universal truth.

My idea, therefore, is that **all these religions are different forces in the economy of God, working for the good of mankind;** and that not one can become dead, not one can be killed. Just as you cannot kill any force in nature, so you cannot kill anyone of these spiritual forces. You have seen that each religion is living. From time to time it may retrograde or go forward. At one time, it may be shorn of a good many of its trappings; at another time it may be covered with all sorts of trappings; but all the same, the soul is ever there, it can never be lost. The ideal which every religion represents is never lost, and so every religion is intelligently on the march.

And that universal religion about which philosophers and others have dreamed in every country already exists. It is here. As the universal brotherhood of man is already existing, so also is universal religion. Which of you, that have travelled far and wide, have not found brothers and sisters in every nation? I have found them all over the world. Brotherhood already exists; only there are numbers of persons who fail to see this and only upset it by crying for new brotherhoods. Universal religion, too, is already existing. If the priests and other people that have taken upon themselves the task of preaching different religions simply cease preaching for a few moments, we shall see it is there. They are disturbing it all the time, because it is to their interest. You see that **priests in every country are very conservative.** Why is it so? **There are very few priests who lead the people; most of them are led by the people and are their slaves and servants.** If you say it is dry, they say it is so; if you say it is black, they say it is black. If the people advance, the priests must advance. They cannot lag behind.

So, before blaming the priests—it is the fashion to blame the priest—you ought to blame yourselves. You only get what you deserve. What would be the fate of a priest who wants to give you new and advanced ideas and lead you forward? His children would probably starve, and he would be clad in rags. He is governed by the same worldly laws as you are. "If you go on," he says, "let us march." Of course, there are exceptional souls, not cowed down by public opinion. They see the truth and truth alone they value. Truth has got hold of them, has got possession of them, as it were, and they cannot but march ahead. They never look backward, and for them there are no people. God alone exists for them, He is the Light before them, and they are following that Light.

I met a Mormon gentleman in this country, who tried to persuade me to his faith. I said, "I have great respect for your opinions, but in certain points we do not agree—I belong to a monastic order, and you believe in marrying many wives. But why don't you go to India to preach?" Then he was astonished. He said, "Why, you don't believe in any marriage at all, and we believe in polygamy, and yet you ask me to go to your country!" I said, "Yes; my countrymen will hear every religious thought wherever it may come from. I wish you would go to India, first, because I am a great believer in sects. Secondly, there are many men in India who are not at all satisfied with any of the existing sects, and on account of this dissatisfaction, they will not have anything to do with religion, and, possibly, you might get some of them." The greater the number of sects, the more chance of people getting religion. In the hotel, where there are all sorts of food, everyone has a chance to get his appetite satisfied. So I want sects to multiply in every country, that more people may have a chance to be spiritual.

Do not think that people do not like religion. I do not believe that. The preachers cannot give them what they need. The same man that may have been branded as an atheist, as a materialist, or what not, may meet a man who gives him the truth needed by him, and he may turn out the most spiritual man in the community. We can eat only in our own way. For instance, **we Hindus eat with our fingers. Our fingers are suppler than yours, you cannot use your fingers the same way. Not only the food should be supplied, but it should be taken in your own particular way. Not only must you have the spiritual ideas, but they must come to you according to your own method.** They must speak your own language, the language of your soul, and then alone they will satisfy you. When the man comes who speaks my language and gives truth in my language, I at once understand it and receive it for ever. This is a great fact.

Now from this we see that there are various grades and types of human minds and what a task religions take upon them! A man brings forth two or three doctrines and claims that his religion ought to satisfy all humanity. He goes out into the world, God's menagerie, with a little cage in hand, and says, "God and the elephant and everybody has to go into this. Even if we have to cut the elephant into pieces, he must go in." Again, there may be a sect with a few good ideas. Its followers say, "All men must come in!" "But there is no room for them." "Never mind! Cut them to pieces; get them in anyhow; if they don't get in, why, they will be damned." No preacher, no sect, have I ever met that pauses and asks, "Why is it that people do not listen to us?" Instead, they curse the people and say, "The people are wicked." They never ask, "How is it that people do not listen to my words? Why cannot I make them see the truth? Why cannot I speak in their language? Why cannot I open their eyes?" Surely, they ought to know better, and when they find people do not listen to them, if they curse anybody, it should be themselves. But it is always the people's fault! They never try to make their sect large enough to embrace everyone.

Therefore we at once see why there has been so much narrow-mindedness, the part always claiming to be the whole; the little, finite unit always laying claim to the infinite. Think of little sects, born within a few hundred years out of fallible human brains, making this arrogant claim of knowledge of the whole of God's infinite truth! Think of the arrogance of it! If it shows anything, it is this, how vain human beings are. And it is no wonder that such claims have always failed, and, by the mercy of the Lord, are always destined to fail. **In this line the Mohammedans were the best off; every step forward was made with the sword—the Koran in the one hand and the sword in the other: "Take the Koran, or you must die; there is no alternative!" You know from history how phenomenal was their success; for six hundred years nothing could resist them, and then there came a time when they had to cry halt.** So will it be with other religions if they follow the same methods. We are such babes! We always forget human nature. When we begin life, we think that our fate will be something extraordinary, and nothing can make us disbelieve that. But when we grow old, we think differently. So with religions.

In their early stages, when they spread a little, they get the idea that they can change the minds of the whole human race in a few years, and go on killing and massacring to make converts by force; then they fail, and begin to understand better. **We see that these sects did not succeed in what they started out to do, which was a great blessing. Just think if one of those fanatical sects had succeeded all over the world, where would man be today?** Now, the Lord be blessed that they did not succeed! **Yet, each one represents a great truth; each religion represents a particular excellence-something which is its soul.**

There is an old story which comes to my mind: There were some ogresses who used to kill people and do all sorts of mischief; but they themselves could not be killed, until someone found out that their souls were in certain birds, and so long as the birds were safe nothing could destroy the ogresses. So, each one of us has, as it were, such a bird, where our soul is; has an ideal, a mission to perform in life.

Every human being is an embodiment of such an ideal, such a mission. Whatever else you may lose, so long as that ideal is not lost, and that mission is not hurt, nothing can kill you. Wealth may come and go, misfortunes may pile mountains high, but if you have kept the ideal entire, nothing can kill you. You may have grown old, even a hundred years old, but if that mission is fresh and young in your heart, what can kill you? But when that ideal is lost and that mission is hurt, nothing can save you. All the wealth, all the power of the world will not save you. And what are nations but multiplied individuals? So, each nation has a mission of its own to perform in this harmony of races; and so long as that nation keeps to that ideal, that nation nothing can kill; but if that nation gives up its mission in life and goes after something else, its life becomes short, and it vanishes.

And so with religions. **The fact that all these old religions are living today proves that they must have kept that mission intact; in spite of all their mistakes,** in spite of all difficulties, in spite of all quarrels, in spite of all the incrustation of forms and figures, the heart of every one of them is sound—it is a throbbing, beating, living heart. They have not lost, anyone of them, the great mission they came for. And it is splendid to study that mission. Take Mohammedanism, for instance. Christian people hate no religion in the world so much as Mohammedanism. They think it is the very worst form of religion that ever existed. **As soon as a man becomes a Mohammedan, the whole of Islam receives him as a brother with open arms, without making any distinction, which no other religion does. If one of your American Indians becomes a Mohammedan, the Sultan of Turkey would have no objection to dine with him. If he has brains, no position is barred to him.** In this country, I have never yet seen a church where the white man and the negro can kneel side by side to pray.

Just think of that: Islam makes its followers all equal—so, that, you see, is the peculiar excellence of Mohammedanism. In many places in the Koran you find very sensual ideas of life. Never mind. **What Mohamme-danism comes to preach to the world is this practical brotherhood of all belonging to their faith. That is the essential part of the Mohammedan religion** and all the other ideas about heaven and of life etc. are not Mohammedanism. They are accretions.

With the Hindus you will find one national idea—spirituality. In no other religion, in no other sacred books of the world, will you find so much energy spent in defining the idea of God. They tried to define the ideal of soul so that no earthly touch might mar it. The spirit must be divine; and spirit understood as spirit must not be made into a man. The same idea of unity, of the realisation of God, the omnipresent, is preached throughout. They think it is all nonsense to say that He lives in heaven, and all that. It is a mere human, anthropomorphic idea. All the heaven that ever existed is now and here. One moment in infinite time is quite as good as any other moment. If you believe in a God, you can see Him even now. We think religion begins when you have realised something. It is not believing in doctrines, nor giving intellectual assent, nor making declarations. If there is a God, have you seen Him? If you say "no", then what right have you to believe in Him? If you are in doubt whether there is a God, why do you not struggle to see Him? Why do you not renounce the world and spend the whole of your life for this one object? Renunciation and spirituality are the two great ideas of India, and it is because India clings to these ideas that all her mistakes count for so little.

With the Christians, the central idea that has been preached by them is the same. "Watch and pray, for the kingdom of Heaven is at hand"—which means, purify your minds and be ready! And that spirit never dies. You recollect that the Christians are, even in the darkest days, even in the most superstitious Christian countries, always trying to prepare themselves for the coming of the Lord, by trying to help others, building hospitals, and so on. So long as the Christians keep to that ideal, their religion lives.

Now an ideal presents itself to my mind. It may be only a dream. I do not know whether it will ever be realised in this world, but sometimes it is better to dream a dream, than die on hard facts. Great truths, even in a dream are good, better than bad facts. So, let us dream a dream.

You know that there are various grades of mind. You may be a matter-of-fact, commonsense rationalist: you do not care for forms and ceremonies; you want intellectual, hard, ringing facts, and they alone will satisfy you. Then there are the Puritans, the Mohammedans, who will not allow a picture or a statue in their place of worship. Very well! But there is another man who is more artistic. He wants a great deal of art-beauty of lines and curves, the colours, flowers, forms; he wants candles, lights, and all the insignia and paraphernalia of ritual, that he may see God. His mind takes God in those forms, as yours takes Him through the intellect. Then, there is the devotional man, whose soul is crying for God: he has no other idea but to worship God, and to praise them. Then again, there is the philosopher, standing outside all these, mocking at them. He thinks, "What nonsense they are! What ideas about God !"

They may laugh at one another, but each one has a place in this world. All these various minds, all these various types are necessary. **If there ever is going to be an ideal religion, it must be broad and large enough to supply food for all these minds. It must supply the strength of philosophy to the philosopher, the devotee's heart to the worshipper; to the ritualist' it will give all that the most marvellous symbolism can convey; to the poet, it will give as much of heart as he can take in and other things besides.** To make such a broad religion, we shall have to go back to the time when religions began and take them all in.

Our watchword, then, will be acceptance, and not exclusion. Not only toleration, for so-called toleration is often blasphemy, and I do not believe in it. **I believe in acceptance.** Why should I tolerate? Toleration means that I think that you are wrong and I am just allowing you to live. Is it not a blasphemy to think that you and I are allowing others to live? I accept all religions that were in the past, and worship with them all; I worship God with everyone of them, in whatever form they worship Him. I shall go to the mosque of the Mohammedan; I shall enter the Christian's church and kneel before the crucifix; I shall enter the Buddhistic temple, where I shall take refuge in Buddha and in his Law. I shall go into the forest and sit down in meditation with the Hindu, who is trying to see the Light which enlightens the heart of everyone.

Not only shall I do all these, but I shall keep my heart open for all that may come in the future. Is God's book finished? Or is it still a continuous revelation going on? It is a marvellous book—these spiritual revelations of the world. The Bible, the Vedas, the Koran, and all other sacred books are but so many pages, and an infinite number of pages remain yet to be unfolded. I would leave it open for all of them. We stand in the present, but open ourselves to the infinite future. We take in all that has been in the past, enjoy the light of the present, and open every window of the heart for all that will come in the future. Salutation to all the prophets of the past, to all the great ones of the present, and to all that are to come in the future!

(Talk delivered at the Universalist Church, Pasadena, California, on Jan. 28, 1900)

India: My Analysis

The Vedic priests base their superior strength on the knowledge of the sacrificial Mantras. By the power of these Mantras, the Devas are made to come down from their heavenly abodes, accept the drink and food offerings, and grant the prayers of the Yajamanas.The kings as well as their subjects are, therefore, looking up to these priests for their welfare during their earthly life. Raja Soma—is worshipped by the priest and is made to thrive by the power of his Mantras. As such, the Devas, whose favourite food is the juice of the Soma plant offered in oblation by the priest, are always kind to him and bestow his desired boons. Thus strengthened by divine grace, he defies all human opposition; for what can the power of mortals do against that of the gods? Even the king, the centre of all earthly power, is a supplicant at his door. A kind look from him is the greatest help; his mere blessing a tribute to the State, pre-eminent above everything else.

Now commanding the king to be engaged in affairs fraught with death and ruin, now standing by him as his fastest friend with kind and wise counsels, now spreading the net of subtle, diplomatic statesmanship in which the king is easily caught—**the priest is seen, often times, to make the royal power totally subservient to him.** Above all, the worst fear is in the knowledge that the name and fame of the royal forefathers and of himself and his family lie at the mercy of the priest's pen. He is the historian. The king might have paramount power, attaining a great glory in his reign, he might prove himself as the father and mother in one to his subjects; but **if the priest is not appeased, his sun of glory goes down with his last breath for ever;** all his worth and usefulness deserving of universal approbation are lost in the great womb of time, like unto the fall of gentle dew on the ocean. Others who inaugurated the huge sacrifices lasting over many years, the performers of the Ashvamedha and so on—those who showered, like incessant rain in the rainy season, countless wealth on the priests—their names, thanks to the grace of priests, are emblazoned in the pages of history. The name of Priyadarshi Dharmashoka, the beloved of the gods, is nothing but a name in the priestly world, while Janamejaya, son of Parikshit, is a household word in every Hindu family.

To protect the State, to meet the expenses of the personal comforts and luxuries of himself and his long retinue, and, above all, to fill to overflowing the coffers of the all powerful priesthood for its propitiation, **the king is continually draining the resources of his subjects, even as the sun sucks up moisture from the earth. His especial prey—his milch cows—are the Vaishyas.**

Neither under the Hindu kings, nor under the Buddhist rule, do we find the common subject—people taking any part in expressing their voice in the affairs of the State. True, Yudhishthira visits the houses of Vaishyas and even Shudras when he is in Varanavata; true, the subjects are praying for the installation of Ramachandra to the regency of Ayodhya; nay, they are even criticising the conduct of Sita and secretly making plans for the bringing about of her exile; but as a recognised rule of the State they have no direct voice in the supreme government. The power of the populace is struggling to express itself in indirect and disorderly ways without any method. The people have not as yet the conscious knowledge of the existence of this power. There is neither the attempt on their part to organise it into a united action, nor have they got the will to do so; there is also a complete absence of that capacity, that skill, by means of which small and incoherent centres of force are united together, creating insuperable strength as their resultant.

Is this due to want of proper laws?—no, that is not it. There are laws, there are methods, separately and distinctly assigned for the guidance of different departments of government, there are laws laid down in the minutest detail for everything, such as the collection of revenue, the management of the army, the administration of justice, punishments and rewards. But at the root of all, is the injunction of the Rishi—the word of divine authority, the revelation of God coming through the inspired Rishi. The laws have, it can almost be said, no elasticity in them. Under the circumstances, it is never possible for the people to acquire any sort of education by which they can learn to combine among themselves and be united for the accomplishment of any object for the common good of the people, or by which they can have the concerted intellect to conceive the idea of popular right in the treasures collected by the king from his subjects, or even such education by which they can be fired with the aspiration to gain the right of representation in the control of State revenues and expenditure. Why should they do such things? Is not the inspiration of the Rishi responsible for their prosperity and progress?

Again, all those laws are in books. Between laws as codified in books and their operation in practical life, there is a world of difference. One Ramachandra is born after thousands of Agnivarnas pass away! Many kings show us the life of Chandashoka; Dharmashokas are rare! The number of kings like Akbar, in whom the subjects find their life, is far less than that of kings like Aurangzeb who live on the blood of their people!

Even if the kings be of as godlike nature as that of Yudhishthira, Ramachandra, Dharmashoka, or Akbar, under whose benign rule the people enjoyed safety and prosperity, and were looked after with paternal care by their rulers, the hand of him who is always fed by another gradually loses the power of taking the food to his mouth. His power of self-preservation can never become fully manifest who is always protected in every respect by another. Even the strongest youth remains but a child if he is always looked after as a child by his parents. Being always governed by kings of godlike nature, to whom is left the whole duty of protecting and providing for the people, they can never get any occasion for under-standing the principles of self-government. Such a nation, being entirely dependent on the king for everything and never caring to exert itself for the common good or for self-defence, becomes gradually destitute of inherent energy and strength. If this state of dependence and protection continues long, it becomes the cause of the destruction of the nation, and its ruin is not far to seek.

Of course, it can be reasonably concluded that, when the government of a country is guided by codes of laws enjoined by Shastras which are the outcome of knowledge inspired by the divine genius of great sages, such a government must lead to the unbroken welfare of the rich and the poor, the wise and the ignorant, the king and the subjects alike. But we have seen already how far the operation of those laws was, or may be, possible in practical life. The voice of the ruled in the government of their land—which is the watchword of the modern Western world, and of which the last expression has been echoed with a thundering voice in the Declaration of the American Government, in the words, "That the government of the people of this country must be by the people and for the good of the people"—cannot however be said to have been totally unrecognised in ancient India. The Greek travellers and others saw many independent small States scattered all over this country, and references are also found to this effect in many places of the Buddhistic literature. And there cannot be the least doubt about it that the germ of self-government was at least present in the shape of the village Panchayat, which is still to be found in existence in many places of India. But the germ remained for ever the germ; the seed though put in the ground never grew into a tree. This idea of self-government never passed beyond the embryo state of the village Panchayat system and never spread into society at large.

In the religious communities, among Sannyasins in the Buddhist monasteries, we have ample evidence to show that self-government was fully developed. Even now, one wonders to see how the power of the Panchayat system, of the principles of self-government, is working amongst the Naga Sannyasins—what deep respect the "Government by the Five" commands from them—what effective individual rights each Naga can exercise within his own sect, what excellent working of the power of organisation and concerted action they have among themselves!

With the deluge which swept the land at the advent of Buddhism, the priestly power fell into decay and the royal power was in the ascendant. Buddhist priests are renouncers of the world, living in monasteries as homeless ascetics, unconcerned with secular affairs. They have neither the will nor the endeavour to bring and keep the royal power under their control through the threat of curses or magic arrows. Even if there were any remnant of such a will, its fulfilment has now become an impossibility. For **Buddhism has shaken the thrones of all the oblation-eating gods and brought them down from their heavenly positions.** The state of being a Buddha is superior to the heavenly positions of many a Brahma or an Indra, who vie with each other in offering their worship at the feet of the Buddha, the God-man! And to this Buddhahood, every man has the privilege to attain; it is open to all even in this life. From the descent of the gods, as a natural consequence, the superiority of the priests who were supported by them is gone.

Accordingly, the reins of that mighty sacrificial horse — the royal power — are no longer held in the firm grasp of the Vedic priest; and being now free, it can roam anywhere by its unbridled will. The centre of power in this period is neither with the priests chanting the Sama hymns and performing the Yajnas according to the Yajur veda; nor is the power vested in the hands of Kshatriya kings separated from each other and ruling over small independent States. But the centre of power in this age is in emperors whose unobstructed sway extend over vast areas bounded by the ocean, covering the whole of India from one end to the other. The leaders of this age are no longer Vishvamitra or Vasishtha, but emperors like Chandragupta, Dharmashoka, and others. There never were emperors who ascended the throne of India and led her to the pinnacle of her glory such as those lords of the earth who ruled over her in paramount sway during the Buddhistic period. **The end of this period is characterised by the appearance of Rajput power on the scene and the rise of Modern Hinduism.** With the rise of Rajput power, on the decline of Buddhism, the sceptre of the Indian empire, dislodged from its paramount power, was again broken into a thousand pieces and wielded by small powerless hands. At this time, the Brahminical (priestly) power again succeeded in raising its head, not as an adversary as before, but this time as an auxiliary to the royal supremacy.

During this revolution, that perpetual struggle for supremacy between priestly and the royal classes, which began from the Vedic times and continued through ages till it reached its climax at the time of the Jain and Buddhist revolutions, has ceased for ever. Now these two mighty powers are friendly to each other; but neither is there any more that glorious Kshatra (warlike) valour of the kings, nor that spiritual brilliance which characterised the Brahmins; each has lost his former intrinsic strength. As might be expected, this new union of the two forces was soon engaged in the satisfaction of mutual self interests, and became dissipated by spending its vitality on extirpating their common opponents, especially the Buddhists of the time, and on similar other deeds. Being steeped in all the vices consequent on such a union, e.g., the sucking of the blood of the masses, taking revenge on the enemy, spoliation of others' property, etc., they in vain tried to imitate the Rajasuya and other Vedic sacrifices of the ancient kings, and only made a ridiculous farce of them. The result was that they were bound hand and foot by a formidable train of sycophantic attendance and its obsequious flatteries, and being entangled in an interminable net of rites and ceremonies with flourishes of Mantras and the like, **they soon became a cheap and ready prey to the Mohammeden invaders from the West.**

That priestly power which began its strife for superiority with the royal power from the Vedic times and continued it down the ages, that hostility against the Kshatra power, Bhagavan Shri Krishna succeeded by his superhuman genius in putting a stop to, at least for the time being, during his earthly existence. That Brahmanya power was almost effaced from its field of work in India during the Jain and Buddhist revolutions, or, perhaps, was holding its feeble stand by being subservient to the strong antagonistic religions. That Brahmanya power, since the appearance of Rajput power, which held sway over India under the Mihira dynasty and others, made its last effort to recover its lost greatness; and in its effort to establish that supremacy, it sold itself at the feet of the fierce hordes of barbarians newly come from Central Asia, and to win their pleasure introduced in the land their hateful manners and customs. Moreover, it, **the Brahmanya power, solely devoting itself to the easy means to dupe ignorant barbarians, brought into vogue mysterious rites and ceremonies backed by its new Mantras and the like; and in doing so, itself lost its former wisdom, its former vigour and vitality,** and its own chaste habits of long acquirement. Thus it turned the whole Aryavarta into a deep and vast whirlpool of the most vicious, the most horrible, the most abominable, barbarous customs; and as the inevitable consequence of countenancing these detestable customs and superstitions, it soon lost all its own internal strength and stamina and became the weakest of the weak. What wonder that it should be broken into a thousand pieces and fall at the mere touch of the storm of Mussulman invasions from the West! That great Brahmanya power fell—who knows, if ever to rise again?

The resuscitation of the priestly power under the Mussulman rule was, on the other hand, an utter impossibility. The Prophet Mohammed himself was dead against the priestly class in any shape and tried his best for the total destruction of this power by formulating rules and injunctions to that effect. Under the Mussulman rule, the king himself was the supreme priest; he was the chief guide in religious matters; and when he became the emperor, he cherished the hope of being the paramount leader in all matters over the whole Mussulman world. To the Mussulman, the Jews or the Christians are not objects of extreme detestation; they are, at the worst, men of little faith. But not so the Hindu. According to him, the Hindu is idolatrous, the hateful Kafir; hence in this life he deserves to be butchered; and in the next, eternal hell is in store for him. The utmost the Mussulman kings could do as a favour to the priestly class—the spiritual guides of these Kafirs—was to allow them somehow to pass their life silently and wait for the last moment. This was again sometimes considered too much kindness! If the religious ardour of any king was a little more uncommon, there would immediately follow arrangements for a great Yajna by way of Kafir-slaughter!

On one side, the royal power is now centred in kings professing a different religion and given to different customs. On the other, the priestly power has been entirely displaced from its influential position as the controller and lawgiver of the society. **The Koran and its code of laws have taken the place of the Dharma Shastras of Manu and others. The Sanskrit language has made room for the Persian and the Arabic.** The Sanskrit language has to remain confined only to the purely religious writings and religious matters of the conquered and detested Hindu, and, as such, has since been living a precarious life at the hands of the neglected priest. The priest himself, the relic of the Brahmanya power, fell back upon the last resource of conducting only the comparatively unimportant family ceremonies, such as the matrimonial etc., and that also only so long and as much as the mercy of the Mohammedan rulers permitted.

In the Vedic and the adjoining periods, the royal power could not manifest itself on account of the grinding pressure of the priestly power. We have seen how, during the Buddhistic revolution, resulting in the fall of the Brahminical supremacy, the royal power in India reached its culminating point. In the interval between the fall of the Buddhistic and the establishment of the Mohammedan empire, we have seen how the royal power was trying to raise its head through the Rajputs in India, and how it failed in its attempt. At the root of this failure, too, could be traced the same old endeavours of the Vedic priestly class to bring back and revive with a new life their original ritualistic days.

Crushing the Brahminical supremacy under his feet, the Mussulman king was able to restore to a considerable extent the lost glories of such dynasties of emperors as the Maurya, the Gupta, the Andhra, and the Kshatrapa.

Thus the priestly power—which sages like Kumarila, Shankara, and Ramanuja tried to reestablish, which for some time was supported by the sword of the Rajput power, and which tried to rebuild its structure on the fall of its Jain and Buddhist adversaries—was under Mohammedan rule laid to sleep for ever, knowing no awakening. In this period, the antagonism or warfare is not between kings and priests, but between kings and kings. At the end of this period, when Hindu power again raised its head, and, to some extent, was successful in regenerating Hinduism through the Mahrattas and the Sikhs, we do not find much play of the priestly power with these regenerations. On the contrary, when the Sikhs admitted any Brahmin into their sect, they, at first, compelled him publicly to give up his previous Brahminical signs and adopt the recognised signs of their own religion.

In this manner, after an age-long play of action and reaction between these two forces, the final victory of the royal power was echoed on the soil of India for several centuries, in the name of foreign monarchs professing an entirely different religion from the faith of the land. But **at the end of this Mohammedan period, another entirely new power made its appearance on the arena and slowly began to assert its prowess in the affairs of the Indian world.**

This power is so new, its nature and workings are so foreign to the Indian mind, its rise so inconceivable, and its vigour so insuperable that though it wields the suzerain power up till now, only a handful of Indians understand what this power is.

We are talking of the occupation of India by England.

From very ancient times, the fame of India's vast wealth and her rich granaries has enkindled in many powerful foreign nations the desire for conquering her. She has been, in fact, again and again conquered by foreign nations. Then why should we say that the occupation of India by England was something new and foreign to the Indian mind?

From time immemorial Indians have seen the mightiest royal power tremble before the frown of the ascetic priest, devoid of worldly desire, armed with spiritual strength—the power of Mantras (sacred formulas) and religious lore—and the weapon of curses. They have also seen the subject people silently obey the commands of their heroic all-powerful suzerains, backed by their arms and armies, like a flock of sheep before a lion. **But that a handful of Vaishyas traders who, despite their great wealth, have ever crouched awe-stricken not only before the king but also before any member of the royal family, would unite, cross for purposes of business rivers and seas, would, solely by virtue of theIr intelligence and wealth, by degrees make puppets of the long-established Hindu and Mohammedan dynasties; not only so, but that they would buy as well the services of the ruling powers of their own country and use their valour and learning as powerful instruments for the influx of their own riches—this is a spectacle entirely novel to the Indians,** as also the spectacle that the descendants of the mighty nobility of a country, of which a proud lord, sketched by the extraordinary pen of its great poet, says to a common man, "Out, dunghill! darest thou brave a nobleman?" would, in no distant future, **consider it the zenith of human ambition to be sent to India as obedient servants of a body of**

merchants, called The East India Company—such a sight was, indeed, a novelty unseen by India before!

According to the prevalence, in greater or lesser degree, of the three qualities of Sattva, Rajas, and Tamas in man, the four castes, the Brahmin, Kashatriya, Vaishya, and Shudra, are everywhere present at all times, in all civilised societies. By the mighty hand of time, their number and power also vary at different times in regard to different countries. In some countries the numerical strength or influence of one of these castes may preponderate over another; at some period, one of the classes may be more powerful than the rest. But from a careful study of the history of the world, it appears that in conformity to the law of nature the four castes the Brahmin, Kshatriya, Vaishya, and Shudra do, in every society, one after another in succession, govern the world.

Among the Chinese, the Sumerians, the Babylonians, the Egyptians, the Chaldeans, the Aryas, the Iranians, the Jews, the Arabs—among all these ancient nations, the supreme power of guiding society is, in the first period of their history, in the hands of the Brahmin or the priest. In the second period, the ruling power is the Kshatriya, that is, either absolute monarchy or oligarchical government by a chosen body of men. Among the modern Western nations, with England at their head, this power of controlling society has been, for the first time, in the hands of the Vaishyas or mercantile communities, made rich through the carrying on of commerce.

Though Troy and Carthage of ancient times and Venice and similar other small commercial States of comparatively modern times became highly powerful, yet, amongst them, there was not the real rising of the Vaishya power in the proper sense of the term.

Correctly speaking, the descendants of the royal family had the sole monopoly of the commerce of those old days by employing the common people and their servants under them to carry-on the trade; and they appropriated to themselves the profits accruing from it. Excepting these few men, no one was allowed to take any part or voice an opinion even in the government of the country and kindred affairs. In the oldest countries like Egypt, the priestly power enjoyed unmolested supremacy only for a short period, after which it became subjugated to the royal power and lived as an auxiliary to it. In China, the royal power, centralised by the genius of Confucius, has been controlling and guiding the priestly power, in accordance with its absolute will, for more than twenty-five centuries; and during the last two centuries, the all-absorbing Lamas of Tibet, though they are the spiritual guides of the royal family, have been compelled to pass their days, being subject in every way to the Chinese Emperor.

In India, the royal power succeeded in conquering the priestly power and declaring its untrammelled authority long after the other ancient civilised nations had done so ; and therefore the inauguration of the Indian Empire came about long after the Chinese, Egyptian, Babylonian, and other Empires had risen. It was only with the Jewish people that the royal power, though it tried hard to establish its supremacy over the priestly, had to meet a complete defeat in the attempt. Not even the Vaishyas attained the ruling power with the Jews. On the other hand, the common subject people, trying to free themselves from the shackles of priestcraft, were crushed to death under the internal commotion of adverse religious movements like Christianity and the external pressure of the mighty Roman Empire.

As in the ancient days the priestly power, in spite of its long-continued struggle, was subdued by the more powerful royal power, so, in modern times, before the violent blow of the newly-risen Vaishya power, many a kingly crown has to kiss the ground, many a sceptre is for ever broken to pieces. Only those few thrones which are allowed still to exercise some power in some of the civilised countries and make a display of their royal pomp and grandeur are all maintained solely by the vast hordes of wealth of these Vaishya communities—the dealers in salt, oil, sugar, and wine—and kept up as a magnificent and an imposing front, and as a means of glorification to the really governing body behind, the Vaishyas.

That mighty newly-risen Vaishya power—at whose command, electricity carries messages in an instant from one pole to another, whose highway is the vast ocean, with its mountain-high waves, at whose instance, commodities are being carried with the greatest ease from one part of the globe to another, and at whose mandate, even the greatest monarchs tremble—on the white foamy crest of that huge wave the all-conquering Vaishya power, is installed the majestic throne of England in all its grandeur.

Therefore the conquest of India by England is not a conquest by Jesus or the Bible as we are often asked to believe. Neither is it like the conquest of India by the Moguls and the Pathans. But behind the name of the Lord Jesus, the Bible, the magnificent palaces, the heavy tramp of the feet of armies consisting of elephants, chariots, cavalry, and infantry, shaking the earth, the sounds of war trumpets, bugles, and drums, and the splendid display of the royal throne, behind all these, there is always the virtual presence of England—that **England whose war flag is the factory chimney, whose troops are the merchant-men, whose battlefields are the market-places of the world,** and whose Empress is the shining Goddess of Fortune herself! It is on this account I have said before that **it is indeed an unseen novelty, this conquest of India by England.** What new revolution will be effected in India by her dash with the new giant power, and as the result of that revolution what new transformation is in store for future India, cannot be inferred from her past history.

I have stated previously that **the four castes, Brahmin, Kshatriya, Vaishya, and Shudra do, in succession,** rule the world. During the period of supreme authority exercised by each of these castes, some acts are accomplished which conduce to the welfare of the people, while others are injurious to them.

The foundation of the priestly power rests on intellectual strength, and not on the physical strength of arms. Therefore, with the supremacy of the priestly power, there is a great prevalence of intellectual and literary culture. Every human heart is always anxious for communication with, and help from, the supersensusous spiritual world. The entrance to that world is not possible for the generality of mankind; only a few great souls who can acquire a perfect control over their sense-organs and who are possessed with a nature preponderating with the essence of Sattva Guna are able to pierce the formidable wall of matter and come face to face, as it were, with the supersensuous—it is only they who know the workings of the kingdom that bring the messages from it and show the way to others. These great souls are the priests, the primitive guides, leaders, and movers of human societies.

The priest knows the gods and communicates with them; he is therefore worshipped as a god. Leaving behind the thoughts of the world, he has no longer to devote himself to the earning of his bread by the sweat of his brow. The best and foremost parts of all food and drink are due as offerings to the gods; and of these gods, the visible proxies on earth are the priests. It is through their mouths that they partake of the offerings. Knowingly or unknowingly, society gives the priest abundant leisure, and he can therefore get the opportunity of being meditative and of thinking higher thoughts.

Hence the development of wisdom and learning originates first with the supremacy of the priestly power. There stands the priest between the dreadful lion—the king—on the one hand, and the terrified flock of sheep—the subject people—on the other. The destructive leap of the lion is checked by the controlling rod of spiritual power in the hands of the priest. The flame of the despotic will of the king, maddened in the pride of his wealth and men, is able to burn into ashes everything that comes in his way; but it is only a word from the priest, who has neither wealth nor men behind him but whose sole strength is his spiritual power, that can quench the despotic royal will, as water the fire.

With the ascendancy of the priestly supremacy are seen the first advent of civilisation, the first victory of the divine nature over the animal, the first mastery of spirit over matter, and the first manifestation of the divine power which is potentially present in this very slave of nature, this lump of flesh, to wit, the human body. The priest is the first discriminator of spirit from matter, the first to help to bring this world in communion with the next, the first messenger from the gods to man, intervening bridge that connects the king with his subjects. **The first offshoot of universal welfare and good is nursed by his spiritual power, by his devotion to learning and wisdom, by his renunciation,** the watchword of his life and, watered even by the flow of his own life-blood. It is therefore that in every land it was He to whom the first and foremost worship was offered. It is therefore that even his memory is sacred to us!

There are evils as well. With the growth of life is sown simultaneously the seed of death. Darkness and light always go together. Indeed, there are great evils which, if not checked in proper time, lead to the ruin of society. The play of power through gross matter is universally experienced; everyone sees, everyone understands, the mighty manifestation of gross material force as displayed in the play of battle-axes and swords, or in the burning properties of fire and lightning. Nobody doubts these things, nor can there ever be any question about their genuineness. But where the repository of power and the centre of its play are wholly mental, where the power is confined to certain special words, to certain special modes of uttering them, to the mental repetition of certain mysterious syllables, or to other similar processes and applications of the mind, there light is mixed with shade, there the ebb and flow naturally disturb the otherwise unshaken faith, and there even when things are actually seen or directly perceived, still sometimes doubts arise as to their real occurrence. Where distress, fear, anger, malice, spirit of retaliation, and the like passions of man, leaving the palpable force of arms, leaving the gross material methods to gain the end in view which everyone can understand, substitute in their stead the mysterious mental processes like Stambhana, Uchchatana, Vashikarana, and Marana for their fructification—there a cloud of smoky indistinctness, as it were, naturally envelops the mental atmosphere of these men who often live and move in such hazy worlds of obscure mysticism. No straight line of action presents itself before such a mind; even if it does, the mind distorts it into crookedness. The final result of all this is insincerity—that very limited narrowness of the heart—and above all, the most fatal is the extreme intolerance born of malicious envy at the superior excellence of another.

The priest naturally says to himself: "Why should I part with the power that has made the Devas subservient to me, has given me mastery over physical and mental illnesses, and has gained for me the service of ghosts, demons, and other unseen spirits? I have dearly bought this power by the price of extreme renunciation. Why should I give to others that to get which I had to give up my wealth, name, fame, in short, all my earthly comforts and happiness?" Again, that power is entirely mental. And how many opportunities are there of keeping it a perfect secret! Entangled in this wheel of circumstances, human nature becomes what it inevitably would: **being used to practise constant self-concealment, it becomes a victim of extreme selfishness and hypocrisy,** and at last succumbs to the poisonous consequences which they bring in their train. In time, the reaction of this very desire to concealment rebounds upon oneself. All knowledge, all wisdom is almost lost for want of proper exercise and diffusion, and what little remains is thought to have been obtained from some supernatural source; and, therefore, far from making fresh efforts to go in for originality and gain knowledge of new sciences, it is considered useless and futile to attempt even to improve the remnants of the old by cleansing them of their corruptions. Thus lost to former wisdom, the former indomitable spirit of self-reliance, the priest, now glorifying himself merely in the name of his forefathers, vainly struggles to preserve untarnished for himself the same glory, the same privilege, the same veneration, and the same supremacy as was enjoyed by his great forefathers. Consequently, his violent collision with the other castes.

According to the law of nature, wherever there is an awakening of a new and stronger life, there it tries to conquer and take the place of the old and the decaying. Nature favours the dying out of the unfit and the survival of the fittest. The final result of such conflict between the priestly and the other classes has been mentioned already.

That renunciation, self-control, and asceticism of the priest which during the period of his ascendancy were devoted to the pursuance of earnest researches of truth are on the eve of his decline employed anew and spent solely in the accumulation of objects of self-gratification and in the extension of privileged superiority over others. That power, the centralisation of which in himself gave him all honour and worship, has now been dragged down from its high heavenly position to the lowest abyss of hell. Having lost sight of the goal, drifting aimless, the priestly power is entangled, like the spider, in the web spun by itself. The chain that has been forged from generation to generation with the greatest care to be put on others' feet is now tightened round its own in a thousand coils, and is thwarting its own movement in hundreds of ways caught in the endless thread of the net of infinite rites, ceremonies, and customs, which it spread on all sides as external means for purification of the body and the mind with a view to keeping society in the iron grasp of these innumerable bonds—the priestly power, thus hopelessly entangled from head to foot, is now asleep in despair!

There is no escaping out of it now. Tear the net, and the priesthood of the priest is shaken to its foundation! There is implanted in every man, naturally, a strong desire for progress; and those who, finding that the fulfilment of this desire is an impossibility so long as one is trammelled in the shackles of priesthood, rend this net and take to the profession of other castes in order to earn money thereby—them, the society immediately dispossesses of their priestly rights. Society has no faith in the Brahminhood of the so-called Brahmins who, instead of keeping the Shikha, part their hair, who, giving up theii ancient habits and ancestral customs, clothe themselves in semi-European dress and adopt the newly introduced usages from the West in a hybrid fashion. Again, in those parts of India, wherever this newcomer, the English Government, is introducing new modes of education and opening up new channels for the coming in of wealth, there hosts of Brahmin ouths are giving up their hereditary priestly profession and trying to earn their livelihood and become rich by adopting the callings of other castes, with the result that the habits and customs of the priestly class, handed down from their distant forefathers, are scattered to the winds and are fast disappearing from the land.

In Gujarat, each secondary sect of the Brahmins is divided into two subdivisions, one being those who still stick to the priestly profession, while the other lives by other professions. There only the first subdivisions, carrying on the priestly profession, are called "Brahmanas", and though the other subdivisions are by lineage descendants from Brahmin fathers, yet the former do not link themselves in matrimonial relation with the latter. For example, by the name of "Nagara Brahmin" are meant only those Brahmins who are priests living on alms; and by the name "Nagara" only are meant those Brahmins who have accepted service under the Government, or those who have been carrying on the Vaishya's profession. But it appears that such distinctions will not long continue in these days in Gujarat. Even the sons of the "Nagara Brahmin" are nowadays getting English education, and entering into Government service, or adopting some mercantile business. Even orthodox Pandits of the old school, undergoing pecuniary difficulties, are sending their sons to the colleges of the English universities or making them choose the callings of Vaidyas, Kayasthas, and other non-Brahmin castes.

If the current of affairs goes on running in this course, then it is a question of most serious reflection, no doubt, how long more will the priestly class continue on India's soil. Those who lay the fault of attempting to bring down the supremacy of the priestly class at the door of any particular person or body of persons other than themselves ought to know that, in obedience to the inevitable law of nature, the Brahmin caste is erecting with its own hands its own sepulchre; and this is what ought to be. It is good and appropriate that every caste of high birth and privileged nobility should make it its principal duty to raise its own funeral pyre with its own hands. Accumulation of power is as necessary as its diffusion, or rather more so. The accumulation of blood in the heart is an indispensable condition for life; its non-circulation throughout the body means death. For the welfare of society, it is absolutely necessary at certain times to have all knowledge and power concentrated in certain families or castes to the exclusion of others, but that concentrated power is focussed for the time being, only to be scattered and broadcast over the whole of society in future. If this diffusion be withheld, the destruction of that society is, without doubt, near at hand.

On the other side, the king is like the lion; in him are present both the good and evil propensities of the lord of beasts. Never for a moment his fierce nails are held back from tearing to pieces the heart of innocent animals, living on herbs and grass, to allay his thirst for blood when occasion arises; again, the poet says, though himself stricken with old age and dying with hunger, the lion never kills the weakest fox that throws itself in his arms for protection. If the subject classes, for a moment, stand as impediments in the way of the gratification of the senses of the royal lion, their death knell is inevitably tolled; if they humbly bow down to his commands, they are perfectly safe. Not only so. Not to speak of ancient days, even in modern times, no society can be found in any country where the effectiveness of individual self-sacrifice for the good of the many and of the oneness of purpose and endeavour actuating every member of the society for the common good of the whole have been fully realised. Hence the necessity of the kings who are the creations of the society itself. They are the centres where all the forces of society, otherwise loosely scattered about, are made to converge, and from which they start and course through the body politic and animate society.

As during the Brahminical supremacy, at the first stage is the awakening of the first impulse for search after knowledge, and later the continual and careful fostering of the growth of that impulse still in its infancy—so, during the Kshatriya supremacy, a strong desire for pleasure pursuits has made its appearance at the first stage, and later have sprung up inventions and developments of arts and sciences as the means for its gratification. Can the king, at the height of his glory, hide his proud head within the lowly cottages of the poor? Or can the common good of his subjects ever minister to his royal appetite with satisfaction?

He whose dignity bears no comparison with anyone else on earth, he who is divinity residing in the temple of the human body—for the common man, to cast even a mere glance at his, the king's, objects of pleasure is a great sin; to think of ever possessing them is quite out of the question. The body of the king is not like the bodies of other people, it is too sacred to be polluted by any contamination; in certain countries it is even believed never to come under the sway of death. A halo of equal sacredness shines around the queen, so she is scrupulously guarded from the gaze of the common folk, not even the sun may cast a glance on her beauty! Hence the rising of magnificent palaces to take the place of thatched cottages. The sweet harmonious strain of artistic music, flowing as it were from heaven, silenced the disorderly jargon of the rabble. Delightful gardens, pleasant groves, beautiful galleries, charming paintings, exquisite sculptures, fine and costly apparel began to displace by gradual steps the natural beauties of rugged woods and the rough and coarse dress of the simple rustic. Thousands of intelligent men left the toilsome task of the ploughman and turned their attention to the new field of fine arts, where they could display the finer play of their intellect in less laborious and easier ways. Villages lost their importance; cities rose in their stead.

It was in India, again, that the kings, after having enjoyed for some time earthly pleasures to their full satisfaction, were stricken at the latter part of their lives with heavy world-weariness, as is sure to follow on extreme sense-gratification; and thus being satiated with worldly pleasures, they retired at their old age into secluded forests, and there began to contemplate the deep problems of life. **The results of such renunciation and deep meditation were marked by a strong dislike for cumbrous rites and ceremonials and an extreme devotion to the highest spiritual truths which we find embodied in the Upanishads, the Gita, and the Jain and the Buddhist scriptures.** Here also was a great conflict between the priestly and the royal powers. Disappearance of the elaborate rites and ceremonials meant a death-blow to the priest's profession. Therefore, naturally, at all times and in every country, the priests gird up their loins and try their best to preserve the ancient customs and usages, while on the other side stand in opposition kings like Janaka, backed by Kshatriya prowess as well as spiritual power. We have dealt at length already on this bitter antagonism between the two parties.

As the priest is busy about centralising all knowledge and learning at a common centre, to wit, himself, so the king is ever up and doing in collecting all the earthly powers and focusing them in a central point, i.e., his own self. Of course, both are beneficial to society. At one time they are both needed for the common good of society, but that is only at its infant stage. But if attempts be made, when society has passed its infant stage and reached its vigorous youthful condition, to clothe it by force with the dress which suited it in its infancy and keep it bound within narrow limits, then either it bursts the bonds by virtue of its own strength and tries to advance, or where it fails to do so, it retraces its footsteps and by slow degrees returns to its primitive uncivilised condition.

Kings are like parents to their subjects, and the subjects are the kings' children. The subjects should, in every respect, look up to the king and stick to their king with unreserved obedience, and the king should rule them with impartial justice and look to their welfare and bear the same affection towards them as he would towards his own children. But what rule applies to individual homes applies to the whole society as well, for society is only the aggregate of individual homes. When the son attains the age of sixteen, the father ought to deal with him as his friend and equal—if that is the rule, does not the infant society ever attain that age of sixteen? It is the evidence of history that at a certain time every society attains its manhood, when a strong conflict ensues between the ruling power and the common people. The life of the society, its expansion and civilisation, depend on its victory or defeat in this conflict.

Christ, the Messenger of Life

The wave rises on the ocean, and there is a hollow. Again another wave rises, perhaps bigger than the former, to fall down again, similarly, again to rise—driving onward. In the march of events, we notice the rise and fall, and we generally look towards the rise, forgetting the fall. But both are necessary, and both are great. This is the nature of the universe. Whether in the world of our thoughts, the world of our relations in society, or, in our spiritual affairs, the same movement of succession, of rises and falls, is going on. Hence great predominances in the march of events, the liberal ideals, are marshalled ahead, to sink down, to digest, as it were, to ruminate over the past—to adjust, to conserve, to gather strength once more for a rise and a bigger rise.

The history of nations also has ever been like that. The great soul, the Messenger of life, Christ, came at a period of the history of his race which we may well designate as a great fall. We catch only little glimpses here and there of the stray records that have been kept of his sayings and doings; for verily it has been well said, that the doings and sayings of that great soul would fill the world if they had all been written down. And the three years of his ministry were like one compressed, concentrated age, which it has taken nineteen hundred years to unfold, and who knows how much longer it will yet take! Little men like you and me are simply the recipients of just a little energy. A few minutes, a few hours, a few years at best, are enough to spend it all, to stretch it out, as it were, to its fullest strength, and then we are gone for ever. But mark this giant that came; centuries and ages pass, yet the energy that he left upon the world is not yet stretched, nor yet expended to its full. It goes on adding new vigour as the ages roll on.

Now what you see in the life of Christ is the life of all the past. The life of every man is, in a manner, the life of the past. It comes to him through heredity, through surroundings, through education, through his own reincarnation—the past of the race. In a manner, the past of the earth, the past of the whole world is there, upon every soul. What are we, in the present, but a result, an effect in the hands of that infinite past? What are we but floating wavelets in the eternal current of events, irresistibly moved forward and onward and incapable of rest? But you and I are only little things, bubbles. There are always some giant waves in the ocean of affairs, and in you and me the life of the past race has been embodied only a little; but there are giants who embody, as it were, almost the whole of the past and who stretch out their hands for the future. These are the signposts here and there which point to the march of humanity; these are verily gigantic. Their shadows covering the earth—they stand undying, eternal! As it has been said by the same Messenger, "No man hath seen God at any time, but through the Son." And that is true. And where shall we see God but in the Son? It is true that you and I, and the poorest of us, the meanest even, embody that God, even reflect that God. The vibration of light is everywhere, omnipresent; bur we have to strike the light of the lamp before we can see the light. The Omnipresent God of the universe cannot be seen until He is reflected by these giant lamps of the earth—the Prophets, the man-Gods, the Incarnations, the embodiments of God.

We all know that God exists, and yet we do not see Him, we do not understand Him. Take one of these great Messengers of light, compare his character with the highest ideal of God that you ever formed, and you will find that your God falls short of the ideal, and that the character of the Prophet exceeds your conceptions. You cannot even form a higher ideal of God than what the actually embodied have practically realised and set before us as an example. Is it wrong, therefore, to worship these as God? Is it a sin to fall at the feet of these man-Gods and worship them as the only divine beings in the world? If they are really, actually, higher than all our conceptions of God, what harm is there in worshipping them? Not only is there no harm, but it is the only possible and positive way of worship. However much you may try by struggle, by abstraction, by whatsoever method you like, still so long as you are a man in the world of men, your world is human, your religion is human, and your God is human. And that must be so. Who is not practical enough to take up an actually existing thing and give up an idea which is only an abstraction, which he cannot grasp, and is difficult of approach except through a concrete medium? Therefore, these incarnations of God have been worshipped in all ages and in all countries.

We are now going to study a little of the life of Christ, the Incarnation of the Jews. When Christ was born, the Jews were in that state which I call a state of fall between two waves; a state of conservatism; a state where the human mind is, as it were, tired for the time being of moving forward and is taking care only of what it has already; a state when the attention is more bent upon particulars, upon details, than upon the great, general, and bigger problems of life; a state of stagnation, rather than a towing ahead; a state of suffering more than of doing. Mark you, I do not blame this state of things. We have no right to criticise it—because had it not been for this fall, the next rise, which was embodied in Jesus of Nazareth would have been impossible. The Pharisees and Sadducees might have been insincere, they might have been doing things which they ought not to have done; they might have been even hypocrites; but whatever they were, these factors were the very cause, of which the Messenger was the effect. The Pharisees and Sadducees at one end were the very impetus which came out at the other end as the gigantic brain of Jesus of Nazareth.

The attention to forms, to formulas, to the everyday details of religion, and to rituals, may sometimes be laughed at; but nevertheless, within them is strength. Many times in the rushing forward we lose much strength. As a fact, the fanatic is stronger than the liberal man. Even the fanatic, therefore, has one great virtue, he conserves energy, a tremendous amount of it. As with the individual so with the race, energy is gathered to be conserved. Hemmed in all around by external enemies, driven to focus in a centre by the Romans, by the Hellenic tendencies in the world of intellect, by waves from Persia, India, and Alexandria—hemmed in physically, mentally, and morally—there stood the race with an inherent, conservative, tremendous strength, which their descendants have not lost even today. And the race was forced to concentrate and focus all its energies upon Jerusalem and Judaism. But all power when once gathered cannot remain collected; it must expend and expand itself. There is no power on earth which can be kept long confined within a narrow limit. It cannot be kept compressed too long to allow of expansion at a subsequent period.

This concentrated energy amongst the Jewish race found its expression at the next period in the rise of Christianity. The gathered streams collected into a body. Gradually, all the little streams joined together, and became a surging wave on the top of which we find standing out the character of Jesus of Nazareth. Thus, every Prophet is a creation of his own times, the creation of the past of his race; he himself is the creator of the future. The cause of today is the effect of the past and the cause for the future. In this position stands the Messenger. In him is embodied all that is the best and greatest in his own race, the meaning, the life, for which that race has struggled for ages; and he himself is the impetus for the future, not only to his own race but to unnumbered other races of the world.

We must bear another fact in mind: that my view of the great Prophet of Nazareth would be from the standpoint of the Orient. Many times you forget, also, that the Nazarene himself was an Oriental of Orientals. With all your attempts to paint him with blue eyes and yellow hair, the Nazarene was still an Oriental. All the similes, the imageries, in which the Bible is written—the scenes, the locations, the attitudes, the groups, the poetry, and symbol,—speak to you of the Orient: of the bright sky, of the heat, of the sun, of the desert, of the thirsty men and animals; of men and women coming with pitchers on their heads to fill them at the wells; of the flocks, of the ploughmen, of the cultivation that is going on around; of the water-mill and wheel, of the mill-pond, of the millstones. All these are to be seen today in Asia.

The voice of Asia has been the voice of religion. The voice of Europe is the voice of politics. Each is great in its own sphere. **The voice of Europe is the voice of ancient Greece.** To the Greek mind, his immediate society was all in all: beyond that, it is Barbarian. None but the Greek has the right to live. Whatever the Greeks do is right and correct; whatever else there exists in the world is neither right nor correct, nor should be allowed to live. It is intensely human in its sympathies, intensely natural, intensely artistic, therefore. **The Greek lives entirely in this world.** He does not care to dream. Even his poetry is practical. **His gods and goddesses are not only human beings, but intensely human,** with all human passions and feelings almost the same as with any of us. **He loves what is beautiful, but, mind you, it is always external nature:** the beauty of the hills, of the snows, of the flowers, the beauty of forms and of figures, the beauty in the human face, and, more often, in the human form—that is what the Greeks liked. And the Greeks being the teachers of all subsequent Europeanism, the voice of Europe is Greek.

There is another type in Asia. Think of that vast, huge continent, whose mountain-tops go beyond the clouds, almost touching the canopy of heaven's blue; a rolling desert of miles upon miles where a drop of water cannot be found, neither will a blade of grass grow; interminable forests and gigantic rivers rushing down into the sea. In the midst of all these surroundings, **the Oriental love of the beautiful and of the sublime developed itself in another direction. It looked inside, and not outside.** There is also the thirst for nature, and there is also the same thirst for power; there is also the same thirst for excellence, the same idea of the Greek and the Barbarian, but it has extended over a larger circle. **In Asia, even today, birth or colour or language never makes a race. That which makes a race is its religion. We are all Christians; we are all Mohammedans; we are all Hindus, or all Buddhists. No matter if a Buddhist is a Chinaman, or is a man from Persia, they think that they are**

brothers, because of their professing the same religion. Religion is the tie, unity of humanity. And then again, **the Oriental, for the same reason, is a visionary, is a born dreamer.** The ripples of the waterfalls, the songs of the birds, the beauties of the sun and moon and the stars and the whole earth are pleasant enough; but they are not sufficient for the oriental mind. He wants to dream a dream beyond. **He wants to go beyond the present.** The present, as it were, is nothing to him. **The Orient has been the cradle of the human race for ages,** and all the vicissitudes of fortune are there—**kingdoms succeeding kingdoms, empires succeeding empires, human power, glory, and wealth,** all rolling down there: **a Golgotha of power and learning.** That is the Orient: a Golgotha of power, of kingdoms, of learning. No wonder, **the oriental mind looks with contempt upon the things of this world and naturally wants to see something that changeth not,** something which dieth not, something which in the midst of this world of misery and death is eternal, blissful, undying. An oriental Prophet never tires of insisting upon these ideals; and, as for Prophets, you may also remember that without one exception, **all the Messengers were Orientals.**

We see, therefore, in the life of this great Messenger of life, the first watchword: "Not this life, but something higher;" and, like the true son of the Orient, he is practical in that. You people of the West are practical in your own department, in military affairs, and in managing political circles and other things. Perhaps the Oriental is not practical in those ways, but he is practical in his own field; he is practical in religion. If one preaches a philosophy, tomorrow there are hundreds who will struggle their best to make it practical in their lives. If a man preaches that standing on one foot would lead one to salvation, he will immediately get five hundred to stand on one foot. You may call it ludicrous; but, mark you, beneath that is their philosophy—that intense practicality. In the West, plans of salvation mean intellectual gymnastics—plans which are never worked out, never brought into practical life. In the West, the preacher who talks the best is the greatest preacher.

So, we find **Jesus of Nazareth, in the first place, the true son of the Orient intensely practical.** He has no faith in this evanescent world and all its belongings. No need of text-torturing, as is the fashion in the West in modern times, no need of stretching out texts until they will not stretch any more. Texts are not India rubber, and even that has its limits. Now, no making of religion to pander to the sense of vanity of the present day! Mark you, let us all be honest. If we cannot follow the ideal, let us confess our weakness, but not degrade it; let not any one try to pull it down. One gets sick at heart at the different accounts of the life of the Christ that Western people give. I do not know what he was or what he was not! One would make him a great politician; another, perhaps, would make of him a great military general; another, a great patriotic Jew; and so on. Is there any warrant in the books for all such assumptions?

The best commentary on the life of a great teacher is his own life. "The foxes have holes, the birds of the air have nests, but the Son of man hath not where to lay his head." That is what Christ says as the only way to salvation; he lays down no other way. Let us confess in sackcloth and ashes that we cannot do that. We still have fondness for "me and mine". We want property, money, wealth. Woe unto us! Let us confess and not put to shame that great Teacher of Humanity! He had no family ties. But do you think that, that Man had any physical ideas in him? Do you think that, this mass of light, this God and not-man, came down to earth to be the brother of animals? And yet, people make him preach all sorts of things. He had no sex ideas! He was a soul! Nothing but a soul—just working a body for the good of humanity; and that was all his relation to the body. In the soul there is no sex. The disembodied soul has no relationship to the animal, no relationship to the body. The ideal may be far away beyond us. But never mind, keep to the ideal. Let us confess that it is our ideal, but we cannot approach it yet.

He had no other occupation in life, no other thought except that one, that he was a spirit. He was a disembodied, unfettered, unbound spirit. And not only so, but he, with his marvellous vision, had found that every man and woman, whether Jew or Gentile, whether rich or poor, whether saint or sinner, was the embodiment of the same undying spirit as himself. Therefore, the one work his whole life showed was to call upon them to realise their own spiritual nature. Give up, he says, these superstitious dreams that you are low and that you are poor. Think not that you are trampled upon and tyrannised over as if you were slaves, for within you is something that can never be tyrannised over, never be trampled upon, never be troubled, never be killed. You are all Sons of God, immortal spirit. "Know", he declared, "the Kingdom of Heaven is within you." "I and my Father are one." Dare you stand up and say, not only that "I am the Son of God", but I shall also find in my heart of hearts that "I and my Father are one"? That was what Jesus o£ Nazareth said. He never talks of this world and of this life. He has nothing to do with it, except that he wants to get hold of the world as it is, give it a push and drive it forward and onward until the whole world has reached to the effulgent Light of God, until everyone has realised his spiritual nature, until death is vanished and misery banished.

We have read the different stories that have been written about him; we know the scholars and their writings, and the higher criticism; and we know all that has been done by study. We are not here to discuss how much of the New Testament is true, we are not here to discuss how much of that life is historical. It does not matter at all whether the New Testament was written within five hundred years of his birth, nor does it matter even, how much of that life is true. But there is something behind it, something we want to imitate. To tell a lie, you have to imitate a truth, and that truth is a fact. You cannot imitate that which never existed. You cannot imitate that which you never perceived. But there must have been a nucleus, a tremendous power that came down, a marvellous manifestation of spiritual power—and of that we are speaking. It stands there. Therefore, we are not afraid of all the criticisms of the scholars.

If I, as an Oriental, have to worship Jesus of Nazareth, there is only one way left to me, that is, to worship him as God and nothing else. Have we no right to worship him in that way, do you mean to say? If we bring him down to our own level and simply pay him a little respect as a great man, why should we worship at all? Our scriptures say, "These great children of Light, who manifest the Light themselves, who are Light themselves, they, being worshipped, become, as it were, one with us and we become one with them."

For, you see, in three ways man perceives God. At first the undeveloped intellect of the uneducated man sees God as far away, up in the heavens somewhere, sitting on a throne as a great Judge. He looks upon Him as a fire, as a terror. Now, that is good, for there is nothing bad in it. You must remember that humanity travels not from error to truth, but from truth to truth; it may be, if you like it better, from lower truth to higher truth, but never from error to truth. Suppose you start from here and travel towards the sun in a straight line. From here the sun looks only small in size. Suppose you go forward a million miles, the sun will be much bigger. At every stage the sun will become bigger and bigger. Suppose twenty thousand photographs had been taken of the same sun, from different standpoints; these twenty thousand photographs will all certainly differ from one another. But can you deny that each is a photograph of the same sun? So all forms of religion, high or low, are just different stages toward that eternal state of Light, which is God Himself. Some embody a lower view, some a higher, and that is all the difference.

Therefore, the religions of the unthinking masses all over the world must be, and have always been, of a God who is outside of the universe, who lives in heaven, who governs from that place, who is a punisher of the bad and a rewarder of the good, and so on. As man advanced spiritually, he began to feel that God was omnipresent, that He must be in him, that He must be everywhere, that He was not a distant God, but clearly the Soul of all souls. As my soul moves my body, even so is God the mover of my soul. Soul within soul. And few individuals who had developed enough and were pure enough, went still further, and at last found God. As the New Testament says, "Blessed are the pure in heart, for they shall see God." And they found at last that they and the Father were one.

You find that all these three stages are taught by the Great Teacher in the New Testament. Note the Common Prayer he taught: "Our Father which art in Heaven, hallowed be Thy name," and so on—a simple prayer, a child's prayer. Mark you, it is the **"Common Prayer"** because it is intended for the uneducated masses. To a higher circle, to those who had advanced a little more, he gave a more **elevated teaching**: "I am in my Father, and ye in me, and I in you." Do you remember that? And then, when the Jews asked him who he was, **he declared that he and his Father were one,** and the Jews thought that that was blasphemy. What did he mean by that? This has been also told by your old Prophets, "Ye are gods and all of you are children of the Most High." Mark the same three stages. You will find that it is easier for you to begin with the first and end with the last.

The Messenger came to show the path: that the spirit is not in forms, that it is not through all sorts of vexations and knotty problems of philosophy that you know the spirit. Better that you had no learning, better that you never read a book in your life. These are not at all necessary for salvation—neither wealth, nor position nor power, not even learning; but what is necessary is that one thing, purity. "Blessed are the pure in heart," for the spirit in its own nature is pure. How can it be otherwise? It is of God, it has come from God. In the language of the Bible, "It is the breath of God." In the language of the Koran, "It is the soul of God."

Do you mean to say that the Spirit of God can ever be impure? But, alas, it has been, as it were, covered over with the dust and dirt of ages, through our own actions, good and evil. Various works which were not correct, which were not true, have covered the same spirit with the dust and dirt of the ignorance of ages. It is only necessary to clear away the dust and dirt, and then the spirit shines immediately. "Blessed are the pure in heart, for they shall see God." "The Kingdom of Heaven is within you." Where goest thou to seek for the Kingdom of God, asks Jesus of Nazareth, when it is there, within you? Cleanse the spirit, and it is there. It is already yours. How can you get what is not yours? It is yours by right. You are the heirs of immortality, sons of the Eternal Father.

This is the great lesson of the Messenger, and **another lesson which is the basis of all religions, is renunciation.** How can you make the spirit pure? By renunciation. A rich young man asked Jesus, "Good Master, what shall I do that I may inherit eternal life?" And Jesus said unto him, "One thing thou lackest; go thy way, sell whatsoever thou hast, and give to the poor, and thou shalt have treasures in heaven: and come, take up thy cross, and follow Me." And he was sad at that saying and went away grieved; for he had great possessions. We are all more or less like that. The voice is ringing in our ears day and night. In the midst of our pleasures and joys, in the midst of worldly things, we think that we have forgotten everything else. Then comes a moment's pause and the voice rings in our ears: "Give up all that thou hast and follow Me." "Whosoever will save his life shall lose it; and whosoever shall lose his life for My sake shall find it." For whoever gives up this life for His sake, finds the life immortal. In the midst of all our weakness there is a moment of pause and the voice rings: "Give up all that thou hast; give it to the poor and follow me."

This is the one ideal he preaches, and this has been the ideal preached by all the great Prophets of the world: renunciation. What is meant by renunciation? That there is only one ideal in morality: unselfishness. Be selfless. The ideal is perfect unselfishness. When a man is struck on the right cheek, he turns the left also. When a man's coat is carried off, he gives away his cloak also.

We should work in the best way we can, without dragging the ideal down. Here is the ideal. When a man has no more self in him, no possession, nothing to call "me" or "mine", has given himself up entirely, destroyed himself as it were—in that man is God Himself; for in him self-will is gone, crushed out, annihilated. That is the ideal man. We cannot reach that state yet; yet, let us worship the ideal, and slowly struggle to reach the ideal, though, maybe, with faltering steps. It may be tomorrow, or it may be a thousand years hence; but that ideal has to be reached. For it is not only the end, but also the means. To be unselfish, perfectly selfless, is salvation itself; for the man within dies, and God alone remains.

One more point. All the teachers of humanity are unselfish. Suppose Jesus of Nazareth was teaching, and a man came and told him, "What you teach is beautiful. I believe that it is the way to perfection, and I am ready to follow it; but I do not care to worship you as the only begotten Son of God." What would be the answer of Jesus of Nazareth? "Very well, brother, follow the ideal and advance in your own way. I do not care whether you give me the credit for the teaching or not. I am not a shopkeeper. I do not trade in religion. I only teach truth, and truth is nobody's property. Nobody can patent truth. Truth is God Himself. Go forward."

But what the disciples say nowadays is: "No matter whether you practise the teachings or not, do you give credit to the Man? If you credit the Master, you will be saved; if not, there is no salvation for you." And thus the whole teaching of the Master is degenerated, and all the struggle and fight is for the personality of the Man. They do not know that in imposing that difference, they are, in a manner, bringing shame to the very Man they want to honour—the very Man that would have shrunk with shame from such an idea. What did he care if there was one man in the world that remembered him or not? He had to deliver his message, and he gave it. And if he had twenty thousand lives, he would give them all up for the poorest man in the world. If he had to be tortured millions of times for a million despised Samaritans, and if for each one of them the sacrifice of his own life would be the only condition of salvation, he would have given his life. And all this without wishing to have his name known even to a single person.

Quiet, unknown, silent, would he work, just as the Lord works. Now, what would the disciple say? He will tell you that you may be a perfect man, perfectly unselfish; but unless you give the credit to our teacher, to our saint, it is of no avail. Why? What is the origin of this superstition, this ignorance? The disciple thinks that the Lord can manifest Himself only once. There lies the whole mistake. God manifests Himself to you in man. But throughout nature, what happens once must have happened before, and must happen in future. There is nothing in nature which is not bound by law; and that means that whatever happens once must go on and must have been going on.

In India they have the same idea of the Incarnations of God. One of their great Incarnations, Krishna, whose grand sermon, the

Bhagavad Gita, some of you might have read, says, "Though I am unborn, of changeless nature, and Lord of beings, yet subjugating My Prakriti, I come into being by My own Maya. Whenever virtue subsides and immorality prevails, then I body Myself forth. For the protection of the good, for the destruction of the wicked, and for the establishment of Dharma, I come into being, in every age." Whenever the world goes down, the Lord comes to help it forward; and so He does from time to time and place to place. In another passage He speaks to this effect: Wherever thou findest a great soul of immense power and purity struggling to raise humanity, know that he is born of My splendour, that I am there working through him.

Let us, therefore, find God not only in Jesus of Nazareth, but in all the great Ones that have preceded him, in all that came after him, and all that are yet to come. Our worship is unbounded and free. They are all manifestations of the same Infinite God. They are all pure and unselfish; they struggled and gave up their lives for us, poor human beings. They each and all suffer vicarious atonement for everyone of us, and also for all that are to come hereafter.

In a sense you are all Prophets; everyone of you is a Prophet, bearing the burden of the world on your own shoulders. Have you ever seen a man, have you ever seen a woman, who is not quietly, patiently, bearing his or her little burden of life? The great Prophets were giants—they bore a gigantic world on their shoulders. Compared with them we are pigmies, no doubt, yet **we are doing the same task; in our little circles, in our little homes, we are bearing our little crosses.** There is no one so evil, no one so worthless, but he has to bear his own cross. But with all our mistakes, with all our evil thoughts and evil deeds, there is a bright spot somewhere, there is still somewhere the golden thread through which we are always in touch with the divine. For, know for certain, that the moment the touch of the divine is lost there would be annihilation. And because none can be annihilated, there is always somewhere in our heart of hearts, however low and degraded we may be, a little circle of light which is in constant touch with the divine.

Our salutations go to all the past Prophets whose teachings and lives we have inherited, whatever might have been their race, clime, or creed! Our salutations go to all those Godlike men and women who are working to help humanity, whatever be their birth, colour, or race! Our salutations go to those who are coming in the future—living Gods—to work unselfishly for our descendants.

(*Talk delivered in Los Angeles, California, 1900*)

The Ether

Classification or grouping of phenomena by their similarities is the first step in scientific knowledge—perhaps it is all. An organized grouping, revealing to us a similarity running through the whole group, and a conviction that under similar circumstances the group will arrange itself in the same form—stretched over all time, past, present and future—is what we call law.

This finding of unity in variety is really what we call knowledge. These different groups of similars are stowed away m the pigeonholes of the mind, and when a new fact comes before us we begin to search for a similar group already existing in one of the pigeonholes of the mind. If we succeed in finding one readymade, we take the newcomer in immediately. If not, we either reject the new fact, or wait till we find more of his kind, and form a new place for the group.

Facts which are extraordinary thus disturb us; but and when we fmd many like them, they cease to disturb, even when our knowledge about their cause remains the same as before.

The ordinary experiences of our lives are no less wonderful than any miracles recorded in any sacred book of the world; nor are we any more enlightened as to the cause of these ordinary experiences than of the so-called miracles. But the miraculous is extraordinary and the everyday experience is ordinary. The "extraordinary" startles the mind, the "ordinary" satisfies.

The field of knowledge is so varied, and the more the difference is from the centre, the more widely the radii diverge.

At the start the different sciences were thought to have no connection whatever with each other; but as more and more knowledge comes in—that is, the more and more we come nearer the centre—the radii are converging more and more, and it seems that they are on the eve of finding a common centre. Will they ever find it?

The study of the mind was, above all, the science to which the sages of India and Greece had directed their attention. All religions are the outcome of the study of the inner man. Here we find the attempt at finding the unity, and in the science of religion, as taking its stand upon general and massive propositions, we find the boldest and the most vigorous manifestation of this tendency at finding the unity.

Some religions could not solve the problem beyond the finding of a duality of causes, one good, the other evil. Others went as far as finding an intelligent personal cause, a few went still further beyond intellect, beyond personality, and found an infinite being.

In those, and only those systems which dared to transcend beyond the personality of a limited human consciousness, we find also an attempt to resolve all physical phenomena into unity.

The result was the "Akasha" of the Hindus and the "Ether" of the Greeks.

This "Akasha" was, after the mind, the first material manifestation, said the Hindu sages, and out of this "Akasha" all this has been evolved.

History repeats itself; and again during the latter part of the nineteenth century, the same theory is coming with more vigour and fuller light.

It is being proved more clearly than ever that as there is a co-relation of physical forces there is also a co-relation of different branches of knowledge, and that behind all these general groups there is a unity of knowledge.

It was shown by Newton that if light consisted of material particles projected from luminous bodies, they must move faster in solids and liquids than in air, in order that the laws of refraction might be satisfied.

Huyghens, on the other hand, showed that to account for the same laws on the supposition that light consisted in the undulating motion of an elastic medium, it must move more slowly in solids and fluids than in gases. Fizeau and Foucault found Huyghens's predictions correct.

Light, then, consists in the vibrating motion of a medium, which must, of course, fill all space. This is called the Ether.

In the fact that the theory of a cosmic ether explains fully all the phenomena of radiation, refraction, diffraction and polarization of light is the strongest argument in favour of the theory.

Of late, gravitation, molecular action, magnetic, electric, and electro-dynamic attractions and repulsions have thus been explained.

Sensible and latent heat, electricity and magnetism themselves have been of late almost satisfactorily explained by the theory ot the all-pervading ether.

Zollner, however, basing his calculations upon the data supplied by the researches of Wilhelm Weber, thinks that the transmission of life force between the heavenly bodies is effected both ways, by the undulation of a medium and by the actual evidence of particles.

Weber found that the molecules, the smallest particles of bodies, were composed of yet smaller particles, which he called the electric particles, and which in the molecules are in a constant circular motion. These electric particles are partly positive, partly negative.

Those of the same electricity repulse; those of different electricity attracting each other, each molecule contains the same amount of electric particles, with a small surplus of either positive or negative quickly changing the balance.

Upon this Zollner builds these propositions:

(1) The molecules are composed of a very great number of particles—the so-called electric particles, which are in constant circular motion around each other within the molecule.

(2) If the inner motion of a molecule increases over a certain limit, then electric particles are emitted. They then travel from one heavenly body through space until they reach another heavenly body, where they are either reflected or absorbed by other molecules.

(3) The electric particles thus traversing space are the ether of the physicist.

(4) These ether particles have a twofold motion: first, their proper motion; second, an undulatory motion, for which they receive the impulse from the ether particles rotating in the molecules.

(5) The motion of the smallest particles corresponds to that of the heavenly bodies.

The corollary is:

The law of attraction which holds good for the heavenly bodies also holds good for the smallest particles.

Under these suppositions, that which we call space is really filled with electric particles, or ether.

Zollner also found the following interesting calculation for the electric atoms:

Velocity: 50,143 geographical miles per second.

Amount of ether particles in a water molecule: 42,000 million.

Distance from each other: 0.0032 millimeter.

So far as it goes, then, the theory of a universal cosmic ether is the best at hand to explain the various phenomena of nature.

As far as it goes, the theory that this ether consists of particles, electric or otherwise, is also very valuable. But on all suppositions, there must be space between two particles of ether, however small; and what fills this inter-ethereal space? If particles are still finer, we require still more fine ethereal particles to fill up the vacuum between every two of them, and so on.

Thus the theory of ether, or material particles in space, though accounting for the phenomena in space, cannot account for space itself.

And thus we are forced to find that the ether which comprehends the molecules explains the molecular phenomena, but itself cannot explain space because we cannot but think of ether as in space. And, therefore, if there is anything which will explain this space, it must be something that comprehends in its infinite being the infinite space itself. And what is there that can comprehend even the infinite space but the Infinite Mind?

(Article published in *New York* Medical Times, Feb. 1895)

The Four Paths of Yoga

Our main problem is to be free. It is evident then that until we realise ourselves as the Absolute, we cannot attain to deliverance. Yet there are various ways of attaining to this realisation. These methods have the generic name of Yoga—to join, to join ourselves to our reality. These Yogas, though divided into various groups, can principally be classed into four; and as each is only a method leading indirectly to the realisation of the Absolute, they are suited to different temperaments. Now it must be remembered that it is not that the assumed man becomes the real man or Absolute. There is no becoming with the Absolute. It is ever free, ever perfect; but the ignorance that has covered its nature for a time is to be removed. Therefore the whole scope of all systems of Yoga and each religion represents one is to clear up this ignorance and allow the Atman to restore its own nature. The chief helps in this liberation are Abhyasa and Vairagya. Vairagya is non-attachment to life, because it is the will to enjoy that brings all this bondage in its train; and Abhyasa is constant practice of anyone of the Yogas.

Karma Yoga. Karma Yoga is purifying the mind by means of work. Now if any work is done, good or bad, it must produce as a result a good or bad effect; no power can stay it, once the cause is present. Therefore, good action producing good Karma, and bad action, bad Karma, the soul will go on in eternal bondage without ever hoping for deliverance. Now Karma belongs only to the body or the mind, never to the Atman (Self) ; only it can cast a veil before the Atman.

The veil cast by bad Karma is ignorance. Good Karma has the power to strengthen the moral powers. And thus it creates non-attachment; it destroys the tendency towards bad Karma and thereby purifies the mind. But if the work is done with the intention of enjoyment, it then produces only that very enjoyment and does not purify the mind or Chitta. Therefore, all work should be done without any desire to enjoy the fruits thereof. All fear and all desire to enjoy here or hereafter must be banished for ever by the Karma-Yogi. Moreover, this Karma without desire of return will destroy the selfishness, which is the root of all bondage. The watchword of the Karma Yogi is "not I, but Thou", and no amount of self-sacrifice is too much for him. But he does this without any desire to go to heaven, or gain name or fame or any other benefit in this world. Although the explanation and rationale of this unselfish work is only in Jnana Yoga, yet the natural divinity of man makes him love all sacrifice simply for the good of others without any ulterior motive, whatever his creed or opinion. Again, with many the bondage of wealth is very great; and Karma Yoga is absolutely necessary for them as breaking the crystallisation that has gathered round their love of money.

Next is **Bhakti Yoga**. Bhakti or worship or love in some form or other is the easiest, pleasantest, and most natural way of man. The natural state of this universe is attraction; and that is surely followed by an ultimate disunion. Even so, love is the natural impetus of union in the human heart; and though itself a great cause of misery, properly directed towards the proper object, it brings deliverance. The object of Bhakti is God. Love cannot be without a subject and an object. The object of love again must be at first a being who can reciprocate our love. Therefore, the God of love must be in some sense a human God. He must be a God of love. Aside from the question whether such a God exists or not, it is a fact that to those who have love in their heart this Absolute appears as a God of love, as personal.

The lower forms of worship, which embody the idea of God as a judge or punisher or someone to be obeyed through fear, do not deserve to be called love, although they are forms of worship gradually expanding into higher forms. We pass on to the consideration of love itself. We will illustrate love by a triangle, of which the first angle at the base is fearlessness. So long as there is fear, it is not love. Love banishes all fear. A mother with her baby will face a tiger to save her child. The second angle is that love never asks, never begs. The third or the apex is that love loves for the sake of love itself. Even the idea of object vanishes. Love is the only form in which love is loved. This is the highest abstraction and the same as the Absolute.

Next is **Raja Yoga**. This Yoga fits in with everyone of these Yogas. It fits inquirers of all classes with or without any belief, and it is the real instrument of religious inquiry. As each science has its particular method of investigation, so is this Raja Yoga the method of religion. This science also is variously applied according to various constitutions. The chief parts are the Pranayama, concentration, and meditation. For those who believe in God, a symbolical name, such as Om or other sacred words received from a Guru, will be very helpful. Om is the greatest meaning, the Absolute. Meditating on the meaning of these holy names while repeating them is the chief practice.

Next is **Jnana Yoga**. This is divided into three parts. First: hearing the truth—that the Atman is the only reality and that everything else is Maya (relativity). Second: reasoning upon this philosophy from all points of view. Third: giving up all further argumentation and realising the truth. This realisation comes from (1) being certain that Brahman is real and everything else is unreal; (2) giving up all desire for enjoyment; (3) controlling the senses and the mind; (4) intense desire to be free. Meditating on this reality always and reminding the soul of its real nature are the only ways in this Yoga. It is the highest, but most difficult. Many persons get an intellectual grasp of it, but very few attain realisation.

Karma Yoga

The grandest idea in the religion of the Vedanta is that we may reach the same goal by different paths; and these paths I have generalised into four, viz., those of work, love, psychology, and knowledge. But these divisions are not very marked and quite exclusive of each other. Each blends into the other. But according to the type which prevails, we name the divisions. It is not that you can find men who have no other faculty than that of work, nor that you can find men who are no more than devoted worshippers only, nor that there are men who have no more than mere knowledge. These divisions are made in accordance with the type or the tendency that may be seen to prevail in a man. We have found that, in the end, all these four paths converge and become one. All religions and all methods of work and worship lead us to one and the same goal.

I have already tried to point out that goal. It is freedom as I understand it. Everything that we perceive around us is struggling towards freedom, from the atom to the man, from the insentient, lifeless particle of matter to the highest existence on earth, the human soul. The whole universe is in fact the result of this struggle for freedom. In all combinations every particle is trying to go on its own way, to fly from the other particles; but the others are holding it in check. Our earth is trying to fly away from the sun, and the moon from the earth. Everything has a tendency to infinite dispersion. All that we see in the universe has for its basis this one struggle towards freedom; it is under the impulse of this tendency that the saint prays and the robber robs. When the line of action taken is not a proper one, we call it evil; and when the manifestation of it is proper and high, we call it good. But the impulse is the same, the struggle towards freedom. The saint is oppressed with the knowledge of his condition of bondage, and he wants to get rid of it; so he worships God. The thief is oppressed with the idea that he does not possess certain things, and he tries to get rid of that want, to obtain freedom from it; so he steals. Freedom is the one goal of all nature, sentient or insentient; and consciously or unconsciously, everything is struggling towards that goal. The freedom which the saint seeks is very different from that which the robber seeks; the freedom loved by the saint leads him to the enjoyment of infinite, unspeakable bliss, while that on which the robber has set his heart only forges other bonds for his soul.

There is to be found in every religion the manifestation of this struggle towards freedom. It is the groundwork of all morality, of unselfishness, which means getting rid of the idea that men are the same as their little body. When we see a man doing good work, helping others, it means that he cannot be confined within the limited circle of "me and mine", there is no limit to this getting out of selfishness. All the great systems of ethics preach absolute unselfishness as the goal. Supposing this absolute unselfishness can be reached by a man, what becomes of him? He is no more the little Mr. So-and-so; he has acquired infinite expansion. The little personality which he had before is now lost to him for ever; he has become infinite, and the attainment of this infinite expansion is indeed the goal of all religions and of all moral and philosophical teachings. The personalist, when he hears this idea philosophically put, gets frightened. At the same time, if he preaches morality, he after all teaches the very same idea himself. He puts no limit to the unselfishness of man. Suppose a man becomes perfectly unselfish under the personalistic system, how are we to distinguish him from the perfected ones in other system? He has become one with the universe and to become that is the goal of all; only the poor personalist has not the courage to follow out his own reasoning to its right conclusion. Karma Yoga is the attaining through unselfish work of that freedom which is the goal of all human nature. Every selfish action, therefore, retards our reaching the goal, and every unselfish action takes us towards the goal; that is why the only definition that can be given of morality is this: *That which is selfish is immoral, and that which is unselfish is moral.*

But, if you come to details, the matter will not be seen to be quite so simple. For instance, environment often makes the details different as I have already mentioned. The same action under one set of circumstances may be unselfish, and under another set quite selfish. So we can give only a general definition, and leave the details to be worked out by taking into consideration the differences in time, place, and circumstances. In one country one kind of conduct is considered moral, and in another the very same is immoral, because the circumstances differ. The goal of all nature is freedom, and freedom is to be attained only by perfect unselfishness; every thought, word, or deed that is unselfish takes us towards the goal, and, as such, is called moral.

That definition holds good in every religion and every system of ethics. In some systems of thought morality is derived from a Superior Being—God. If you ask why a man ought to do this and not that, their answer is: "Because such is the command of God." But whatever be the source from which it is derived, their code of ethics also has the same central idea—not to think of self but to give up self. And yet some persons, in spite of this high ethical idea, are frightened at the thought of having to give up their little personalities. We may ask the man who clings to the idea of little personalities to consider the case of a person who has become perfectly unselfish, who has no thought for himself, who does no deed for himself, who speaks no word for himself, and then say where his "himself" is. That "himself" is known to him only so long as he thinks, acts, or speaks for himself. If he is only conscious of others, of the universe, and of the all, where is his "himself'? It is gone for ever.

Karma Yoga, therefore, is a system of ethics and religion intended to attain freedom through unselfishness, and by good works. **The Karma Yogi need not believe in any doctrine whatever. He may not believe even in God,** may not ask what his soul is, nor think of any metaphysical speculation. **He has got his own special aim of realising selflessness; and he has to work it out himself.** Every moment of his life must be realisation, because he has to solve by mere work, without the help of doctrine or theory, the very same problem to which the Jnani applies his reason and inspiration and the Bhakta his love.

Now comes the next question: **What is this work? What is this doing good to the world? Can we do good to the world? In an absolute sense, no; in a relative sense, yes.** No permanent or everlasting good can be done to the world; if it could be done, the world would not be this world. We may satisfy the hunger of a man for five minutes, but he will be hungry again. Every pleasure with which we supply a man may be seen to be momentary. No one can permanently cure this ever-recurring fever of pleasure and pain. **Can any permanent happiness be given to the world?** In the ocean we cannot raise a wave without causing a hollow somewhere else. The sum total of the good things in the world has been the same throughout in its relation to man's need and greed. It cannot be increased or decreased.

Take the history of the human race as we know it today. Do we not find the same miseries and the same happiness, the same pleasures and pains, the same differences in position? Are not some rich, some poor, some high, some low, some healthy, some unhealthy? All this was just the same with the Egyptians, the Greeks, and the Romans in ancient times as it is with the Americans today. So far as history is known, it has always been the same; yet at the same time we find that, running along with all these incurable differences of pleasure and pain, there has ever been the struggle to alleviate them. Every period of history has given birth to thousands of men and women who have worked hard to smooth the passage of life for others. And how far have they succeeded? We can only play at driving the ball from one place to another. We take away pain from the physical plane, and it goes to the mental one. It is like that picture in Dante's hell where the misers were given a mass of gold to roll up a hill. Every time they rolled it up a little, it again rolled down. All our talks about the millennium are very nice as schoolboys' stories, but they are no better than that. All nations that dream of the millennium also think that, of all peoples in the world, they will have the best of it then for themselves. This is the wonderfully unselfish idea of the millennium!

We cannot add happiness to this world; similarly, we cannot add pain to it either. The sum total of the energies of pleasure and pain displayed here on earth will be the same throughout. We just push it from this side to the other side, and from that side to this, but it will remain the same, because to remain so is its very nature. This ebb and flow, this rising and falling, is in the world's very nature; it would be as logical to hold otherwise as to say that we may have life without death. This is complete nonsense, because the very idea of life implies death and the very idea of pleasure implies pain. The lamp is constantly burning out, and that is its life. If you want to have life, you have to die every moment for it. Life and death are only different expressions of the same thing looked at from different standpoints; they are the failing and the rising of the same wave, and the two form one whole. One looks at the "fall" side and becomes a pessimist, another looks at the "rise" side and becomes an optimist. When a boy is going to school and his father and mother are taking care of him, everything seems blessed to him; his wants are simple, he is a great optimist. But the old man, with his varied experience, becomes calmer, and is sure to have his warmth considerably cooled down. So, old nations, with signs of decay all around them, are apt to be less hopeful than new nations. There is a proverb in India: "A thousand years a city, and a thousand years a forest." This change of city into forest and vice versa is going on everywhere, and it makes people optimists or pessimists according to the side they see of it.

The next idea we take up is **the idea of equality**. These millennium ideas have been great motive powers to work. Many religions preach this as an element in them—that God is coming to rule the universe, and that then there will be no difference at all in conditions. The people who preach this doctrine are mere fanatics, and fanatics are indeed the sincerest of mankind. Christianity was preached just on the basis of the fascination of this fanaticism, and that is what made it so attractive to the Greek and the Roman slaves. They believed that under the millennial religion there would be no more slavery, that there would be plenty to eat and drink; and, therefore, they flocked round the Christian standard. Those who preached the idea first were of course ignorant fanatics, but very sincere.

In modern times this millennial aspiration takes the form of equality—of liberty, equality, and fraternity. This is also fanaticism. True equality has never been and never can be on earth. How can we all be equal here? This impossible kind of equality implies total death. What makes this world what it is? Lost balance. In the primal state, which is called chaos, there is perfect balance. How do all the formative forces of the universe come then? By struggling, competition, conflict. Suppose that all the particles of matter were held in equilibrium, would there be then any process of creation? We know from science that it is impossible. Disturb a sheet of water, and there you find every particle of the water trying to become calm again, one rushing against the other; and in the same way all the phenomena which we call the universe—all things therein—are struggling to get back to the state of perfect balance. Again a disturbance comes, and again we have combination and creation.

Inequality is the very basis of creation. At the same time the forces struggling to obtain equality are as much a necessity of creation as those which destroy it.

Absolute equality, that which means a perfect balance of all the struggling forces in all the planes, can never be in this world. Before you attain that state, the world will have become quite unfit for any kind of life, and no one will be there. We find, therefore, that all these ideas of the millennium and of absolute equality are not only impossible but also that, if we try to carry them out, they will lead us surely enough to the day of destruction. **What makes the difference between man and man? It is largely the difference in the brain.** Nowadays no one but a lunatic will say that we are all born with the same brain power. We come into the world with unequal endowments; we came as greater men or as lesser men, and there is no getting away from that prenatally determined condition.

The American Indians were in this country for thousands of years, and a few handfuls of your ancestors come to their land. What difference they have caused in the appearance of the country! Why did not the Indians make improvements and build cities, if all were equal? With your ancestors a different sort of brain power came into the land, different bundles of past impressions came, and they worked out and manifested themselves. Absolute non-differentiation is death. **So long as this world lasts, differentiation there will and must be,** and the millennium of perfect equality will come only when a cycle of creation comes to its end. Before that, equality cannot be. **Yet this idea of realising the millennium is a great motive power. Just as inequality is necessary for creation itself, so the struggle to limit it is also necessary.** If there were no struggle to become free and get back to God, there would be no creation either. It is the difference between these two forces that determines the nature of the motives of men. There will always be these motives to work, some tending towards bondage and others towards freedom.

This world's wheel within wheel is a terrible mechanism: if we put our hands in it, as soon as we are caught we are gone. We all think that when we have done a certain duty, we shall be at rest; but before we have done a part of that duty, another is already in waiting. **We are all being dragged along by this mighty, complex world-machine.** There are only two ways out of it; one is to give up all concerns with the machine, to let it go and stand aside, to give up our desires. That is very easy to say, but is almost impossible to do. I do not know whether in twenty millions of men one can do that. **The other way is to plunge into the world and learn the secret of work, and that is the way of Karma Yoga.** Do not fly away from the wheels of the world-machine, but stand inside it and learn the secret of work. Through proper work done inside, it is also possible to come out. Through this machinery itself is the way out.

We have now seen what work is. It is a part of nature's foundation, and goes on always. Those that believe in God understand this better, because they know that God is not such an incapable being as will need our help. Although this universe will go on always, our goal is freedom, our goal is unselfishness; and according to Karma Yoga, that goal is to be reached through work. All ideas of making the world perfectly happy may be good as motive powers for fanatics; but we must know that fanaticism brings forth as much evil as good. The Karma Yogi asks why you require any motive to work other than the inborn love of freedom. Be beyond the common worldly motives. **"To work you have the right, but not to the fruits thereof." Man can train himself to know and to practise that, says the Karma Yogi.** When the idea of doing good becomes a part of his very being, then he will not seek for any motive outside. Let us do good because it is good to do good; he who does good work even in order to get to heaven binds himself down, says the Karma Yogi. Any work that is done with any the least selfish motive, instead of making us free, forges one more chain for our feet.

So the only way is to give up all the fruits of work, to be unattached to them. Know that this world is not we, nor are we this world; that we are really not the body; that we really do not work. We are the Self, eternally at rest and at peace. Why should we be bound by anything? It is very good to say that we should be perfectly non-attached, but what is the way to do it? **Every good work we do without any ulterior motive, instead of forging a new chain, will break one of the links in the existing chains. Every good thought that we send to the world without thinking of any return, will be stored up there and break one link in the chain, and make us purer and purer,** until we become the purest of mortals. Yet all this may seem to be rather quixotic and too philosophical, more theoretical than practical. I have read many arguments against the Bhagavad-Gita, and many have said that without motives you cannot work. They have never seen unselfish work except under the influence of fanaticism, and, therefore, they speak in that way.

Let me tell you in conclusion a few words about one man who actually carried this teaching of Karma Yoga into practice. That man is Buddha. He is the one man who ever carried this into perfect practice. All the prophets of the world, except Buddha, had external motives to move them to unselfish action. The prophets of the world, with this single exception, may be divided into two sets, one set holding that they are incarnations of God come down on earth, and the other holding that they are only messengers from God; and both draw their impetus for work from outside, expect reward from outside, however highly spiritual may be the language they use. But Buddha is the only prophet who said, "I do not care to know your various theories about God. What is the use of discussing all the subtle doctrines about the soul? Do good and be good. And this will take you to freedom and to whatever truth there is." He was, in the conduct of his life, absolutely without personal motives; and what man worked more than he? Show me in history one character who has soared so high above all.

The whole human race has produced but one such character, such high philosophy, such wide sympathy. This great philosopher, preaching the highest philosophy, yet had the deepest sympathy for the lowest of animals, and never put forth any claims for himself. He is the ideal Karma Yogi, acting entirely without motive, and the history of humanity shows him to have been the greatest man ever born; beyond compare the greatest combination of heart and brain that ever existed, the greatest soul-power that has even been manifested. He is the first great reformer the world has seen. He was the first who dared to say, "Believe not because some old manuscripts are produced, believe not because it is your national belief, because you have been made to believe it from your childhood; but reason it all out, and after you have analysed it, then, if you find that it will do good to one and all, believe it, live up to it, and help others to live up to it." He works best who works without any motive, neither for money, nor for fame, nor for anything else; and when a man can do that, he will be a Buddha, and out of him will come the power to work in such a manner as will transform the world. This man represents the very highest ideal of Karma Yoga.

Bhakti Yoga

Now we shall consider the Yoga through devotion. But you must remember that no one system is necessary for all. I want to set before you many systems, many ideals, in order that you may find one that will suit you; if one does not, perhaps another may.

We want to become harmonious beings, with the psychical, spiritual, intellectual, and working (active) sides of our nature equally developed. Nations and individuals typify one of these sides or types and cannot understand more than that one. They get so built up into one ideal that they cannot see any other. The ideal is really that we should become manysided. Indeed the cause of the misery of the world is that we are so onesided that we cannot sympathise with one another. Consider a man looking at the sun from beneath the earth, up the shaft of a mine; he sees one aspect of the sun. Then another man sees the sun from the earth's level, another through mist and fog, another from the mountain top. To each the sun has a different appearance. So there are many appearances, but in reality there is only one sun. There is diversity of vision, but one object; and that is the sun.

Each man, according to his nature, has a peculiar tendency and takes to certain ideals and a certain path by which to reach them. But the goal is always the same to all. The Roman Catholic is deep and spiritual, but he has lost breadth. The Unitarian is wide, but he has lost spirituality and considers religion as of divided importance. What we want is the depth of the Roman Catholic and the breadth of the Unitarian. We must be as broad as the skies, as deep as the ocean; we must have the zeal of the fanatic, the depth of the mystic, and the width of the agnostic. The word "toleration" has acquired an unpleasant association with the conceited man who, thinking himself in a high position, looks down on his fellow-creatures with pity. This is a horrible state of mind. We are all travelling the same way, towards the same goal, but by different paths made by the necessities of the case to suit diverse minds. We must become manysided, indeed we must become protean in character, so as not only to tolerate, but to do what is much more difficult, to sympathise, to enter into another's path, and feel with him in his aspirations and seeking after God.

There are two elements in every religion—a positive and a negative. In Christianity, for instance, when you speak of the Incarnation, of the Trinity, of salvation through Jesus Christ, I am with you. I say, "Very good, that I also hold true." But when you go on to say, "There is no other true religion, there is no other revelation of God," then I say, "Stop, I cannot go with you when you shut out, when you deny." Every religion has a message to deliver, something to teach man; but when it begins to protest, when it tries to disturb others, then it takes up a negative and therefore a dangerous position, and does not know where to begin or where to end.

Every force completes a circuit. The force we call man starts from the Infinite God and must return to Him. This return to God must be accomplished in one of two ways—either by slowly drifting back, going with nature, or by our own inward power, which causes us to stop on our course, which would, if left alone, carry us in a circuit back to God, and violently turn round and find God, as it were, by a short cut. This is what the Yogi does.

I have said that every man must choose his own ideal which is in accord with his nature. This ideal is called a man's Ishta. You must keep it sacred, and therefore secret, and when you worship God, worship according to your Ishta. How are we to find out the particular method? It is very difficult, but as you persevere in your worship, it will come of itself. Three things are the special gifts of

God to man—the human body, the desire to be free, and the blessing of help from one who is already free. Now, we cannot have devotion without a Personal God. There must be the lover and the beloved. God is an infinitised human being. It is bound to be so, for so long as we are human, we must have a humanised God, we are forced to see a Personal God and Him only. Consider how all that we see in this world is not the object pure and simple, but the object plus our own mind. The chair plus the chair's reaction on your mind is the real chair. You must colour everything with your mmd, and then alone you can see it. (Example: The white, square, shiny, hard box, seen by the man with three senses, then by the man with four senses, then by him with five senses. The last alone sees it with all the enumerated qualities, and each one before has seen an additional one to the previous man. Now suppose a man with six senses sees the same box, he would see still another quality added.)

Because I see love and knowledge, I know the universal cause is manifesting that love and knowledge. How can that be loveless which causes love in me? We cannot think of the universal cause without human qualities. **To see God as separate from ourselves in the universe is necessary as a first step.** There are three visions of God: the lowest vision, when God seems to have a body like ourselves (see Byzantine art); a higher vision when we invest God with human qualities; and then on and on, till we come to the highest vision, when we see God.

But remember that in all these steps we are seeing God and God alone; there is no illusion in it, no mistake. Just as when we saw the sun from different points, it was still the sun and not the moon or anything else.

We cannot help seeing God as we are—infinitised, but still as we are. Suppose we tried to conceive God as the

Absolute, we should have again to come back to the relative state in order to enjoy and love.

The devotion to God as seen in every religion is divided into two parts: the devotion which works through forms and ceremonies and through words, and that which works through love. In this world we are bound by laws, and we are always striving to break through these laws, we are always trying to disobey, to trample on nature. For instance, nature gives us no houses, we build them. Nature made us naked, we clothe ourselves. Man's goal is to be free, and just in so far as we are incompetent to break nature's laws shall we suffer. We only obey nature's law in order to be outlawed—beyond law. The whole struggle of life is not to obey. (That is why I sympathise with Christian Scientists, for they teach the liberty of man and the divinity of soul.) The soul is superior to all environment. "The universe is my father's kingdom; I am the heir-apparent"—that is the attitude for man to take. "My own soul can subdue all."

We must work through law before we come to liberty. External helps and methods, forms, ceremonies, creeds, doctrines, all have their right place and are meant to support and strengthen us until we become strong. Then they are no more necessary. They are our nurses, and as such indispensable in youth. Even books are nurses, medicines are nurses. But we must work to bring about the time when man shall recognise his mastery over his own body. Herbs and medicines have power over us as long as we allow them; when we become strong, these external methods are no more necessary.

Worship through Words and Love

Body is only mind in a grosser form, mind being composed of finer layers and the body being the denser layers; and when man has perfect control over his mind, he will also have control over his body. Just as each mind has its own peculiar body, so to each word belongs a particular thought. We talk in double consonants when we are angry—"stupid", "fool", "idiot", etc.; in soft vowels when we are sad—"Ah me! " These are momentary feelings, of course; but there are eternal feelings, such as love, peace, calmness, joy, holiness; and **these feelings have their word-expression in all religions,** the word being only the embodiment of these, man's highest feelings. **Now the thought has produced the word, and in their turn these words may produce the thoughts or feelings.** This is where the help of words come in. Each of such words covers one ideal. These **sacred mysterious words we all recognise and know,** and yet if we merely read them in books, they have no effect on us. **To be effective, they must be charged with spirit,** touched and used by one who has himself been touched by the Spirit of God and who now lives. It is only he who can set the current in motion. The "laying on of hands" is the continuation of that current which was set in motion by Christ. The one who has the power of transmitting this current is called a Guru. With great teachers the use of words is not necessary—as with Jesus. But the "small fry" transmit this current through words.

Do not look on the faults of others. You cannot judge a man by his faults. (Example: Suppose we were to judge of an apple tree by the rotten, unripe, unformed apples we find on the ground. Even so do the faults of a man not show what the man's character is.) Remember, the wicked are always the same all over the world. The thief and the murderer are the same in Asia and Europe and America. They form a nation by themselves. It is only in the good and the pure and the strong that you find variety. Do not recognise wickedness in others. Wickedness is ignorance, weakness. What is the good of telling people they are weak? Criticism and destruction are of no avail. We must give them something higher; tell them of their own glorious nature, their birthright. Why do not more people come to God? The reason is that so few people have any enjoyments outside their five senses. The majority *cannot* see with their eyes nor hear with their ears in the inner world.

We now come to *Worship through Love.*

It has been said, "It is good to be born in a church, but not to die in it." The tree receives support and shelter from the hedge that surrounds it when young; but unless the hedge is removed, the growth and strength of that tree will be hindered. Formal worship, as we have seen, is a necessary stage, but gradually by slow growth we outgrow it and come to a higher platform. When love to God becomes perfect, we think no more of the qualities of God—that He is omnipotent, omnipresent, and all those big adjectives. We do not *want* anything of God, so we do not care to notice these qualities. Just all we want is love of God. But anthropomorphism still follows us. **We cannot get away from our humanity, we cannot jump out of our bodies; so we must love God as we love one another.**

There are five steps in human love:

1. The lowest, most commonplace, when we look up to our Father for protection, food, etc.
2. The love which makes us want to serve. Man wants to serve God as his master, the longing to serve dominating every other feeling; and we are indifferent whether the master is good or bad, kind or unkind.
3. The love of a friend, the love of equals—companions, playmates. Man feels God to be his companion.
4. Motherly love. God is looked upon as a child. In India this is considered a higher love than the foregoing, because it has absolutely no element of fear.
5. The love of husband and wife; love for love's sake—God the perfect, beloved one.

It has been beautifully expressed: "Four eyes meet, a change begins to come into two souls; love comes in the middle between these two souls and makes them one."

When a man has this last and most perfect form of love, then all desires vanish, forms and doctrines and churches drop away, even the desire for freedom—the end and aim of all religions is freedom from birth and death and other things—is given up. The highest love is the love that is sexless, for it is perfect unity that is expressed in the highest love, and sex differentiates bodies. It is therefore only in spirit that union is possible. The less we have of the physical idea, the more perfect will be our love; at last all physical thought will be forgotten, and the two souls will become one. We love, love always. Love comes and penetrates through the forms and sees beyond. It has been said, "The lover sees Helen's beauty in an Ethiopian's brow." The Ethiopian is the suggestion and upon that suggestion the man throws his love. As the oyster throws over the irritants, it finds in its shell the substance that turns the irritants into beautiful pearls, so man throws out love, and it is always man's highest ideal that he loves, and the highest ideal is always selfless; so man loves love. God is love, and we love God—or love love. We only *see* love, love cannot be expressed. "A dumb man eating butter" cannot tell you what butter is like. Butter is butter, and its qualities cannot be expressed to those who have not tasted it. Love for love's sake cannot be expressed to those who have not felt it.

Love may be symbolised by a triangle. The first angle is, love never begs, never asks for anything; the second, love knows no fear; the third and the apex, love for love's sake.

Through the power of love the senses become finer and higher. The perfect love is very rare in human relations, for human love is almost always interdependent and mutual. But God's love is a constant stream, nothing can hurt or disturb it. When man loves God as his highest ideal, as no beggar, wanting nothing, then is love carried to the extreme of evolution, and it becomes a great power in the universe. It takes a long time to get to these things and we have to begin by that which is nearest to our nature; some are born to service, some to be mothers in love. Anyhow, the result is with God. We must take advantage of nature.

On Doing Good to the World

We are asked: What good is your Religion to society? Society is made a test of truth. Now this is very illogical. Society is only a stage of growth through which we are passing. We might just as well judge the good or utility of a scientific discovery by its use to the baby. It is simply monstrous. If the social state were permanent it would be the same as if the baby remained a baby. There can be no perfect man-baby; the words are a contradiction in terms, so there can be no perfect society. Man must and will grow out of such early stages. Society is good at a certain stage, but it cannot be our ideal; it is a constant flux. The present mercantile civilisation must die, with all its pretensions and humbug-all a kind of "Lord Mayor's Show".

What the world wants is thought-power through individuals. My Master used to say, "Why don't you help your own lotus flower to bloom? The bees will then come of themselves." The world needs people who are mad with the love of God. You must believe in yourself, and then you will believe in God. The history of the world is that of six men of faith, six men of deep pure character. We need to have three things; the heart to feel, the brain to conceive, the hand to work. First we must go out of the world and make ourselves fit instruments. Make yourself a dynamo. *Feel* first for the world. At a time when all men are ready to work, where is the man of *feeling?* Where is the feeling that produced an Ignatius Loyola? Test your love and humility. That man is not humble or loving who is jealous. Jealousy is a terrible horrible sin; it enters a man so mysteriously. Ask yourself, does your mind react in hatred or jealousy? Good works are continually being undone by the tons of hatred and anger which are being poured out on the world. If you are pure, if you are strong, you, one man, are equal to the whole world.

The brain to conceive the next condition of doing good works is only a dry Sahara after all; it cannot do anything alone unless it has the *feeling* behind it. Take love, which has never failed; and then the brain will conceive, and the hand will work righteousness. Sages have dreamed of and have *seen* the vision of God. "The pure in heart shall see God." All the great ones claim to have *seen* God. Thousands of years ago has the vision been seen, and the unity which lies beyond has been recognised; and now the only thing we can do is to fill in these glorious outlines.

I once knew a Yogi, a very old man, who lived in a hole in the ground all by himself. All he had was a pan or two to cook his meals in. He ate very little, and wore scarcely anything, and spent most of his time meditating.

With him all people were alike. He had attained to non-injuring. What he saw in everything, in every person, in every animal, was the Soul, the Lord of the Universe. With him, every person and every animal was "my Lord". He never addressed any person or animal in any other way. Well, one day a thief came his way and stole one of his pans. He saw him and ran after him. The chase was a long one. At last the thief from exhaustion had to stop, and the Yogi, running up to him, fell on his knees before him and said, "My Lord, you do me a great honour to come my way. Do me the honour to accept the other pan. It is also yours." This old man is dead now. He was full of love for everything in the world. He would have died for an ant. Wild animals instinctively knew this old man to be their friend. Snakes and ferocious animals would go into his hole and sleep with him. They all loved him and never fought in his presence.

Never talk about the faults of others, no matter how bad they may be. Nothing is ever gained by that. You never help one by talking about his fault; you do him an injury, and injure yourself as well.

All regulations in eating, practising, etc., are all right so long as they are complementary to a spiritual aspiration but they are not ends in themselves; they are only helps.

Never quarrel about religion. All quarrels and disputations concerning religion simply show that spirituality is not present. Religious quarrels are always over the husks. When purity, when spirituality goes, leaving the soul dry, quarrels begin, and not before.

Raja Yoga

Prana

The theory of creation is that matter is subject to five conditions: ether, luminous ether, gaseous, liquid, and solid. They are all evoked out of one primal element, which is very finest ether.

The name of the energy in the universe is Prana, which is the force residing in these elements. Mind is the great instrument for using the Prana. Mind is material. Behind the mind is Atman which takes hold of the Prana. Prana is the driving power of the world, and can be seen in every manifestation of life. The body is mortal and the mind is mortal; both, being compounds, must die. Behind all is the Atman which never dies. The Atman is pure intelligence controlling and directing Prana. But the intelligence we see around us is always imperfect. When intelligence is perfect, we get the Incarnation—the Christ. Intelligence is always trying to manifest itself, and in order to do this it is creating minds and bodies of different degrees of development. In reality, and at the back of all things, every being is equal.

Mind is very fine matter; it is the instrument for manifesting Prana. Force requires matter for manifestation.

The next point is how to use this Prana. We all use it but how sadly we waste it! The first doctrine in the preparatory stage is that all knowledge is the outcome of experience. Whatever is beyond the five senses must also be experienced in order to become true to us.

Our mind is acting on three planes: the subconscious, conscious, and superconscious. Of men, the Yogi alone is superconscious. The whole theory of Yoga is to go beyond the mind. These three planes can be understood by considering the vibrations of light or sound. There are certain vibrations of light too slow to become visible; then as they get faster, we see them as light; and then they get too fast for us to see them at all. The same with sound.

How to transcend the senses without disturbing the health is what we want to learn. The Western mind has stumbled into acquiring some of the psychic gifts which in them are abnormal and are frequently the sign of disease. The Hindu has studied and made perfect this subject of science, which all may now study without fear or danger.

Mental healing is a fine proof of the superconscious state; for the thought which heals is a sort of vibration in the Prana, and it does not go as a thought but as something higher for which we have no name.

Each thought has three states. First, the rising or beginning, of which we are unconscious; second, when the thought rises to the surface; and third, when it goes from us. **Thought is like a bubble rising to the surface. When thought is joined to will, we call it power.** That which strikes the sick person whom you are trying to help is not thought, but power. The self-man running through it all is called in Sanskrit Sutratma, the "Thread-self".

The last and highest manifestation of Prana is love. The moment you have succeeded in manufacturing love out of Prana, you are free. It is the hardest and the greatest thing to gain. You must not criticise others; you must criticise yourself. If you see a drunkard, do not criticise him; remember he is you in another shape. He who has not darkness sees no darkness in others. What you have inside you is that you see in others. This is the surest way of reform. If the would-be reformers who criticise and see evil would themselves stop creating evil, the world would be better. Beat this idea into yourself.

The body must be properly taken care of. The people who torture their flesh are demoniacal. Always keep your mind joyful; if melancholy thoughts come, kick them out. A Yogi must not eat too much, but he also must not fast; he must not sleep too much, but he must not go without any sleep. In all things only the man who holds the golden mean can become a Yogi.

What is the best time for practice in Yoga? The junction time of dawn and twilight, when all nature becomes calm. Take help of nature. Take the easiest posture in sitting. Have the three parts straight—the ribs, the shoulders, and the head—leaving the spine free and straight, no leaning backwards or forwards. Then mentally hold the body as perfect, part by part. Then send a current of love to all the world; then pray for enlightenment. And lastly, join your mind to your breath and gradually attain the power of concentrating your attention on its movements. The reason for this will be apparent by degrees.

The Ojas

The "Ojas" is that which makes the difference between man and man. The man who has much Ojas is the leader of men. It gives a tremendous power of attraction. **Ojas is manufactured from the nerve-currents.** It has this peculiarity: **it is most easily made from that force which manifests itself in the sexual powers.** If the powers of the sexual centres are not frittered away and their energies wasted action is only thought in a grosser state, they can be manufactured into Ojas. The two great nerve-currents of the body start from the brain, go down on each side of the spinal cord, but they cross in the shape of the figure 8 at the back of the head. Thus the left side of the body is governed by the right side of the head. At the lowest point of the circuit is the sexual centre, the Sacral Plexus. The energy conveyed by these two currents of nerves comes down, and a large amount is continually being stored in the Sacral Plexus. The last bone in the spine is over the Sacral Plexus and is described in symbolic language as a triangle; and as the energy is stored up beside it, this energy is symbolised by a serpent.

Consciousness and sub-consciousness work through these two nerve-currents. But superconsciousness takes off the nerve-current when it reaches the lower end of the circuit, and instead of allowing it to go up and complete the circuit, stops and forces it up the spinal cord as Ojas from the Sacral Plexus. The spinal cord is naturally closed, but it can be opened to form a passage for this Ojas. As the current travels from one centre of the spinal cord to another, you can travel from one plane of existence to another. This is why the human being is greater than others, because all planes, all experiences, are possible to the spirit in the human body. We do not need another; for man can, if he likes, finish in his body his probation and can after that become pure spirit. When the Ojas has gone from centre to centre and reaches the Pineal Gland a part of the brain to which science can assign no function, man then becomes neither mind nor body, he is free from all bondage.

The great danger of psychic powers is that man stumbles, as it were, into them and knows not how to use them rightly. He is without training and without knowledge of what has happened to him. **The danger is that in using these psychic powers, the sexual feelings are abnormally roused as these powers are in fact manufactured out of the sexual centre. The best and safest way is to avoid psychic manifestations, for they play the most horrible pranks on their ignorant and untrained owners.**

To go back to symbols. Because this movement of the Ojas up the spinal cord feels like a spiral one, it is called the "snake". The snake, therefore, or the serpent, rests or the bone or triangle. When it is roused, it travels up the spinal cord; and as it goes from centre to centre, a new natural world is opened inside us—the Kundalini is roused.

Pranayama

Prana stands in metaphysics for the sum total of the energy that is in the universe. This universe, according to the theory of the philosophers, proceeds in the form of waves; it rises, and again it subsides, melts away, as it were; then again it proceeds out in all this variety; then again it slowly returns. So it goes on like a pulsation. The whole of this universe is composed of matter and force; and according to Sanskrit philosophers, everything that we call matter, solid and liquid, is the outcome of one primal matter which they call Akasha or ether; and the primordial force, of which all the forces that we see in nature are manifestations, they call Prana. It is this Prana acting upon Akasha, which creates this universe, and after the end of a period, called a cycle, there is a period of rest. One period of activity is followed by a period of rest; this is the nature of everything. When this period of rest comes, all these forms that we see in the earth, the sun, the moon, and the stars, all these manifestations melt down until they become ether again. They become dissipated as ether.

All these forces, either in the body or in the mind as gravitation, attraction, motion, thought, become dissipated, and go off into the primal Prana. We can understand from this the importance of Pranayama. Just as this ether encompasses us everywhere and we are interpenetrated by it, so everything we see is composed of this ether, and we are floating in the ether like pieces of ice floating in a lake. They are formed of the water of the lake and float in it at the same time. So everything that exists is composed of this Akasha and is floating in this ocean. In the same way we are surrounded by this vast ocean of Prana—force and energy. It is this Prana by which we breathe and by which the circulation of the blood goes on; it is the energy in the nerves and in the muscles, and the thought in the brain. All forces are different manifestations of this same Prana, as all matter is a different manifestation of the same Akasha. We always find the causes of the gross in the subtle. The chemist takes a solid lump of ore and analyses it; he wants to find the subtler things out of which that gross is composed. So with our thought and our knowledge, the explanation of the grosser is in the finer. The effect is the gross and the cause the subtle. This gross universe of ours, which we see, feel, and touch, has its cause and explanation behind in the thought. The cause and explanation of that is also further behind.

So in this human body of ours, we first find the gross movements, the movements of the hands and lips; but where are the causes of these? The finer nerves, the movements of which we cannot perceive at all, so fine that we cannot see or touch or trace them in any way with our senses, and yet we know they are the cause of these grosser movements. These nerve movements, again, are caused by still finer movements, which we call thought; and that is caused by something finer still behind, which is the soul of man, the Self, the Atman. In order to understand ourselves we have first to make our perception fine. No microscope or instrument that was ever invented will make it possible for us to see the fine movements that are going on inside; we can never see them by any such means. **So the Yogi has a science that manufactures an instrument for the study of his own mind, and that instrument is in the mind. The mind attains to powers of finer perception which no instrument will ever be able to attain.**

To attain to this power of superfine perception we have to begin from the gross. And as the power becomes finer and finer, we go deeper and deeper inside our own nature; and all the gross movements will first be tangible to us, and then the finer movements of the thought; he will be able to trace the thought before its beginning, trace it where it goes and where it ends. For instance, in the ordinary mind a thought arises. The mind does not know how it began or whence it comes. The mind is like the ocean in which a wave rises, but although the man sees the wave, he does not know how the wave came there, whence its birth, or whether it melts down again; he cannot trace it any further. But when the interception becomes finer, we can trace this wave long, long before it comes to the surface; and we will be able to trace it for a long distance after it has disappeared, and then we can understand psychology as it truly is. Nowadays men think this or that and write many volumes, which are entirely misleading, because they have not the power to analyse their own minds and are talking of things they have never *known*, but only theorised about.

All science must be based on facts, and these facts must be observed and generalised. Until you have some facts to generalise upon, what are you going to do? So all these attempts at generalising are based upon knowing the things we generalise. A man proposes a theory, and adds theory to theory, until the whole book is a patchwork of theories, not one of them with the least meaning. The science of Raja Yoga says, first you must gather facts about your own mind, and that can be done by analysing your mind, developing its finer powers of perception and seeing for yourselves what is happening inside; and when you have got these facts, then generalise; and then alone you will have the real science of psychology.

As I have said, to come to any finer perception we must take the help of the grosser end of it. The current of action which is manifested on the outside is the grosser. If we can get hold of this and go on further and further, it becomes finer and finer, and at last the finest. So this body and everything we have in this body are not different existences, but, as it were, various links in the same chain proceeding from fine to gross. You are a complete whole; this body is the outside manifestation, the crust, of the inside; the external is grosser and the inside finer; and so finer and finer until you come to the Self. And at last, when we come to the Self, we come to know that it was only the Self that was manifesting all this; that it was the Self which became the mind and became the body; that nothing else exists but the Self, and all these others are manifestations of that Self in various degrees, becoming grosser and grosser. So we will find by analogy that in this whole universe there is the gross manifestation, and **behind that is the finer movement, which we can call the will of God. Behind that even, we will find that Universal Self. And then we will come to know that the Universal Self becomes God and becomes this universe;** and that it is not that this universe is one and God another and the Supreme Self another, but that they are different states of the manifestation of the same Unity behind.

All this comes of our Pranayama. **These finer movements that are going on inside the body are connected with the breathing; and if we can get hold of this breathing and manipulate it and control it, we will slowly get to finer and finer motions, and thus enter, as it were, by getting hold of that breathing, into the realms of the mind.**

The first breathing is simply an exercise for the time being. Some of these breathing exercises, again, are difficult, because these require a great deal of dieting and other restrictions. So we will take the simpler ones. This breathing consists of three parts. The first is breathing in, which is called in Sanskrit Puraka, filling; and the second part is called Kumbhaka, retaining, filling the lungs and stopping the air from coming out; the third is called Rechaka, breathing out. The first exercise is simply breathing in and stopping the breath and throwing it out slowly. Then there is one step more in the breathing. These three parts of breathing make one Pranayama. This breathing should be regulated by numbers. Breathe in four seconds, then hold the breath for eight seconds, then again throw it out slowly in four seconds. Then begin again, and do this four times in the morning and four times in the evening.

There is one thing more. Instead of counting by one, two, three, and all such meaningless things, it is better to repeat any word that is holy to you. In our country we have symbolical words, "Om" for instance, which means God. If that be pronounced instead of one, two, three, four, it will serve your purpose very well. One thing more. This breathing should begin through the left nostril and should turn out through the right nostril, and the next time it should be drawn in through the right and thrown out through the left. Then reverse again, and so on. In the first place you should be able to drive your breathing through either nostril at will, just by the power of the will. After a time you will find it easy. We must stop the one nostril while breathing through the other with the finger and during the retention, of course, both nostrils.

The first two lessons should not be forgotten. The first thing is to hold yourselves straight; second to think of the body as sound and perfect, as healthy and strong. Then throw a current of love all around, think of the whole universe being happy. Then if you believe in God, pray. Then breathe.

In many of you certain physical changes will come, twitchings all over the body, nervousness; some of you will feel like weeping, sometimes a violent motion will come. Do not be afraid; these things have to come as you go on practising. The whole body will have to be rearranged as it were. New channels for thought will be made in the brain, nerves which have not acted in your whole life will begin to work, and a whole new series of changes will come in the body itself.

Thought, Imagination and Meditation

The same faculty that we employ in dreams and thoughts, namely, imagination, will also be the means by which we arrive at

Truth. 'When the imagination is very powerful, the object becomes visualised. Therefore by it we can bring our bodies to any state of health or disease. When we see a thing, the particles of the brain fall into a certain position like the mosaics of a kaleidoscope. Memory consists in getting back this combination and the same setting of the particles of the brain. The stronger the will, the greater will be the success in resetting these particles of the brain. There is only one power to cure the body, and that is in every man. Medicine only rouses this power. Disease is only the manifest struggle of that power to throw off the poison which has entered the body. Although the power to overthrow poison may be roused by medicine, it may be more permanently roused by the force of thought. Imagination must hold to the thought of health and strength in order that in case of illness the memory of the ideal of health may be roused and the particles rearranged in the position into which they fell when healthy. The tendency of the body is then to follow the brain.

The next step is when this process can be arrived at by another's mind working on us. Instances of this may be seen every day. Words are only a mode of mind acting on mind. Good and evil thoughts are each a potent power, and they fill the universe. As vibration continues so thought remains in the form of thought until translated into action. For example, force is latent in the man's arm until he strikes a blow, when he translates it into activity. We are the heirs of good and evil thought. If we make ourselves pure and the instruments of good thoughts, these will enter us. The good soul will not be receptive to evil thoughts. Evil thoughts find the best field in evil people; they are like microbes which germinate and increase only when they find a suitable soil. Mere thoughts are like little wavelets; fresh impulses to vibration come to them simultaneously, until at last one great wave seems to stand up and swallow up the rest.

These universal thought-waves seem to recur every five hundred years, when invariably the great wave typifies and swallows up the others. It is this which constitutes a prophet. He focuses in his own mind the thought of the age in which he is living and gives it back to mankind in concrete form. Krishna, Buddha, Christ, Mohammed, and Luther may be instanced as the great waves that stood up above their fellows (with a probable lapse of five hundred years between them). Always the wave that is backed by the greatest purity and the noblest character is what breaks upon the world as a movement of social reform. Once again in our day there is a vibration of the waves of thought and the central idea is that of the Immanent God, and this is everywhere cropping up in every form and every sect. In these waves, construction alternates with destruction; yet the construction always makes an end of the work of destruction. Now, as a man dives deeper to reach his spiritual nature, he feels no longer bound by superstition. The majority of sects will be transient, and last only as bubbles because the leaders are not usually men of character. Perfect love, the heart never reacting, this is what builds character. There is no allegiance possible where there is no character in the leader, and perfect purity ensures the most lasting allegiance and confidence.

Take up an idea, devote yourself to it, struggle on in patience, and the sun will rise for you.

Four Exercises

To return to imagination:

We have to visualise the Kundalini. The symbol is the serpent coiled on the triangular bone.

Then practise the breathing as described before, and, while holding the breath, imagine that breath like the current which flows down the figure 8 ; when it reaches the lowest point, imagine that it strikes the serpent on the triangle and causes the serpent to mount up the channel within the spinal cord. Direct the breath in thought to this triangle.

We have now finished the physical process and from this point it becomes mental.

The first exercise is called the "gathering-in". The mind has to be gathered up or withdrawn from wandering.

After the physical process, let the mind run on and do not restrain it; but keep watch on your mind as a witness watching its action. This mind is thus divided into two—the player and the witness. Now strengthen the witnessing part and do not waste time in restraining your wanderings. The mind must think; but slowly and gradually, as the witness does its part, the player will come more and more under control, until at last you cease to play or wander.

2nd Exercise: Meditation—which may be divided into two. We are concrete in constitution and the mind must think in forms. Religion admits this necessity and gives the help of outward forms and ceremonies. You cannot meditate on God without some form. One will come to you, for thought and symbol are inseparable. Try to fix your mind on that form.

3rd Exercise: This is attained by practising meditation and is really "one-pointedness". The mind usually works in a circle; make it remain on one point.

The last is the result. When the mind has reached this, all is gained—healing, clairvoyance, and all psychic gifts. In a moment you can direct this current of thought to anyone, as Jesus did, with instantaneous result.

People have stumbled upon these gifts without previous training, but I advise you to wait and practise all these steps slowly; then you will get everything under your control. You may practise healing a little if love is the motive, for that cannot hurt. Man is very short-sighted and impatient. All want power, but few will wait to gain it for themselves. He distributes but will not store up. It takes a long time to earn and but a short time to distribute. Therefore store up your powers as you acquire them and do not dissipate them.

Every wave of passion restrained is a balance in your favour. It is therefore good policy not to return anger for anger, as with all true morality. Christ said, "Resist not evil," and we do not—understand it until we discover that *it* is not only moral but actually the best policy, for anger is loss of energy to the man who displays it. You should not allow your minds to come into those brain-combinations of anger and hatred.

When the primal element is discovered in chemical science, the work of the chemist will be finished. When unity is discovered, perfection in the science of religion is reached, and this was attained thousands of years ago. Perfect unity is reached when man says, "I and my Father are one".

Jnana Yoga

This is the rational and philosophic side of Yoga and very difficult, but I will take you slowly through it.

Yoga means the method of joining man and God. When you understand this, you can go on with your own definitions of man and God, and you will find the term Yoga fits in with every definition. Remember always, there are different Yogas for different minds and that if one does not suit you, another may. All religions are divided into theory and practice. The Western mind has given itself up to the theory and only sees the practical part of religion as good works. **Yoga is the practical part of religion and shows that religion is a practical power apart from good works.**

At the beginning of the nineteenth century man tried to find God through reason, and Deism was the result. What little was left of God by this process was destroyed by Darwinism and Millism. Men were then thrown back upon historical and comparative religion. They thought, religion was derived from element worship (see Max Müller on the sun myths etc.); others thought that religion was derived from ancestor worship (see Herbert Spencer). But taken as a whole, these methods have proved a failure. Man cannot get at Truth by external methods.

"If I know one lump of clay, I know the whole mass of clay." The universe is all built on the same plan. The individual is only a part, like the lump of clay. If we know the human soul—which is one atom—its beginning and general history, we know the whole of nature. Birth, growth, development, decay, death—this is the sequence in all nature and is the same in the plant and the man. The difference is only in time. The whole cycle may be completed in one case in a day, in the other in three score years and ten; the methods are the same. **The only way to reach a sure analysis of the universe is by the analysis of our own minds. A proper psychology is essential to the understanding of religion.** To reach Truth by reason alone is impossible, because imperfect reason cannot study its own fundamental basis. Therefore **the only way to study the mind is to get at facts,** and then intellect will arrange them and deduce the principles. The intellect has to build the house; but it cannot do so without bricks and *it* cannot make bricks. **Jnana Yoga is the surest way of arriving at facts.**

First we have the physiology of mind. We have organs of the senses, which are divided into organs of action and organs of perception. By organs I do not mean the external sense-instruments. The ophthalmic centre in the brain is the organ of sight, not the eye alone. So with every organ, the function is internal. Only when the mind reacts, is the object truly perceived. The sensory and motor nerves are necessary to perception.

Then there is the mind itself. It is like a smooth lake which when struck, say, by a stone, vibrates. The vibrations gather together and react on the stone, and all through the lake they will spread and be felt. The mind is like the lake; it is constantly being set in vibrations, which leave an impression on the mind; and the idea of the Ego, or personal self, the "I", is the result of these impressions. This "I" therefore is only the very rapid transmission of force and is in itself no reality.

The mind-stuff is a very fine material instrument used for taking up the Prana. When a man dies, the body dies; but a little bit of the mind, the seed, is left when all else is shattered; and this is the seed of the new body called by St Paul "the spiritual body". This theory of the materiality of the mind accords with all modern theories. The idiot is lacking in intelligence because his mind-stuff is injured. Intelligence cannot be in matter nor can it be produced by any combinations of matter. **Where then is intelligence? It is behind matter; it is the Jiva, the real Self, working through the instrument of matter. Transmission of force is not possible without matter, and as the Jiva cannot travel alone, some part of mind is left as a transmitting medium when all else is shattered by death.**

How are perceptions made? The wall opposite sends an impression to me, but I do not see the wall until my mind reacts, that is to say, the mind cannot know the wall by mere sight. The reaction that enables the mind to get a perception of the wall is an intellectual process. In this way the whole universe is seen through our eyes plus mind (or perceptive faculty); it is necessarily coloured by our own individual tendencies. The *real* wall, or the *real* universe, is outside the mind, and is unknown and unknowable. Call this universe X, and our statement is that **the seen universe is X plus mind.**

What is true of the external must also apply to the internal world. Mind also wants to know itself, but this Self can only be known through the medium of the mind and is, like the wall, unknown. This self we may call Y, and the statement would then be, **Y plus mind is the inner self.** Kant was the first to arrive at this analysis of mind, but it was long ago stated in the Vedas. We have thus, as it were, mind standing between X and Y and reacting on both.

If X is unknown, then any qualities we give to it are only derived from our own mind. Time, space, and causation are the three conditions through which mind perceives. Time is the condition for the transmission of thought, and space for the vibration of grosser matter. Causation is the sequence in which vibrations come. Mind can only cognise through these. Anything therefore, beyond mind must be beyond time, space, and causation.

To the blind man the world is perceived by touch and sound. To us with five senses it is another world. If any of us developed an electric sense and the faculty of seeing electric waves, the world would appear different. Yet the world, as the X to all of these, is still the same. As each one brings his own mind, he sees his own world. There is X plus one sense; X plus two senses, up to five, as we know humanity. The result is constantly varied, yet X remains always unchanged. Y is also beyond our minds and beyond time, space, and causation.

But, you may ask, "How do we know there are two things, X and Y, beyond time, space, and causation?" Quite true, time makes differentiation, so that, as both are really beyond time, they must be really one. When mind sees this one, it calls it variously—X, when it is the outside world, and Y, when it is the inside world. This unit exists and is looked at through the lens of minds.

The Being of perfect nature, universally appearing to us, is God, is Absolute. The undifferentiated is the perfect condition; all others must be lower and not permanent.

What makes the undifferentiated appear differentiated to mind? This is the same kind of question as what is the origin of evil and free will? The question itself is contradictory and impossible, because the question takes for granted cause and effect. There is no cause and effect in the undifferentiated; the question assumes that the undifferentiated is in the same condition as the differentiated. "Whys" and "wherefores" are in mind only. The Self is beyond causation, and It alone is free. Its light it is which percolates through every form of mind. With every action I assert I am free, and yet every action proves that I am bound. The real Self is free, yet when mixed with mind and body, It is not free. The will is the first manifestation of the real Self; the first limitation therefore of this real Self is the will. Will is a compound of Self and mind. Now, no compound can be permanent, so that when we will to live, we must die. Immortal life is a contradiction in terms, for life, being a compound, cannot be immortal. True Being is undifferentiated and *eternal.* How does this Perfect Being become mixed up with will, mind, thought—all defective things? It never has become mixed. You are the real you (the Y of our former statement); you never were will; you never have changed; you as a person never existed; It is illusion. Then on what, you will say, do the phenomena of illusion rest? This is a bad question. Illusion never rests on Truth, but only on illusion. Everything struggles to go back to what was before these illusions, to be free in fact. What then is the value of life? It is to give us experience. Does this view do away with evolution? On the contrary, it explains it. It is really the process of refinement of matter allowing the real Self to manifest Itself. It is as if a screen or a veil were between us and some other object. The object becomes clear as the screen is gradually withdrawn. The question is simply one of manifestation of the higher Self.

Abstract Unity

To know the Om is to know the secret of the universe. The object of Jnana Yoga is the same as that of Bhakti and Raja Yogas, but the method is different. This is the Yoga for the strong, for those who are neither mystical nor devotional, but rational. As the Bhakti Yogi works his way to complete oneness with the Supreme through love and devotion, so the Jnana Yogi forces his way to the realisation of God by the power of pure reason. He must be prepared to throw away all old idols, all old beliefs and superstitions, all desire for this world or another, and be determined only to find freedom. Without Jnana (knowledge) liberation cannot be ours. It consists in knowing what we really are, that we are beyond fear, beyond birth, beyond death. The highest good is the realisation of the Self. It is beyond sense, beyond thought. The *real* "I" cannot be grasped. It is the eternal subject and can never become the object of knowledge, because knowledge is only of the related, not of the Absolute. All sense-knowledge is limitation, it is an endless chain of cause and effect. This world is a relative world, a shadow of the real; still, being the plane of equipoise where happiness and misery are about evenly balanced, it is the only plane where man can realise his true Self and know that he is Brahman.

This world is "the evolution of nature and the manifestation of God." It is our interpretation of Brahman or the Absolute, seen through the veil of Maya or appearance. The world is not zero, it has a certain reality it only *appears* because Brahman *is*.

How shall we know the knower? The Vedanta says, "We are It, but can never know It, because It can never become the object of knowledge." Modern science also says that It cannot be known. We can, however, have glimpses of It from time to time. When the delusion of this world is once broken, it will come back to us, but no longer will it hold any reality for us. We shall know it as a mirage. To reach behind the mirage is the aim of all religions. That man and God are one is the constant teaching of the Vedas, but only few are able to penetrate behind the veil and reach the realisation of this truth.

The first thing to be got rid of by him who would be a Jnani is fear. Fear is one of our worst enemies. Next, **believe in nothing until you *know* it.** Constantly tell yourself, "I am not the body, I am not the mind, I am not thought, I am not even consciousness; I am the Atman." When you can throwaway *all*, only the true Self will remain. **The Jnani's meditation is of two sorts: (I) to deny and**

think away everything we are *not;* (2) to insist upon what we really are — the Atman, the One Self-Existence, Knowledge, and Bliss. The true rationalist must go on and fearlessly follow his reason to its farthest limits. It will not answer to stop anywhere on the road. When we begin to deny, *all* must go until we reach what cannot be thrown away or denied, which is the real "I". That "I" is the witness of the universe, it is unchangeable, eternal, infinite. Now, layer after layer of ignorance covers it from our eyes, but it remains ever the same.

Two birds sat on one tree. The bird at the top was calm, majestic, beautiful, perfect. The lower bird was always hopping from twig to twig, now eating sweet fruits and being happy, now eating bitter fruits and being miserable. One day, when he had eaten a fruit more bitter than usual, he glanced up at the calm majestic upper bird and thought, "How I would like to be like him!" and he hopped up a little way towards him. Soon he forgot all about his desire to be like the upper bird, and went on as before, eating sweet and bitter fruits and being happy and miserable. Again he looked up, again he went up a little nearer to the calm and majestic upper bird. Many times was this repeated until at last he drew very near the upper bird; the brilliancy of his plumage dazzled him, seemed to absorb him, and finally, to his wonder and surprise, he found there was only one bird — he was the upper bird all the time and had but just found it out.

Man is like that lower bird, but if he perseveres in his efforts to rise to the highest ideal he can conceive of, he too will find that he was the Self all the time and the other was but a dream. To separate ourselves utterly from matter and all belief in its reality is true Jnana. **The Jnani must keep ever in his mind the "Om Tat Sat", that is, Om the only real existence. Abstract unity is the foundation of Jnana Yoga.** This is called Advaitism ("without dualism or dvaitism"). This is the cornerstone of the Vedanta philosophy, the Alpha and the Omega. "Brahman alone is true, all else is false and I am Brahman." Only by telling ourselves this until we make it a part of our very being, can we rise beyond all duality, beyond both good and evil, pleasure and pain, joy and sorrow, and know ourselves as the One, eternal, unchanging, infinite — the "One without a second."

The Jnana Yogi must be as intense as the narrowest sectarian, yet as broad as the heavens. **He must absolutely control his mind, be able to be a Buddhist or a Christian, to have the power to consciously divide himself into all these different ideas and yet hold fast to the eternal harmony.** Constant drill alone can enable us to get this control. All variations are in the One, but we must learn not to identify ourselves with what we do, and to hear nothing, see nothing, talk of nothing but the thing in hand. We must put in our whole soul and be intense. Day and night tell yourself, "I am He, I am He.

The greatest teacher of the Vedanta philosophy was Shankaracharya. By solid reasoning he extracted from the Vedas the truths of Vedanta, and on them built up the wonderful system of Jnana that is taught in his commentaries. He unified all the conflicting descriptions of Brahman and showed that there is only one Infinite Reality. He showed too that as man can only travel slowly on the upward road, all the varied presentations are needed to suit his varying capacity. **We find something akin to this in the teachings of Jesus, which he evidently adapted to the different abilities of his hearers.** First he taught them of a Father in heaven and to pray to Him. Next he rose a step higher and told them, "I am the vine, you are the branches," and lastly he gave them the highest truth: "I and my Father are one," and "The Kingdom of Heaven is within you." Shankara taught that three things were the great gifts of God: (1) human body, (2) thirst after God, and (3) a teacher who can show us the light. When these three great gifts are ours, we may know that our redemption is at hand. Only knowledge can free and save us, but with knowledge must go virtue.

The essence of Vedanta is that there is but one Being and that every soul is that Being in full, not a part of that Being. All the sun is reflected in each dew-drop. Appearing in time, space, and causality, this Being is man, as we know him, but behind all appearance is the one Reality. Unselfishness is the denial of the lower or apparent self. We have to free ourselves from this miserable dream that we are these bodies. We must *know* the truth, "I am He". We are not drops to fall into the ocean and be lost; each one is the *whole,* infinite ocean, and will know it when released from the fetters of illusion.

Infinity cannot be divided, the "One without a second" can have no second, all *is* that One. This knowledge will come to all, but we should struggle *to* attain it now, because until we have it, we cannot really give mankind the best help. The Jivanmukta ('the living free' or 'one who knows') alone is able to give real love, real charity, real truth, and it is truth alone that makes us free. Desire makes slaves of us, it is an insatiable tyrant and gives its victims no rest; but the Jivanmukta has conquered all desire by rising to the knowledge that he is the One and there is nothing left to wish for.

The mind brings before us all our delusions—body, sex, creed, caste, bondage; so we have to tell the truth to the mind incessantly, until it is made to realise it. Our real nature is all bliss, and all the pleasure we know is but a reflection, an atom, of that bliss we get from touching our real nature. *That* is beyond both pleasure and pain. It is the "witness" of the universe, the unchanging reader before whom turn the leaves of the book of life.

Through practice comes Yoga, through Yoga comes knowledge, through knowledge love and through love, bliss.

"Me and mine" is a superstition; we have lived in it so long that it is well-nigh impossible to shake it off. Still we must get rid of it if we would rise to the highest. We must be bright and cheerful, long faces do not make religion. Religion should be the most joyful thing in the world, because it is the best. Asceticism cannot make us holy. Why should a man who loves God and who is pure be sorrowful? He should be like a happy child:, be truly a child of God. The essential thing in religion is making the heart pure; the Kingdom of Heaven is within us, but only the pure in heart can see the King. While we think of the world, it is only the world for us; but let us come to it with the feeling that the world is God, and we shall have God. This should be our thought towards everyone and everything—parents, children, husbands, wives, friends, and enemies. Think how it would change the whole universe for us if we could consciously fill it with God! See nothing but God! All sorrow, all struggle, all pain would be for ever lost to us!

Jnana is "creedlessness", but that does not mean that it despises creeds. It only means that a stage above and beyond

creeds has been gained. The Jnani seeks not to destroy, but to help all. As all rivers roll their waters into the sea and become one, so all creeds should lead to Jnana and become one.

The reality of everything depends upon Brahman, and only as we really grasp this truth, have we any reality. When we cease to see any differences, then we know that "I and the Father are One."

Jnana is taught very dearly by Krishna in the Bhagavad-Gita. This great poem is held to be the crown jewel of all Indian literature. It is a kind of commentary on the Vedas. It shows us that our battle for spirituality must be fought out in this life; so we must not flee from it, but rather compel it to give us all that it holds. As the Gita typifies this struggle for higher things, it is highly poetical to lay the scene in a battlefield. Krishna in the guise of a charioteer to Arjuna, leader of one of the opposing armies, urges him not to be sorrowful, not to fear death, since he knows he is immortal, that nothing which changes can be in the *real* nature of man, Through chapter after chapter, Krishna teaches the higher truths of philosophy and religion to Arjuna. It is these teachings which make this poem so wonderful; practically the whole of the Vedanta philosophy is included in them. The Vedas teach that the soul is infinite and in no way affected by the death of the body. **The soul is a circle whose circumference is nowhere, but whose centre is in some body. Death (so-called) is but a change of centre. God is a circle whose circumference is nowhere and whose centre is everywhere,** and when we can get out of the narrow centre of body, we shall realise God—our true Self.

The present is only a line of demarcation between the past and the future; so we cannot rationally say that we care only for the present, as it has no existence apart from the past and the future. It is all one complete whole, the idea of time being merely a condition imposed upon us by the form of our understanding.

Jnana teaches that the world should be given up, but not on that account to be abandoned. To be *in* the world, but not *of* it, is the true test of the Sannyasin. This idea of renunciation has been in some form common to nearly all religions. Jnana demands that we look upon all alike, that we see only "sameness". Praise and blame, good and bad, even heat and cold, must be equally acceptable to us. In India there are many holy men of whom this is literally true. They wander on the snow-clad heights of the Himalayas or over the burning desert sands, entirely unclothed and apparently entirely unconscious of any difference in temperature.

Just Existence

We have first of all to give up this superstition of body; we are not the body. Next must go the further superstition that we are mind. We are not mind; it is but the "silken body", not any part of the soul. The mere word "body" applied to nearly all things, includes something common among all bodies. This is *existence.* Our bodies are symbols of thought behind, and the thoughts themselves are in their turn symbols of Something behind them, that is, the one Real Existence, the Soul of our soul, the Self of the universe, the Life of our life, our true Self. As long as we believe ourselves to be even the least different from God, fear remains with us; but when we know ourselves to be the One, fear goes: of what can we be afraid? By sheer force of will the Jnani rises beyond body, beyond mind, making this universe zero. Thus he destroys Avidya and knows his true Self, the Atman. Happiness and misery are, only in the senses, they cannot touch our real Self. The soul is beyond time, space, and causality—therefore unlimited, omni-present.

The Jnani has to come out of all forms, to get beyond all rules and books, and be his own book. Bound by forms, we crystallise and die. Still the Jnani must never condemn those who cannot yet rise above forms. He must never even think of another, "I am holier than thou".

These are the marks of the true Jnana Yogi: (I) He desires nothing, save to know. (2) All his senses are under perfect restraint; he suffers everything without murmuring, equally content if his bed be the bare ground under the open sky, or if he is lodged in a king's palace. He shuns no suffering, he stands and bears it—he has given up all but the Self. (3) He knows that all but the One is unreal. (4) He has an intense desire for freedom. With a strong will, he fixes his mind on higher things and so attains to peace. If we know not peace, what are we more than the brutes? He does everything for others—for the Lord—giving up all fruits of work and looking for no result, either here or hereafter. What can the universe give us more than our own soul? Possessing that, we possess *all.* The Vedas teach that the Atman, or Self, is the One Undivided Existence. It is beyond mind, memory, thought or even consciousness as we know it. From it are all things. It is that through which, or because of which, we see, hear, feel and think. The goal of the universe is to realise oneness with the "Om" or One Existence. The Jnani has to be free from all forms; he is neither a Hindu, a Buddhist nor a Christian but he is all three. All action is renounced, given up to the Lord ; then no action has power to bind. The Jnani is a tremendous regionalist; he denies everything. He tells himself day and night: "There are no beliefs, no sacred words, no heaven, no hell, no creed, no church—there is only the Atman." When everything has been thrown away until what cannot be thrown away is reached, that is the Self. The Jnani takes nothing for granted; he analyses by pure reason and force of will until **he reaches Nirvana which is the extinction of all relativity. No description or even conception of this state is possible.** Jnana is never to be judged by any earthly result. Be not like the vulture which soars almost beyond sight but which is ever ready to sweep downwards at the sight of a bit of carrion. Ask not for healing or longevity or prosperity, ask only to be free.

We are "Existence, Knowledge, Bliss" (Sachchidananda). Existence is the last generalisations in the universe; so we exist and we know it; and bliss is the natural result af existence without alloy. Now and then we know a moment af supreme bliss, when we ask nothing, give nothing, and know nothing but bliss. Then it passes and we again see the panorama af the universe going on before us and we know it is but a "mosaic work set upon God, who is the background of all things." When we return to earth and see the Absolute as relative, we see Sachchidananda as Trinity—Father, Son, Holy Ghost. Sat—the creating principle; Chit—the guiding principle; Ananda—the realising principle, which joins us again to the One. No one can know "existence" (Sat) except through "knowledge" (Chit), and hence the force of the saying of Jesus, No man can see the Father save through the Son. The Vedanta teaches that Nirvana can be attained here and now, that we do not have to wait for death to reach it. Nirvana is the realisation of the Self, and after having once, if only for an instant, known this, never again can one be deluded by the mirage of personality. Having eyes, we must see the apparent; but all the time we *know* it for what it is, we have found out its true nature. It is the "screen" that hides the Self which is unchanging. The screen opens and we find the Self behind it—all change is in the screen. In the saint the screen is thin and the Reality can almost shine through; but in the sinner it is thick, and we are apt to lose sight of the truth that the Atman is there, as well as behind the saint.

All reasoning ends only in finding Unity; so we first use analysis, then synthesis. In the world of science, the forces are gradually narrowed down in the search for one underlying force. When physical science can perfectly grasp the final unity, it will have reached an end, for reaching unity we find rest. Knowledge is final.

Religion, the most precious of all sciences, long ago discovered that final unity, to reach which is the object of Jnana Yoga. There is but one Self in the universe, of which all lower selves are but manifestations. The Self, however, is infinitely more than all of its manifestations. All is the Self or Brahman. The saint, the sinner, the lamb, the tiger, even the murderer, as far as they have any reality, can be nothing else, because there is nothing else. "That which exists is One, sages call It variously." Nothing can be higher than this knowledge, and in those purified by Yoga it comes in flashes to the soul. The more one has been purified and prepared by Yoga and meditation, the clearer are these flashes of realisation. This was discovered 4,000 years ago, but has not yet become the property of the race; it is still the property of some individuals only.

Of Human Understanding

All men, so-called, are not yet really human beings. Every one has to judge of this world through his own mind. The higher understanding is extremely difficult. The concrete is more to most people than the abstract. As an illustration of this, a story is told of two men in Bombay—one a Hindu and the other a Jain—who were playing chess in the house of a rich merchant of Bombay. The house was near the sea, the game long; the ebb and flow of the tide under the balcony where they sat attracted the attention of the players. One explained it by a legend that the gods in their play threw the water into a great pit and then threw it out again. The other said: No, the gods draw it up to the top of a high mountain to use it, and then when they have done with it, they throw it down again. A young student present began to laugh at them and said, "Do you not know that the attraction of the moon causes the tides?" At this, both men turned on him in a fury and inquired if he thought they were fools. Did he suppose that they believed the moon had any ropes to pull up the tides, or that it could reach so far? They utterly refused to accept any such foolish explanation.

At this juncture the host entered the room and was appealed to by both parties. He was an educated man and of course knew the truth, but seeing plainly the impossibility of making the chess-players understand it, he made a sign to the student and then proceeded to give an explanation of the tides that proved eminetly satisfactory to his ignorant hearers. "You must know," he told them, "that afar off in the middle of the ocean, there is a huge mountain of sponge—you have both seen sponge, and know what I mean. This mountain of sponge absorbs a great deal of the water and then the sea falls; by and by the gods come down and dance on the mountain and their weight squeezes all the water out and the sea rises again. This, gentlemen, is the cause of the tides, and you can easily see for yourselves how reasonable and simple is this explanation." The two men who ridiculed the power of the moon to cause the tides, found nothing incredible in a mountain of sponge danced upon by the gods! The gods were real to them, and they had actually seen sponge; what was more likely than their joint effect upon the sea!

"Comfort" is no test of truth; on the contrary, truth is often far from being "comfortable". If one intends to really find truth, one must not cling to comfort. It is hard to let all go, but the Jnani *must* do it. He must become pure, kill out all desires and cease to identify himself with the body. Then and then only, the higher touch can shine in his soul. Sacrifice is necessary, and this immolation of the lower self is the underlying truth that has made sacrifice a part of all religions. All the propitiatory offerings to the gods were but dimly understood types of the only sacrifice that is of any real value, the surrender of the apparent self, through which alone we can realise the higher Self, the Atman. The Jnani must not try to preserve the body, nor even wish to do so. He must be strong and follow truth, even though the universe fall. Those who follow "fads" can never do this. It is a life-work, nay, the work of a hundred lives! Only the few dare to realise the God within, to renounce heaven and Personal God and all hope of reward. A firm will is needed to do this; to be even vacillating is a sign of tremendous weakness.

Man always *is* perfect, or he never could become so ; but he had to realise it. If man were bound by external causes, he could only be mortal. Immortality can only be true of the unconditioned. Nothing can act on the Atman—the idea is pure delusion; but man must identify himself with that, not with body or mind. Let him know that he is the witness of the universe, then he can enjoy the beauty of the wonderful panorama passing before him. Let him even tell himself, "I am the universe, I am Brahman." When man *really* identifies himself with the One, the Atman, everything is possible to him and all matter becomes his servant. As Shri Ramakrishna has said: After the butter is churned, it can be put in water or milk and will never mix with either; so when man has once realised the Self, he can no more be contaminated by the world.

"From a balloon, no minor distinctions are visible, so when man rises high enough, he will not see good and evil people." "Once the pot is burned, no more can it be shaped; so with the mind that has once touched the Lord and has had a baptism of fire, no more can it be changed." Philosophy in Sanskrit means "clear vision," and religion is practical philosophy. Mere theoretic, speculative philosophy is not much regarded in India. There is no church, no creed, no dogma. The two great divisions are the "Dvaitists" and the "Advaitists." The former say, "The way to salvation is through the mercy of God; the law of causation, once set in motion, can never be broken; only God, who is not bound by this law, by His mercy helps us to break it." The latter say, "Behind all this nature is something that is free; and finding that which is beyond all law gets us freedom; and freedom is salvation."

Dualism is only one phase, Advaitism goes to the ultimate. To become pure is the shortest path to freedom. Only that is ours which we earn. No authority can save us, no beliefs. If there is a God, all can find Him. No one needs to be told it is warm; each one can discover it for himself. So it should be with God. He should be a fact in the consciousness of all men. The Hindus do not recognise "sin", as it is understood by the Western mind. Evil deeds are not "sins", we are not offending some Ruler in committing these; we are simply injuring ourselves, and we must suffer the penalty. It is not a sin to put one's finger in the fire, but he who does so will surely suffer just as much as if it were. All deeds produce certain results, and "every deed returns to the doer". "Trinitarianism" is an advance on "Unitarianism," which is dualism, God and man for ever separate. The first step upwards is when we recognise ourselves as the children of God; the last step is when we realise ourselves as the One, the Atman.

Illogical Questions

The question why there cannot be eternal bodies is in itself illogical, as "body" is a term applied to a certain combination of elements, changeable and in its very nature impermanent. When we are not passing through changes, we will not have bodies (so-called). "Matter" beyond the limit of time, space, and causality will not be matter at all. Time and space exist only in us, we are the one Permanent Being. All forms are transitory, that is why all religions say, "God has no form." Menander was a Greco-Bactrian king. He was converted to Buddhism about 150 B.C. by one of the Buddhist missionary monks and was called by them "Milinda." He asked a young monk, his teacher, "Can a perfect man (such as Buddha) be in error or make mistakes?" The young monk's answer was: The perfect man can remain in ignorance of minor matters not in his experience, but he can *never* be in error as to what his insight has actually realised. He is perfect here and now. He knows the whole mystery, the Essence of the universe, but he may not know the mere external variation through which that Essence is manifested in time and space. He knows the *clay* itself, but has not had experience of every shape it may be wrought into. The perfect man knows the Soul itself, but not every form and combination of its manifestation.

He would have to attain more relative knowledge just as we do, though on account of his Immense power, he would learn it far more quickly.

The tremendous "searchlight" of a perfectly controlled mind, when thrown on any subject, would rapidly reduce it to possession. It is very important to understand this, because it saves so much foolish explanation as to how a Buddha or a Jesus could be mistaken in ordinary relative Knowledge, as we well know they were. The disciples should not be blamed as having put down the sayings erroneously. It is humbug to say that one thing is true and another untrue in their statements. Accept the whole account, or reject it. How can *we* pick out the true from the false?

If a thing happens once, it can happen again. If any human being has ever realised perfection, we too can do so. If we cannot become perfect here and now, we never can in any state or heaven or condition imagine. If Jesus Christ was not perfect, then the religion bearing his name falls to the ground. If he was perfect, then we too can become perfect. The perfect man does not reason or "know", as we count "knowing", for all our knowledge is mere comparison, and there is no comparison, no classification, possible in the Absolute. Instinct is less liable to error than reason, but reason is higher and leads to intuition, which is higher still. Knowledge is the parent of intuition, which like instinct, is also unerring, but on a higher plane. There are three grades of manifestation in living beings: (1) subconscious—mechanical, unerring; (2) conscious—knowing, erring; (3) superconscious—intuitional, unerring; and these are illustrated in an animal, man, and God. For the man who has become perfect, nothing remains but to apply his understanding. He lives only to help the world, desiring nothing for himself. What distinguishes is negative—the positive is ever wider and wider. What we have in common in the widest of all, and that is "Being."

"Law is a mental shorthand to explain a series of phenomena"; but law as an entity, so to speak, does not exist. We use the word to express the regular succession of certain occurrences in the phenomenal world. We must not let law become a superstition, a something inevitable, to which we must submit. Error must accompany reason, but the very struggle to conquer error makes us gods. Disease is the struggle of nature to cast out something wrong; so sin is the struggle of the divine in us to throw off the animal. We must "sin"—that is, make mistakes—in order to rise to Godhood.

Do not pity anyone. Look upon all as your equal, cleanse yourself of the primal sin of inequality. We are all equal and must not think, "I am good and you are bad, and I am trying to reclaim you." Equality is the sign of the free. Jesus came to publicans and sinners and lived with them. He never set himself on a pedestal. Only sinners see sin. See not man, see only the Lord. We manufacture our own heaven and can make a heaven even in hell. Sinners are only to be found in hell, and as long as we see them around us, we are there ourselves. Spirit is not in time, nor in space. Realise "I am Existence Absolute, Knowledge Absolute, Bliss Absolute—I am He, I am He." Be glad at birth, be glad at death, rejoice always in the love of God. Get rid of the bondage of body; we have become slaves to it and learnt to hug our chains and love our slavery; so much so that we long to perpetuate it, and go on with "body" "body" for ever. Do not cling to the idea of "body," do not look for a future existence in any way like this one; do not love or want the body, even of those dear to us. This life is our teacher, and dying only makes room to begin over again. Body is our schoolmaster, but to commit suicide is folly, it is only killing the "schoolmaster." Another will take his place. So until we have learnt to transcend the body, we must have it, and losing one, will get another. Still we must not identify ourselves with the body, but look upon it only as an instrument to be used in reaching perfection. Hanuman, the devotee of Rama, summed up his philosophy in these words: When I identify myself with the body, O Lord, I am Thy creature, eternally separate from Thee. When I identify myself with the soul, I am a spark of that Divine Fire which Thou art. But when I identify myself with the Atman, I and Thou art one.

Therefore the Jnani strives to realise the Self and nothing else.

Thought and Reason

Thought is all important, for "what we think we become." There was once a Sannyasin, a holy man, who sat under a tree and taught the people. He drank milk, and ate only fruit, and made endless "Pranayamas," and felt himself to be very holy. In the same village lived an evil woman. Every day the Sannyasin went and warned her that her wickedness would lead her to hell. The poor woman, unable to change her method of life which was her only means of livelihood, was still much moved by the terrible future depicted by the Sannyasin. She wept and prayed to the Lord, begging Him to forgive her because she could not help herself. By and by both the holy man and the evil woman died. The angels came and bore her to heaven, while the demons claimed the soul of the Sannyasin. "Why is this!" he exclaimed, "have I not lived a most holy life, and preached holiness to everybody? Why should I be taken to hell while this wicked woman is taken to heaven?" "Because," answered the demons, "while she was forced to commit unholy acts, her mind was always fixed on the Lord and she sought deliverance, which has now come to her. But you, on the contrary, while you performed only holy acts, had your mind always fixed on the wickedness of others. You saw only sin, and thought only of sin, so now you have to go to that place where only sin is." The moral of the story is obvious: The outer life avails little. The heart must be pure and the pure heart sees only good, never evil. **We should never try to be guardians of mankind, or to stand on a pedestal as saints reforming sinners.** Let us rather purify ourselves, and the result must be that in so doing we shall help others.

Physics is bounded on both sides by metaphysics. So it is with reason—it starts from non-reason and ends with non-reason. If we push inquiry far enough in the world of perception, we must reach a plane beyond perception. Reason is really stored up and classified perception, preserved by memory. We can never imagine or reason beyond our sense-perceptions. Nothing beyond reason can be an object of sense-knowledge. We feel the limited character of reason, yet it does bring us to a plane: where we get a glimpse of something beyond. The question then arises: Has man an instrument that transcends reason? It is very probable that in man there is a power to reach beyond reason; in fact the saints in all ages assert the existence of this power in themselves. But it is impossible in the very nature of things to translate spiritual ideas and perceptions into the language of reason, and these saints, each and all, have declared their inability to make known their spiritual experiences. Language can, of course, supply no words for them, so that it can only be asserted that these are actual experiences and can be had by all. Only in that way can they become known, but they can never be described.

Religion is the science which learns the transcendental in nature through the transcendental in man. We know as yet but little of man, consequently but little of the universe. When we know more of man, we shall probably know more of the universe. Man is the epitome of all things and all knowledge is in him; Only for the infinitesimal portion of the universe, which comes into sense-perception, are we able to find a reason; never can we give the reason for any fundamental principle. Giving a reason for a thing is simply to classify it and put it in a pigeonhole of the mind. When we meet a new fact, we at once strive to put it in some existing category and the attempt to do this is to reason. When we succeed in placing the fact, it gives a certain amount of satisfaction, but we can never go beyond the physical plane in this classification. That man can transcend the limits of the senses is the emphatic testimony of all past ages. The Upanishads told 5,000 years ago that the realisation of God could never be had through tre senses. So far, modern agnosticism agrees, but the Vedas go further than the negative side and assert in the plainest terms that man can and does transcend this sense-bound, frozen universe. He can, as it were, find a hole in the ice, through which he can pass and reach the whole ocean of life. Only by so transcending the world of sense, can he reach his true Self and realise what he really is.

Jnana is never sense-knowledge. **We cannot *know* Bahman, but we *are* Brahman, the whole of it, not a piece.** The unextended can never be divided. The apparent variety is but the reflection seen in time and space, as we see the sun reflected in a million dew-drops, though we know that the sun itself is one and not many. In Jnana we have to lose sight of the variety and see only the Unity. Here there is no subject, no knowing, no thou or he or I, only the one, absolute Unity. We *are* his all the time; once free, ever free. **Man is *not* bound by the law of causation. Pain and misery are not in man, they are but as the passing cloud throwing its shadow over the sun, but the cloud passes, the sun is unchanged; and so it is with man.** He is not born, he does not die, he is not in time and space. These ideas are mere reflections of the mind, but we mistake them for the reality and so lose sight of the glorious truth they obscure. **Time is but the method of our thinking, we are the eternally present tense.** Good and evil have existence only in relation to us. One cannot be had without the other, because neither has meaning or existence apart from the other. As long as we recognise duality, or separate God and man, so long we must see good and evil. Only by going to the centre, by unifying ourselves with God can we escape the delusions of the senses. When we let go the eternal fever of desire, the endless thirst that gives us no rest, when we have for ever quenched desire, we shall escape both good and evil, because we shall have transcended both. The satisfaction of desire only increases it, as oil poured on fire but makes it burn more fiercely. The further from the centre, the faster goes the wheel, the less the rest. Draw near the centre, check desire, stamp it out, let the false self go, then our vision will clear and we shall see God. Only through renunciation of this life and of all life to come (heaven etc.), can we reach the point where we stand firmly on the true Self. While we hope for anything, desire still rules us. Be for one moment really "hopeless", and the mist will clear. For what to hope when one is the all of existence? **The secret of Jnana is to give up all and be sufficient unto ourselves. Say "not", and you become "not"; say "is", and you become "is".** Worship the Self within, naught else exists. All that binds us is Maya—delusion.

The Self is the condition of all in the universe, but It can never be conditioned. As soon as we know that we are It, we are free. As mortals we are not and never can be free. Free mortality is a contradiction in terms, for mortality implies change, and only the changeless can be free. The Atman alone is free, and that is our real essence. We feel this inner freedom; in spite of all theories, all beliefs, we know it, and every action proves that we know it. The will is not free, its apparent freedom is but a reflection from the Real. If the world were only an endless chain of cause and effect, where could one stand to help it? There must needs be a piece of dry land for the rescuer to stand on, else how can he drag anyone out of the rushing stream and save him from doing? Even the fanatic who cries "I am a worm" thinks that he is on the way to become a saint. He sees the saint even in the worm.

There are two ends or aims of human life, real knowing, Vijnana, and bliss. Without freedom, these two are impossible. They are the touchstone of all life. We should feel the Eternal Unity so much, that we should weep for all sinners, knowing that it is *we* who are sinning. The eternal law is self-sacrifice, not self-assertion. What self to assert when all is one? There are no "rights", all is love. **The great truths that Jesus taught have never been lived. Let us try his method and see if the world will not be saved. The contrary method has nearly destroyed it. Selflessness only, not selfishness, can solve the question.** The idea of "right" is a limitation; there is really no "mine" and "thine", for I am thou and thou art I. We have "responsibility", not "rights". We should say, "I am the universe," not "I am John" or "I am Mary." These limitations are all delusions and are what holds us in bondage, for as soon as I think, "I am John", I want exclusive possession of certain things and begin to say "me and mine", and continually make new distinctions in so doing.

So our bondage goes on increasing with every fresh distinction, and we get further and further away from the, central Unity, the undivided Infinite. There is only one Individual, and each of us is That. Oneness alone is love and fearlessness; separation leads us to hatred and fear. Oneness fulfils the law. Here, on earth, we strive to enclose little spaces and exclude outsiders, but we cannot do that in the sky, though that is what sectarian religion tries to do when it says, "Only *this* way leads to salvation, all others are wrong." Our aim should be to wipe out these little enclosures to widen the boundaries uoil they are lost sight of, and to realise that all religions lead to God. This little puny self must be sacrificed. This is the truth symbolised by baptism into a new life, the death of the old man, the birth of the new—the perishing of the false self, the realisation of the Atman, the one Self of the universe.

Karma Kanda, Jnana Kanda

The two great divisions of the Vedas are Karma Kanda—the portion pertaining to doing or work, and Jnana Kanda—the portion treating of knowing, true knowledge. In the Vedas we can find the whole process of the growth of religious ideas. This is because when a higher truth was reached, the lower perception that led to it, was still preserved. This was done, because the sages realised that the world of creation being eternal, there would always be those who needed the first steps to knowledge, that the highest philosophy, while open to all, could never be grasped by all. **In nearly every other religion, only the last or highest realisation of truth has been preserved,** with the natural consequence that the older ideas were lost, while the newer ones were only understood by the few and gradually came to have no meaning for the many.

We see this result illustrated in the growing revolt against old traditions and authorities. Instead of accepting them, the man of today boldly challenges them to give reasons for their claims, to make clear the grounds upon which they demand acceptance. **Much in Christianity is the mere application of new names and meanings to old pagan beliefs and customs.** If the old sources had been preserved and the reasons for the transitions fully explained, many things would have been clearer. The Vedas preserved the old ideas and this fact necessitated huge commentaries to explain them and why they were kept. It also led to many superstitions, through clinging to old forms after all sense of their meaning had been lost. In many ceremonials, words are repeated which have survived from a now forgotten language and to which no real meaning can now be attached. **The idea of evolution was to be found in the Vedas long before the Christian era; but until Darwin said it was true, it was regarded as a mere Hindu superstition.**

All external forms of prayer and worship are included in the Karma Kanda. These are good when performed in a spirit of unselfishness and not allowed to degenerate into mere formality. They purify the heart. The Karma Yogi wants everyone to be saved before himself. His only salvation is to help others to salvation. "To serve Krishna's servants is the highest worship." One great saint prayed, "Let me go to hell with the sins of the whole world, but let the world be saved." This true worship leads to intense self-sacrifice. It is told of one sage that he was willing to give all his virtues to his dog, that it might go to heaven, because it had long been faithful to him, while he himself was content to go to hell.

The Jnana Kanda teaches that knowledge alone can save, in other words, that he must become "wise unto salvation". Knowledge is first objective, the Knower knowing Himself. The Self, the only subject, is in manifestation seeking only to know Itself. The better the mirror, the better reflection it can give; so man is the best mirror, and the purer the man, the more clearly he can reflect God. Man makes the mistake of separating himself from God and identifying himself with the body. This mistake arises through Maya, which is not exactly delusion but might be said to be seeing the real as something else and not as it is. This identifying of ourselves with the body leads to inequality, which inevitably leads to struggle and jealousy, and so long as we see inequality, we can never know happiness. "Ignorance and inequality are the two sources of all misery," says Jnana.

When man has been sufficiently buffeted by the world, he awakes to a desire for freedom; and searching for means of escape from the dreary round of earthly existence, he seeks knowledge, learns what he really is, and is free. Better that he looks at the world as a huge machine, but takes good care to keep his fingers out of the wheels. Duty ceases for him who is free; what power can constrain the free being? He does good, because it is his nature, not because any fancied duty commands it. This does not apply to those who are still in the bondage of the senses. Only for him, who has transcended the lower self, is this freedom. He stands on his own soul, obeys no law; he is free and perfect. He has undone the old superstitions and got out of the wheel. Nature is but the mirror of our own selves. There is a limit to the working power of human beings, but no limit to desire; so we strive to get hold of the working powers of others and enjoy the fruits of their labours, escaping work ourselves. Inventing machinery to work for us can never increase well-being, for in gratifying desire, we only find it, and then we want more and more without end. Dying, still filled with ungratified desires, we have to be born again and again in the vain search for satisfaction. "Eight millions of bodies have we had, before we reached the human," say the Hindus. Jnana says, "Kill desire and so get rid of it." That is the only way. Cast out all causation and realise the Atman. Only freedom can produce true morality. If there were only an endless train of cause and effect, Nirvana could not be. It is extinction of the seeming self, bound by this chain. That is what constitutes freedom, to get beyond causality.

Our true nature is good, it is free, the pure being that can never be or do wrong. When we read God with our eyes and minds, we call Him this or that; but in reality there is but One, all variations are our interpretations of that One. **We *become* nothing; we *regain* our true Self.** Buddha's summary of misery as the outcome of "ignorance and caste"—inequality—has been adopted by the Vedantists, because it is the best ever made. It manifests the wonderful insight of this greatest among men. Let us then be brave and sincere: whatever path we follow with devotion, must take us to freedom. Once lay hold of one link of the chain and the whole must come after it by degrees. Water the root of the tree and the whole tree is watered. It is of little advantage to waste time to water each leaf. In other words, seek the Lord and getting Him we get all. Churches, doctrines, forms—these are merely the hedges to protect the tender plant of religion; but later on they must all be broken down, that the little plant may become a tree. **So the various religious sects, Bibles, Vedas, and scriptures are just "tubs" for the little plant;** but it has to get out of the tub and fill the world.

We must learn to feel ourselves as much in the sun, in the stars, as here. Spirit is beyond all time and space; every eye seeing is my eye; every mouth praising the Lord is my mouth; every sinner is I.

We are confined nowhere, we are not body. The universe is our body. We are just the pure crystal reflecting all, but itself ever the same. We are magicians waying magic wands and creating scenes before us at will, but we have to go behind appearances and know the Self. This world is like water in a kettle, beginning to boil; first a bubble comes, then another, then many until all is in ebullition and passes away in steam. **The great teachers are like the bubbles as they begin—here one, there one; but in the end every creature has to be a bubble and escape.** Creation, ever new, will bring new water and go through the process all over again. **Buddha and Christ are the two greatest "bubbles" the world has known.** They were great souls who having realised freedom helped others to escape. Neither was perfect, but they are to be judged by their virtues, never by their defects. Jesus fell short, because he did not always live up to his own highest ideal; and above all, because he did not give woman an equal place with man. **Woman did everything for, yet not one was made an apostle. This was doubtless owing to his Semitic origin. The great Aryans, Buddha among the rest, have always put woman in an equal position with man. For them sex in religion did not exist.** In the Vedas and Upanishads, women taught the highest truths and received the same veneration as men.

Three qualities

Both happiness and misery are chains, the one golden, the other iron; but both are equally strong to bind us and hold us back from realising our true nature. The Atman knows neither happiness nor misery. These are merely "states", and states must ever change. The nature of the soul is bliss and peace unchanging. We have not to *get* it ; we *have* it; let us wash away the dross from our eyes and see it. We must stand ever on the Self and look with perfect calmness upon all the panorama of the world. It is but baby's play and ought never to disturb us. If the mind is pleased by praise, it will be pained by blame. All pleasures of the senses or even of the mind are evanescent, but within ourselves is the one true unrelated pleasure, dependent on nothing outside **"The pleasure of the Self is what the world calls religion." The more our bliss is within,**

the more spiritual we are. Let us not depend upon the world for pleasure.

Some poor fish-wives, overtaken by a violent storm, found refuge in the garden of a rich man. He received them kindly, fed them, and left them to rest in a summer-house, surrounded by exquisite flowers which filled all the air with their rich perfume. The women lay down in this sweet-smelling paradise, but could not sleep. They missed something out of their lives and could not be happy without it. At last one of the women arose and went to the place where they had left their fish baskets, brought them to the summer-house, and then once more happy in the familiar smell, they were all soon sound asleep.

Let not the world be our "fish-basket" which we have to depend upon for enjoyment. This is Tamasika, or being bound by the lowest of the three qualities or Gunas. Next higher come the egotistical who talk always about "I", "I". Sometimes they do good work and may become spiritual. These are Rajasika or active. Highest come the introspective nature Sattvika, those who live only in the Self. These three qualities are in every human being in varying proportions, and different ones predominate at different times. We must strive to overcome Tamas with Rajas and then to submerge both in Sattva.

Creation is not a "making" of something, it is the struggle to regain equilibrium, as when atoms of cork are thrown to the bottom of a pail of water: they rush to the top singly and in clusters, and when all have reached the top and equilibrium has been regained, all motion or "life" ceases. So with creation; if equilibrium were reached, all change would cease and life, so-called, would end. Life must be accompanied with evil, for when the balance is regained, the world must end, as sameness and destruction are one. There is no possibility of ever having pleasure without pain, or good without evil, for **living itself is just the lost equilibrium.** What we want is freedom, not life, nor pleasure, nor good. Creation is eternal, without beginning, without end, the ever moving ripple in an infinite lake. There are yet unreached depths and others where stillness has been regained, but the ripple is ever progressing, the struggle to regain the balance is eternal. **Life and death are but different names for the same fact,** they are the two sides of one coin. **Both are Maya, the inexplicable state of striving at one point to live and a moment later to die.** Beyond all this is the true nature," the Atman. We enter into creation, and then, for us, it becomes living. **Things are dead in themselves, only we give them life, and then, like fools, we turn round and are afraid of them or enjoy them!** The world is neither true nor untrue, it is the shadow of truth.

"Imagination is the gilded shadow of truth," says the poet. The internal universe, the Real, is infinitely greater than the external one, which is but the shadowy projection of the true one. When we see the "rope", we do not see the "serpent", and when the "serpent" is, the "rope" is not. Both cannot exist at the same time; so while we see the world we do not realise the Self, it is only an intellectual concept. In the realisation of Brahman, the personal "I" and all sense of the world is lost. The Light does not know the darkness, because it has no existence in the light; so Brahman is all. While we recognise a God, it is really only the Self that we have separated from ourselves and worship as outside of us ; but all the time it is our own true Self, the one and only God. **The nature of the brute is to remain where he is, of man to seek good and avoid evil, of God to neither seek nor avoid, but just to be blissful eternally. Let us be Gods,** let us make our hearts like an ocean, to go beyond all the trifles of the world and see it only as a picture. We can then enjoy it without being in any way affected by it. Why look for good in the world, what can we find there? The best it has to offer is only as if children playing in a mud puddle found a few glass beads. They lose them again and have to begin the search anew. Infinite strength is religion and God. We are only souls if we are free, there is immortality only if we are free, there is God only if He is free.

Until we give up the world manufactured by the ego, never can we enter the Kingdom of Heaven. None ever did, none ever will. To give up the world is to utterly forget the ego, to know it not at all, living in the body but not being ruled by it. **This rascal ego must be obliterated.** Power to help mankind is with the silent ones who only live and love and withdraw their own personality entirely. They never say "me" or "mine", they are only blessed in being the instruments to help others. They are wholly identified with God, asking nothing and not *consciously* doing anything. They are the true Jivanmuktas—the absolutely selfless, their little personality thoroughly blown away, ambition non-existent. They are all principle, with no personality. The more we sink the "little self", the more God comes. Let us get rid of the little "I" and let only the great "I" live in us. Our best work and our greatest influence is when we are without a thought of self. It is the "desireless" who bring great results to pass. Bless men when they revile you. Think how much good they are doing by helping to stamp out the false ego. Hold fast to the real Self, **think only pure thoughts, and you will accomplish more than a regiment of mere preachers.** Out of purity and silence comes the world of power.

Expression is necessarily degeneration, because spirit can only be expressed by the "letter", and as St. Paul said, "the letter killeth". Life cannot be in the "letter" which is only a reflection. Yet, principle must be clothed in matter to be "known". We lose sight of the Real in the covering and come to consider that as the Real, instead of as the symbol. This is an almost universal mistake. Every great teacher knows this and tries to guard against it; but humanity, in general, is prone to worship the *seen* rather than the unseen. This is why a succession of prophets have come to the world to point again and again to the principle behind the personality and to give it a new covering suited to the times. Truth remains ever unchanged, but it can only be presented in a "form"; so from time to time a new "form" or expression is given to Truth, as the progress of mankind makes them ready to receive it.

Free, Finally

When we free ourselves from name and form, especially when we no longer need a body of any kind, good or bad, coarse or fine, then only do we escape from bondage. "Eternal progression" would be eternal bondage. We must get beyond all differentiation and reach eternal "sameness" or homogeneity or Brahman. The Atman is the unity of all personalities and is unchangeable, the "One without a second". It is not life, but it is coined into life. It is beyond life and death and good and bad. It is the Absolute Unity. **Dare to seek Truth even through hell.** Freedom can never be true of name and form, of the related. No form can say, "I am free as a form." Not until all idea of form is lost, does freedom come. If our freedom hurts others, we are not free. We must not hurt others. While real perception is only one, relative perceptions must be many. The fountain of all knowledge is in everyone of us—as in the highest angel. **Real religion is one; all quarrel is with the forms, the symbols, the "illustrations".** The millennium exists already for those who find it. The truth is, we have lost ourselves and think the world to be lost. "Fool! Hearest not thou? In thine own heart, day and night, is singing that Eternal Music—Sachchidananda, Soham, Soham, (Existence, Knowledge, and Bliss, I am He, I am He)!"

To try to think without a phantasm is to try to make the impossible possible. Each thought has two parts—the thinking and the word, and we must have both. Neither idealists nor materialists are able to explain the world; to do that, we must take both idea and expression. All knowledge is of the reflected as we can only see our own faces reflected in a mirror. So no one can know his Self or Brahman; but each is that Self and must see it reflected in order to make it an object of knowledge. This seeing the illustrations of the unseen Principle is what leads to idolatry so-called. The range of idols is wider than is usually supposed. They range from wood and stone to great personalities as Jesus or Buddha.

The introduction of idols into India was the result of Buddha's constantly inveighing against a Personal God. The Vedas knew them not, but the reaction against the loss of God as Creator and Friend led to making idols of the great teachers, and **Buddha himself became an idol and is worshipped as such by millions of people. Violent attempts at reform always end in retarding true reform.** To worship is inherent in every man's nature; only the highest philosophy can rise to pure abstraction. So man will ever personify his God in order to worship Him. This is very good, as long as the symbol, be it what it may, is worshipped as a symbol of the Divinity behind and not in and for itself. Above all, we need to free ourselves from the superstition of believing because "it is in the books." To try to make everything—science, religion, philosophy, and all—conform to what any book says, is a most horrible tyranny.

Book-worship is the worst form of idolatry. There was once a stag, proud and free and he talked in a lordly fashion to his child, "Look at me, see my powerful horns! With one thrust I can kill a man; it is a fine thing to be a stag." Just then the sound of the huntsman's bugle was heard in the distance, and the stag precipitately fled, followed by his wondering child. When they had reached a place of safety, he inquired, "Why do you fly before man, O my father, when you are so strong and brave?" The stag answered, "My child, I know I am strong and powerful, but when I hear that sound, something seizes me and makes me fly whether I will or no." So with us. We hear the "bugle sound" of the laws laid down in the books, habits and old superstitions lay hold of us; and before we know it, we are fast bound and forget our real nature which is freedom.

Knowledge exists eternally. The man who discovers a spiritual truth is what we call "inspired", and what he brings to the world is revelation. But revelation too is eternal and is not to be crystallised as final and then blindly followed. **Revelation may come to any man who has fitted himself to receive it**. Perfect purity is the most essential thing, for only "the pure in heart shall see God". Man is the highest being that exists and this is the greatest world, for here can man realise freedom. **The highest concept we can have of God is man. Every attribute we give Him belongs also to man, only in a lesser degree.** When we rise higher and want to get out of this concept of God, we have to get out of the body, out of mind and imagination, and leave this world out of sight. When we rise to be the absolute, we are no longer in the world—all is Subject, without object.

Man is the apex of the only "world" we can ever know. Those who have attained "sameness" or perfection, are said to be "living in God". All hatred is "killing the self by the self"; therefore, **love is the law of life.** To rise to this is to be perfect; but the more "perfect" we are, the less work can we do. The Sattvika see and know that all this world is mere child's play and do not trouble themselves about that. We are not much disturbed when we see two puppies fighting and biting each other. We know it is not a serious matter. The perfect one knows that this world is Maya. **Life is called Samsara—it is the result of the conflicting forces acting upon us.** Materialism says, "The voice of freedom is a delusion." Idealism says, "The voice that tells of bondage is but a dream." Vedanta says, "We are free and not free at the same time." That means that we are never free on the earthly plane, but ever free on the spiritual side. The Self is beyond both freedom and bondage. We *are* Brahman, we *are* immortal knowledge beyond the senses, we *are* Bliss Absolute.

❑❑❑